WBI DEVELOPMENT ST

The Role of Parliament in Curbing Corruption

Edited by
Rick Stapenhurst
Niall Johnston
Riccardo Pellizo

The World Bank
Washington, DC

©2006 The International Bank for Reconstruction and Development / The World Bank
1818 H Street NW
Washington DC 20433
Telephone: 202-473-1000
Internet: www.worldbank.org
E-mail: feedback@worldbank.org

1 2 3 4 09 08 07 06

This volume is a product of the staff of the International Bank for Reconstruction and Development / The World Bank. The findings, interpretations, and conclusions expressed in this volume do not necessarily reflect the views of the Executive Directors of The World Bank or the governments they represent.

The World Bank does not guarantee the accuracy of the data included in this work. The boundaries, colors, denominations, and other information shown on any map in this work do not imply any judgement on the part of The World Bank concerning the legal status of any territory or the endorsement or acceptance of such boundaries.

Rights and Permissions
The material in this publication is copyrighted. Copying and/or transmitting portions or all of this work without permission may be a violation of applicable law. The International Bank for Reconstruction and Development / The World Bank encourages dissemination of its work and will normally grant permission to reproduce portions of the work promptly.

For permission to photocopy or reprint any part of this work, please send a request with complete information to the Copyright Clearance Center Inc., 222 Rosewood Drive, Danvers, MA 01923, USA; telephone: 978-750-8400; fax: 978-750-4470; Internet: www.copyright.com.

All other queries on rights and licenses, including subsidiary rights, should be addressed to the Office of the Publisher, The World Bank, 1818 H Street NW, Washington, DC 20433, USA; fax: 202-522-2422; e-mail: pubrights@worldbank.org.

ISBN-10: 0-8213-6723-4
ISBN-13: 978-0-8213-6723-0
e-ISBN: 0-8213-6724-2
DOI: 10.1596/ 978-0-8213-6723-0

Library of Congress Cataloging-in-Publication Data

The role of parliament in curbing corruption / edited by Rick Stapenhurst, Niall
Johnston, Riccardo Pelizzo.
     p. cm. — (WBI development studies)
  Includes bibliographical references.
  ISBN-13: 978-0-8213-6723-0
  ISBN-10: 0-8213-6723-4
  ISBN-10: 0-8213-6724-2 (electronic)
  1. Political corruption—Developing countries—Prevention.   2. Legislative
bodies—Developing countries.   3. Economic development   I. Stapenhurst, Rick.
II. Johnston, Niall, 1961–   III. Pelizzo, Riccardo.
  JF1525.C66R65 2006
  364.1'323091724—dc22

                                                                                     2006023024

Contents

Part II. Legislation

Part III. Oversight and Financial Control

Part IV. Representation

Part V. Corruption in Political Parties and Parliament

Part VI. International Parliamentary Links

Appendixes

Boxes

Figures

Tables

Foreword

This book comes at a very opportune time in the dialogue around development. Starting in the early 1990s, there has been increasing concern about corruption, not only about the impact of corruption and governance in general on development but also about the ethical dimensions of behavior and the role that individuals, firms, and institutions play in governing such behavior. Many countries have adopted anti-corruption policies, but there is evidence from data that little progress has been made. Any progress in curbing corruption must come from a broad-based coalition of actors: the three branches of government (executive, legislative, and judicial), civil society, the media, and the private sector.

The World Bank Institute (WBI, or the Institute) has been involved in the diagnostic, policy advice, and capacity development support to countries on the issues of corruption and governance. Recognizing that corruption is a complex phenomenon, the Institute has been using an action-learning approach, helping countries solve problems in their own settings, using their own experience to learn from what works and what does not, and engaging them with other countries who are struggling with similar issues and who have made progress in addressing issues of particular relevance to their country constraints.

Our partner in our work to strengthen government accountability through enhanced parliamentary oversight is the Commonwealth Parliamentary Association (CPA). As a network of, and professional development association for, some 16,000 parliamentarians across the Commonwealth, the CPA has made considerable progress in recent years in working in what might be termed "applied parliamentary development," as well as continuing its traditional role of promoting parliamentary practice and procedure. In that context, the Association focuses on the role of parliaments and parliamentarians in the process of curbing corruption.

This book was conceived after observing a major gap in the level of knowledge around the world on the role that the institution of parliament plays in development. Responding to research findings and country demands, WBI's Parliamentary Strengthening Program and the CPA organized a series of conferences over a period of three years. These conferences, held at and organized in collaboration with Wilton Park, assembled leading experts, Members of Parliament, and parliamentary staff from all over the world to share experiences and discuss the roles, tools, and strategies that parliamentarians have at their disposal to fight corruption. The main focus of the conferences was on the primary areas of interest of, and leverage for, parliaments regarding anti-corruption.

The first conference was held June 10–13, 2002. It presented an overview of the issues and challenges facing parliaments and governments in their efforts to reduce corruption, including cultural perceptions, pay and conditions of public service, and access to information. It thus set the stage for detailed examination of issues in later conferences: party political funding, election systems, parliamentary codes of conduct, the importance of coalition building, and the need for independent anti-corruption commissions. It considered international initiatives to combat corruption, including United Nations (UN) and other conventions against corruption and the formation of the Global Organization of Parliamentarians Against Corruption (GOPAC).

The second conference was held March 3–6, 2003, and focused on the role of parliaments in curbing corruption in Central and Eastern Europe. This conference looked at the impact of corruption on economic development. It also introduced key points of entry in curbing corruption, with a special look at the role of transparency in awarding contracts and what tools can be used to promote such transparency. In addition, the roles of the media and civil society organizations in reducing corruption were seen as key. International bodies and parliaments were also viewed as critical in dealing with global issues such as fighting money laundering.

The third and final conference was held June 7–10, 2004, and it focused primarily on political institutions, with special attention to financing politics, but it also looked at ethical and behavioral issues for curbing corruption, including parliamentary ethics. Participants exchanged experiences on the nature of corruption, paying particular attention to the relationship between corruption, party finances, and the violation of party finance regulations. The costs of corruption, with a particular focus on the impact of corruption on democracy, governance, and poverty, generated much interest. Participants also shared tools to curb corruption, looking especially at public accounts committees and codes of conduct for Members of Parliament.

This book provides an overview of the main findings and recommendations on the role of parliamentarians in curbing corruption, based on a collection of experiences and lessons shared during these conferences. It would be of particular interest to donor agencies seeking to ensure that development assistance is effectively used, to client countries trying to make headway in curbing corruption, to practitioners who are looking for "how-to" guidance, and to academics (particularly in the areas of public administration, political science, and business ethics).

I would like to thank Finland's Ministry of Forgeign Affairs, the United Kingdom's Department for International Development, and the Canadian International Development Agency for their support to WBI's Parliamentary Strengthening Program and the publication of this book.

Frannie A. Léautier
Vice President
World Bank Institute

Preface

Corruption is a disease that threatens the hopes of the poor: for a better future for themselves and their children. It drains finances that might otherwise go to programs that bring education within reach of poor children, or that offer health care to an ailing farmer or a young mother.

Parliamentarians have been entrusted with the enormous responsibility of amplifying the voices of citizens in the halls of government—and ensuring that governments are making decisions that best serve the interests of their people. Parliamentarians can also play a vital role in empowering citizens to call to task governments that don't do enough to stop corruption.

For nearly a decade now, the World Bank Group has been at the forefront of diagnosing corruption as part of its mission to fight poverty. Since that time, the World Bank has supported more than 600 anti-corruption programs and governance initiatives in partner countries. For example, the Bank has conducted in-depth country governance and corruption surveys and diagnostics; developed multi-pronged anti-corruption strategies; and assisted both governmental and nongovernmental institutions in building their capacity.

Initially, the World Bank's anti-corruption efforts emphasized strengthening "horizontal" accountability at the government level through building up the judiciary, audit institutions, ombuds offices and anti-corruption agencies. In recent years, these efforts have been complemented by an emphasis on "vertical" accountability to citizens through institutions like the media and civil society.

The parliament is an important institution which cuts across both vertical and horizontal accountability. In most countries, parliament has the constitutional mandate to both oversee government and to hold government to account. At the same time, parliaments can play a key role in promoting horizontal accountability—amplifying the voices of citizens—through such mechanisms as constituency outreach, public hearings, and parliamentary commissions.

This book addresses the role of parliament in curbing corruption. It examines some of the papers presented at three conferences organized jointly by the World Bank Institute and the Commonwealth Parliamentary Association over the past four years, supplemented by specially commissioned chapters. It covers such topics as parliament and anti-corruption legislation, effective financial scrutiny, parliament and supreme audit institutions, the role of the media in curbing corruption, and building parliamentary networks, among others.

It is my hope that *The Role of Parliament in Curbing Corruption* will offer useful insights for parliamentarians and parliamentary staff, development practitioners, students of development, and those interested in curbing corruption and improving governance in rich and poor countries alike—and in the process remove one the biggest barriers obstructing access by the poor to the opportunities they deserve.

Paul Wolfowitz
President
The World Bank Group

1

Introduction: Parliamentarians Fighting Corruption

Rick Stapenhurst, Martin Ulrich, and Severin Strohal

Parliamentarians from around the world met in the Chamber of the Canadian House of Commons October 13–16, 2002, and formed the Global Organization of Parliamentarians Against Corruption (GOPAC). At this meeting, corruption was identified as the greatest threat to the democratic ideal of self-government, endangering representative institutions selected in free elections by a broadly enfranchised people. Corruption was not only seen as a threat to democracy but also perceived to undermine economic development, violate social justice, and destroy trust in state institutions. In addition, if most commentators were right, corruption is getting worse in many countries and becoming an increasingly widespread phenomenon.

Citizens bear the heavy economic and social costs of corruption. In a democracy that works, they look to their parliament—the people they select to set the framework of law and oversee its implementation—for help. This does not imply that corruption is caused by a weak parliament or parliamentary inaction; rather, because the causes of corruption are many and complex, it suggests that parliament plays an essential leadership role in combating corruption. Especially in systems in which the executive is not directly elected, parliament becomes the most direct instrument citizens have to influence the executive, the locus of most state corruption.

To date, most efforts to curb corruption focus on the executive and judicial branches of government. This chapter will, after an initial introduction to the topic, outline how anti-corruption policies should be extended to

- include each of the core governance responsibilities of parliament (legislation, oversight, and representation),
- address issues related to party-political financing and parliamentary ethics, and
- strengthen international parliamentary networks fighting corruption.

Setting the Context

Before this chapter proceeds to describe the roles of the legislature in curbing corruption, it will be necessary to grasp the context in which it flourishes and the broader anti-corruption policies in which the parliament's work should be set.

1

Defined by the World Bank (1997, 17) and Transparency International (TI) as "abuse of public power for private benefits," corruption is a global phenomenon.[1] Daniel Kaufmann and Phyllis Dininio in chapter 2 provide an initial overview of the origins, typology, and costs of corruption. Rooted in the weakness of public institutions and exacerbated by poverty, corruption is the exploitation by public officials of their power in delivering public goods for private payoffs (Heidenheimer and Johnston 2002; Coolidge and Rose-Ackerman 1997; Klitgaard 1988). On the demand side, businesses, households, and private individuals engage in corruption to obtain access and advancements in markets, goods, and services that are otherwise unavailable or scarce (Johnston 1986). The phenomenon itself can take a variety of forms, ranging from grand to administrative corruption, from bribery to embezzlement, and from fraud to petty corruption. Corruption thrives in an environment where public servants have little regular incentives (low or irregular payment of salaries [or both], no health insurance, and so forth) and work within weak accountability structures. Chapter 2 and Daniel Lederman, Norman Loayza, and Rodrigo R. Soares in chapter 3 identify numerous other factors that increase the probability of corruption, such as the following:

- Missing mechanisms to ensure government accountability and transparency (that is, oversight bodies, active opposition parties, independent media, free and fair elections)
- Weak law enforcement structures (such as an effective prosecution, specialized anti-corruption agencies, and an independent and well-resourced judiciary)
- Missing regulatory frameworks (legislation, codes of conduct, and audit requirements)
- Low levels of education and literacy
- An unprofessional civil service (exposure to nepotism and patronage)
- Lack of private sector competition in service provision

These factors are interrelated and lead to a vicious circle of bad governance, corruption, and poverty.

At the same time, the factors noted in chapters 2 and 3 also outline some of the priority areas for anti-corruption policies. Extensive and broad in application, they should seek to increase the openness, accountability, and transparency of government. After a careful study of the specific country context, such efforts might include the reform of the public sector, require greater participation of civil society in policy making, lead to increased competitiveness in the provision of goods and services, and necessitate the strengthening of institutionalized watchdogs.

However, it is rare that any such anti-corruption efforts will be successful if they are not backed by political will. In chapter 4, Sahr Kpundeh and Phyllis Dininio identify six indicators of such commitment, including the home-grown nature of the initiative, the level of public participation in the reform process, and the amount of resources dedicated to the effort. Even if political will can actually be mobilized to translate anti-corruption rhetoric into action, such commitment often unravels in the face of numerous obstacles. Legislators, for example, encounter many opportunities to engage in corruption either to ensure their reelection (vote buying, illicit

---

[1] See Transparency International's reports on the state of corruption in different areas of the world at www.transparency.org.

party financing) or to obtain private financial gain from their work (some committees, such as the appropriations committee, may be particularly prone to kickbacks). Kpundeh and Dininio conclude that broad-based coalitions and specialized and well-resourced institutions are necessary to bolster the legislature's resolve, exercise pressure, and sustain the political will of the country's leadership in curbing corruption. It therefore becomes clear that anti-corruption policies and reforms are successful only if they follow a holistic approach, address each of the root causes, and encompass a broad coalition of relevant actors, including government bodies, parliament, civil society, and the private sector).

Facing the extensive origins of corruption, as well as the complexity of anti-corruption measures, parliaments will have to fully exploit their constitutionally provided roles and tools and live up to their responsibilities to enact and oversee effective national anti-corruption efforts.

Legislative Role

Of the core roles of parliament, it is likely that the legislative role is the best understood and most similar among countries. Parliaments, constrained only by their constitutions, have the authority to enact any laws they wish and can therefore create the necessary legal framework to prevent and curb corruption. They can enact laws to address what they consider inappropriate behavior by citizens, businesses, and other organizations, and they can provide for surveillance and penalties. In addition, parliaments can focus on bolstering integrity in governance—a broader perspective than fighting corruption—by establishing not only incentives to encourage appropriate private sector behavior but also regimes for financial and public service management, transparency, and accountability in the government sector. Thus, to the extent that better laws would solve the problem of corruption, parliaments—if they reflect well the interests of the citizens and are not captured by other forces—can be part of the solution. Yet Fred Matiangi provides (see his case study on the role of parliament in curbing corruption in Kenya, which is an annex to chapter 5) an illustration of many of the difficulties that parliaments face when they enact legislation.

However, while appropriate laws may be a necessary component in a country's arsenal of policies and interventions to curb corruption, they are never sufficient. If they were, corruption could be easily eradicated. As Jeremy Pope points out in chapter 5, it rarely is a lack of anti-corruption legislation that impedes such efforts; rather, it is often the weak qualitative formulation and the lack of implementation of such laws that need special attention. Legislation must follow a key set of principles—such as compliance with human rights standards—in clear language, minimizing areas of discretion and adapted to the local circumstances. In civil as well as criminal law, parliaments should address some particularly relevant issues—such as conflicts of interest, nepotism, and statutes of limitation—not only to provide for the necessary punitive measures but also to promote an administrative and social environment adverse to corruption.

However, depending on how laws are enacted and the credibility of the electoral process, the laws might be seen as more or less legitimate. Moreover, an appropriate legislative base might not be enacted if the public and parliamentarians are unaware of the costs and benefits of doing so. In addition, the government might well be able to put pressure on parliament—or on a sufficient number of parliamentarians—to impede the enactment of certain legislation. Finally, parliament will have to oversee the implementation of the legislation by the executive.

Oversight

Parliaments can also curb corruption by fulfilling another key responsibility: holding the government accountable. This can be achieved through effective participation in the budgetary process, the exercise of parliamentary oversight through anti-corruption commissions, cooperation with supreme audit institutions, and promoting a media-friendly environment.

Financial Control

Because financial integrity is central to anti-corruption efforts, it is helpful to devote direct attention to parliament's role in the budget cycle. The budget cycle, which involves the government, public service, civil society, and the legislature, comprises four stages: drafting, legislation, implementation, and audit (see Joachim Wehner's study in chapter 6). In most countries, the ultimate control over the national budget rests with parliament, which may delegate responsibility to government for budget formulation. This "power of the purse" constrains governments to tax and spend in only specific ways and seeks to ensure disciplined management of funds, disciplined reporting, and transparency. It is one of the most powerful parliamentary tools for holding governments to account. It also provides a means for parliamentarians to be heard on how (and how much) money is to be obtained and spent. Once the budget has been allocated, the parliament—and its specialized committees (such as the public accounts committee)—considers the audit findings provided by supreme audit institutions and provides recommendations for the next budget. To ensure transparency and accountability, such a budget cycle must fulfill three conditions. First, there must be a disciplined and transparent assignment of authority for the disbursal of funds granted by parliament. Second, there should be a requirement for clear standards of expenditure measurement, their application, and the results associated with those expenditures—all in relation to the authorities granted and the commitments made when the authorities were granted. Third, there should be publicly accessible controls. Such a regime of parliamentary financial control is a key part of integrity in governance.

These powers are important, but even in mature democracies, parliamentarians lament their loss of influence in financial and budgetary matters. Their power varies, depending not only on the constitutional provisions regarding its role but also on a number of other factors. Typically, an enormous amount of money is being processed, the expertise and detailed information on its application and use rest within the executive, extremely complex financial instruments are applied, and pressures to employ shortcuts to respond to crises are compelling. In addition, in some countries, finances are so stressed that financial management is reduced to cash flow management. Apart from issues of sufficient material and human resource, there is the question of the timing of the budget. It should be tabled sufficiently in advance of the fiscal year to allow for effective scrutiny and analysis. Another variable is the access to information, which is crucial for parliament to exercise its financial control function, because only accurate, reliable, and timely information can guarantee a proper analysis and evaluation of proposals. Political dynamics and power relationships between the executive and the legislative and between government and the opposition constitute a final important variable. For all these reasons (many of which are examined more closely by Joachim Wehner in chapter 6), parliamentarians struggle to understand the application and use of public resources, to influence their use, and to communicate financial matters and any concerns to their constituents.

This leads directly to other oversight practices employed by parliament, including the work of parliamentary agents (such as auditors and ombudsmen), mandatory executive reporting on certain operations and performance, or the direct authority to question ministers publicly on the operations of their departments. This also includes the authority to review departmental and program performance (usually by parliamentary committees) by calling for witnesses and documents, and doing all of this in a transparent fashion in cooperation with outside bodies. Also, in some countries, parliaments have the authority to review and approve appointments of certain public officials. These practices vary considerably and take various institutional forms, even among jurisdictions with apparently similar oversight structures. Two oversight tools are of particular interest here: supreme audit institutions and anti-corruption commissions.

Specialized Agencies

As the complexity of government has grown, complicated by globalization on one side and devolution and decentralization of power on the other, and as the range of financial instruments used in public finance has expanded, the need for professional expertise and resources has led to the creation of specialized parliamentary investigation and accountability agencies in many countries. The best-known of these agencies are supreme audit institutions (SAIs). The role of SAIs and their relation to parliamentary oversight committees are studied by Rick Stapenhurst and Jack Titsworth in chapter 7. Although their mandates vary considerably, particularly among the differing governance systems, SAIs can help to deter waste and corruption by attesting to the financial accuracy of the data provided by the government; checking whether the executive's spending has complied with applicable provisions, laws, and regulations; and reviewing the government's performance (that is, whether it has delivered public services in an effective manner). To be effective, an SAI should feature a clear mandate, be independent, continuously update its expertise, and be allowed to report its results to specialized parliamentary committees such as the public accounts committee—which should then consider making recommendations to parliament for enactment. In addition, the need for specialist supporting organizations that are adequately resourced and independent of the executive is growing.

There has been a lot of debate surrounding the role and efficiency of anti-corruption commissions, another institution helping parliament to control corruption. Explaining and analyzing different types of commissions in chapter 9, John R. Heilbrunn points out the necessary prerequisites for such commissions to be successful. Indeed, sometimes created as hollow constructs, their sole purpose can be to delay meaningful legal reforms and satisfy the call for reforms from international donors. To ensure their effectiveness, they should be the result of a broad-based appeal by constituents. Moreover, to work successfully, anti-corruption commissions must be independent, part of a broader anti-corruption strategy, embedded in a reporting hierarchy encompassing the legislative and executive, and have the government enact its recommendations.

Public Questioning and Media Involvement

As the fourth estate, an independent and attentive media can to a great extent support these parliamentary oversight efforts. Indeed, as Rod Macdonell and Milica Pesic discuss in chapter 8, the media owe it to themselves and to society to participate in the fight against corruption and often do so effectively. Parliament can follow up on public exposure of corrupt officials, the prompting of investigations, and the exhibition of commercial wrongdoing by the media. While ministers may be obligated to respond, they do not always answer the questions posed by parliament. Nonetheless, where there are independent media, such behavior attracts public attention and thereby reinforces parliamentary oversight. At the same time, parliament has a key role to play in ensuring a free and vibrant media to permit such oversight. Chapter 6 lists and explains several ways for parliament to do so: it can promote a diverse media landscape, ensure the protection of journalists, push for free access to information, support media accountability, and so forth. An excellent example of such fruitful cooperation occurred during the aftermath of the war in the 1990s in Uganda (see the case study by John Smith). The collaboration between an active and representative parliament and a free and independent media, able to challenge the government and provide coverage of corruption scandals, allowed MPs to tackle several high profile cases of fraud.

Together, these four approaches to oversight—financial control, specialized agencies, public questioning, and media involvement—can be a powerful antidote to corruption. They are more effective to the degree that they have professional staff support and independent media to ensure that the public is well informed as to what is occurring—ultimately under their "authority." However, where parliament itself is dominated by a corrupt executive or lacks representative legitimacy, these theoretical oversight powers might well not exist in practice. Thus, as with legislative power, they are only part of the parliamentary toolbox for curbing corruption.

Representation

Representation is a combination of public deliberation and consensus building within parliament, as well as the engagement of citizens on matters of public policy. Although it is perhaps less tangible than the other parliamentary roles, representation is an important parliamentary instrument for building integrity in public governance. It occurs through a number of different channels, such as the participation of civil society or the formation of political parties, and can have the effect of empowering citizens to reject corrupt practices and expose politicians and officials who engage in corrupt activity. In this way, parliamentarians can help establish public standards for appropriate behavior.

In the most direct sense, parliamentarians, as representatives of the people, are mandated to represent the wishes and concerns of their constituents. Especially in many developing countries, it is likely that a large number of these constituents will be poor. However, because corruption threatens and affects the poor in the worst way, parliamentarians, as their representatives, must prevent it. It falls to them to travel back regularly to their home regions to organize forums of discussions, listen to their constituents, understand the causes and effects of corruption, include this information and awareness in the formulation of anti-corruption policies, and monitor their impact. However, parliamentary practices and support services, regardless of party affiliation, might affect the capacity of individual parliamentarians to pursue a public leadership role in fighting corruption. Where public resources are provided to individual Members to maintain an office in their districts and funds for travel to retain regular face-to-face contact, this aspect of representation is likely to be more effective. Such constituency services are crucial for parliamentarians to retain the necessary legitimacy and public endorsement to pursue their policies.

From this primary aspect of representation flows a secondary—but not less important—one. Just as much as a diverse media landscape can support the parliament in its oversight role, broad coalitions between parliament and a vibrant civil society can be helpful in curbing corruption. As Michael Johnston points out in chapter 10, parliament can help to channel the interests and concerns of civil society into an open debate, the passing of legislation, and the creation of political will to fight corruption. Again, this will allow the parliament to gain credibility and legitimacy in the eyes of the population, thereby deepening its roots and extending the social basis supporting the anti-corruption efforts. Such coalitions require a number of conditions to develop: the mobilization of the main stakeholders suffering from corruption, autonomy from the ruling power, and a mix of incentives; yet they might be effective by creating synergies through pooling resources, the strengthening of political will, and the increased flow of information.

Legislators are often members of another representative political institution: political parties. Indeed, parties, usually based on mass membership, aggregate a diverse set of interests and mold them into a distinctive political and electoral platform that Members of Parliament will then seek to translate into policies. Increasingly, in countries plagued by fraud and economic mismanagement, anti-corruption is becoming a concern for political parties; however, as will be mentioned below, they often take part in corruption themselves. Riccardo Pelizzo argues in chapter 11 that it is only when political parties are strongly institutionalized that they will be able to effectively and credibly translate their anti-corruption platform into policies. This involves, among other measures, an increased outreach to the public, the training and education of party officials, and more democratic procedures for the selection of candidates and leaders.

As complex as the phenomenon of corruption is itself, so is the role of parliament in anti-corruption efforts. It is only by taking leadership and effectively making anti-corruption part of its legislative, oversight, and representative responsibilities that such policies stand a chance of bearing fruit.

Corruption in Political Parties and Parliament

Little can be achieved by legislators on a national level if they do not first confront the specter of corruption within their ranks. Two particular sets of issues come to mind: political party financing and codes of conduct for parliamentarians.

As the strength of political parties has increased over time, they have become a locus of administrative power and therefore a potential agent of corruption, particularly where their accountability to their members and the entire electorate is weak. Riccardo Pelizzo illustrates this point in chapter 11, showing how the weak institutionalization of political parties in many developing countries increases the temptation to quell financial needs by illegal means. This problem is particularly acute during the electoral competition of political parties for power, leading to a race for financial resources, engendering the problem of party political funding, examined by Michael Pinto-Duschinsky in chapter 12. Corruption scandals in campaign financing, often implicating the parliamentarians themselves, abound and can take a multitude of forms such as vote buying, contributions from criminal sources, illegal use of state sources, and so forth. In many countries, this problem is compounded by traditions of patron-client relationships. The attitude of the electorate then becomes another issue: although they might be condemning corruption in general, they might still sell their votes. Also, in some cases, candidates for office believe that they have no other choice but to engage in illicit fund raising if they must pay for campaigning without public subsidies (Bryan and Baer 2005). Although the problem might never be completely solved, it is up to the legislators to formulate laws regulating campaign finances, including regulations on the disclosure of interests, spending and contribution limits, and the provision of public subsidies. It is also up to parliamentarians to pressurize the government to enforce such laws, establish ethics committees to monitor the political campaigns, and so forth.

The legitimacy of democracy does not only depend on the integrity of political parties. Parliamentarians themselves must adhere to strictly ethical behavior. Rick Stapenhurst and Riccardo Pelizzo give a detailed overview of the origins, nature, and conditions for effective implementation of ethical regimes in chapter 13. Covering everything from conflicts of interest and the disclosure of assets to rules on postgovernmental employment and nepotism, codes of conduct and codes of ethics perform two functions: internally, they improve the behavior of legislators; externally, they restore the often-shattered public confidence in parliamentarians. To be effective, such codes must be accompanied by enforcement mechanisms and be based on a shared understanding by parliamentarians of what is appropriate behavior and what is not, because otherwise they amount to little else then empty promises. A practical insight into the development and application of codes of conduct is provided with Sir Philip Mawer's case study of the House of Commons' Parliamentary Codes of Conduct and Registers of Members' Interests in the United Kingdom. One of the key aspects of this code is the open and publicly accessible disclosure of the assets of Members of Parliament (MPs), which provide the population with the knowledge of the interests that might affect the MP's decision making. Another important element is the relatively effective means of enforcement. Although ethical problems still do occur, it seems that this code has managed to restore public confidence in the parliamentary system in many ways.

International Parliamentary Links

So far, this chapter has considered corruption as a national phenomenon. However, it clearly does not stop at national borders; on the contrary, because it is of global reach and shares many common traits around the world, parliamentary representation and cooperation at a regional or global level can support the legislators' efforts to fight corruption.

The creation of networks between parliamentarians has proved to be a very valuable tool to this end. They allow the bundling of advocacy efforts, the development of a community of practitioners to share experiences and best practices, as well as strong peer-support mechanisms. John Williams looks at the evolution and functions of two of these in chapter 14: the Global Organization of Parliamentarians Against Corruption (GOPAC) and the Parliamentary Network on the World Bank (PNoWB). On one hand, GOPAC is an example of a single-purpose network, aiming to combat and prevent corruption through the strengthening of integrity in governance. It does so by providing its membership with a platform to exchange information, relevant training, and crucial peer-support mechanisms. Founded in 2002, it has already achieved considerable results and developed a number of regional and national chapters around the world. PNoWB, on the other hand, was created to strengthen parliamentary involvement and say in development issues. Through a diverse range of activities, it seeks to increase transparency, accountability, and parliamentary participation in international development. This chapter also highlights that to be successful, these and other parliamentary networks aim to stick to some guiding principles such as maintaining a minimum of continuity, a strong focus, a committed leadership, and access to appropriate expertise.

In a similar way, parliamentarians can curb corruption through their role in the global governance system. Many international organizations have developed parliamentary forums, such as the European Parliament (in the case of the European Union) or the Commonwealth Parliamentary Association (in the case of the Commonwealth). Although their power varies to a great degree, each can make an important contribution by adding anti-corruption efforts to its agenda. In appendix 1, Kimmo Kiljunen provides a broader look at the importance of parliamentary assemblies in international organizations. He argues that if citizens are to regain confidence in the ability of their governments to effectively manage globalization, the transparency, openness, and accountability of international organizations must be increased through specialized international legislative committees and greater involvement of parliaments in guiding the work of their governments in international affairs. (The reports of these conferences, prepared by Nicholas Hopkinson [Deputy Director at Wilton Park] and Riccardo Pelizzo, are presented in appendix 2.)

Conclusion

Corruption has a disastrous impact on economic growth and development and is a symptom of the weakness of economic, social, and political institutions. Parliamentarians have therefore a responsibility to curb it. Although governance structures (for example, parliamentary or congressional forms of government) do influence how parliamentarians can best fight corruption, they are not the key determinants. Public expectations regarding the role of the state and particular histories of political development in each country are also influential factors in actual corruption. The challenge is tailoring the individual instruments and packaging them into a coherent strategy in specific countries. Doing so requires a thorough understanding of the individual circumstances, as well as the practical lessons learned from other jurisdictions.[2]

---

[2] GOPAC, supported by the World Bank Institute, is updating Controlling Corruption: A Parliamentarian's Handbook.

Although corruption is fortunately now getting public attention in many areas of the world and a consensus is emerging that parliament, in addition to the executive and the judiciary, must play its role vigorously to successfully combat corruption, not enough attention has yet been paid to this role. However, as this introduction has shown, parliaments have an extensive array of tools at their disposal, ranging from their legislative to their oversight powers, from engaging in powerful coalitions with civil society to cooperating on an international level. The following chapters will seek to illustrate the importance of credible parliamentary engagement to effectively fight corruption.

Bibliography

Bryan, Shary, and Denise Baer, eds. 2005. *Money in Politics*. Washington, DC: NDI.

Coolidge, Jacqueline, and Susan Rose-Ackerman. 1988. "High-Level Rent Seeking and Corruption in African Regimes." Policy Working Paper 1780, 20–45, World Bank, Washington, DC.

Heidenheimer, Arnold, and Michael Johnston, eds. 2002. *Political Corruption: Readings in Comparative Analysis*. New Brunswick, NJ: Transaction Books.

Johnston, Michael. 1986. "The Political Consequences of Corruption: A Reassessment." Comparative Politics 18 (4): 467–80.

Klitgaard, Robert. 1988. *Controlling Corruption*. Berkeley: University of California Press.

World Bank. 1997. *Helping Countries Combat Corruption: The Role of the World Bank*. Washington, DC: World Bank.

Part I
Governance
in the Developing World

2

Corruption: A Key Challenge for Development

Daniel Kaufmann and Phyllis Dininio

Introduction

Not so long ago, corruption remained an issue on the fringe of international development. Development practitioners and leaders from developing countries avoided the issue because it was considered a matter of a country's internal politics and not an impediment to development. Some academics even made the claim that corruption facilitated development by greasing the wheels of a rigid administration (Huntington 1968; Neff 1964).[1] The "Washington Consensus" (or development paradigm) of the early 1990s made no mention of corruption control or governance in its list of 10 key reforms. To the extent that it was considered, the paradigm suggested that corruption control was a by-product of development (Naím 1994; Kuczynski and Williamson 2003).

The 1996 Annual Meetings of the International Monetary Fund (IMF) and the World Bank, however, marked a turning point in the development community's approach to corruption. On that occasion, the President of the World Bank placed the corruption issue center stage as a key challenge for development (Wolfensohn 2005). This speech prompted the launch or expansion of anti-corruption initiatives by the World Bank and other development agencies, complementing the work of the nongovernmental organization (NGO) in the anti-corruption arena, Transparency International (TI).

At the same time, new empirical research reshaped some of the thinking about corruption. New data refuted the corruption-as-grease claim and, instead, showed how corruption engenders more distortions and intrusions in the economy as public officials look for more ways to extract corrupt payments (World Bank 1997, 103; Kaufmann 1997). Moreover, this research showed little evidence of higher incomes in a country leading to better governance. By contrast, the data suggest a strong causal effect running from control of corruption to higher income levels (Mauro

---

[1] In his seminal work on modernization, Huntington made the well-known claim: "In terms of economic growth, the only thing worse than a society with a rigid, overcentralized, dishonest bureaucracy is one with a rigid, overcentralized, honest bureaucracy. A society which is relatively uncorrupt . . . may find a certain amount of corruption a welcome lubricant easing the path to modernization."

1997) and to such development outcomes as lower infant mortality rates and higher rates of literacy (Kaufmann 2000). This body of work challenges the notion that governance is a "luxury good" that automatically accrues with wealth accumulation—an assertion often used as a justification for complacency. Instead, the research affirms that concerted efforts to improve governance and address corruption are required even during periods of robust growth.

Until recently, many of the efforts to fight corruption have centered on public sector and judicial reform. The somewhat thornier challenge of addressing imbalances of power in the polity and economy is only now receiving more attention. Practitioners today acknowledge that increasing political and economic competition may be a necessary, if insufficient, element of addressing grand corruption. In this regard, legislators can play a pivotal role. Legislators can use their legislative, financial, oversight, and representative powers to foster political and economic competition and curb corruption. As the other chapters in this volume make clear, legislators can also use their powers to advance the more traditional objective of strengthening their country's accountability framework.

Costs of Corruption

The emerging research on corruption has affirmed its significant negative impact on economic growth. Mauro's examination of more than 100 countries offered a quantitative estimate of this effect. He found that if a given country were to improve its corruption score by 2.38 points on a 10-point scale, its annual per capita gross domestic product (GDP) growth would rise by more than half a percentage point (Mauro 1997, 91).

Corruption can weaken economic growth through many channels. Unsound policies, unpredictable processes, and distorted public expenditures resulting from vested interests lead to macroeconomic instability, weakened property rights, reduced competition, inefficient allocation of resources, deteriorated physical infrastructure, and smaller expenditures on education (Hellman, Jones, and Kaufmann 2000; Tanzi and Davoodi 1997; Mauro 1997). For business, corruption increases risks and uncertainty, entails payments that represent a kind of tax, and requires more management time spent negotiating with public officials. As a result, it dampens investment (Mauro 1997; Wei 1998) and pushes firms into the unofficial economy (Friedman et al. 2000; Johnson et al. 2000). Where rent seeking provides more lucrative opportunities than productive work does, the allocation of talent within the economy also deteriorates (Murphy, Shleifer, and Vishny 1991).

The economic costs of corruption fall disproportionately on the poor. As highlighted by the work of Hernando de Soto (2000), administrative barriers and weak property rights make it difficult for the poor to escape from poverty through small-scale entrepreneurial activity. Bribes demanded by public officials also represent a regressive tax because they constitute a greater share of small firms' income than that of larger firms. Moreover, corruption undermines the delivery of public services such as health care and education on which the poor depend. Low government revenues, a diversion of public spending to areas that profit the elite (like large defense contracts), and leakage of funds and supplies in health and education systems contribute to deteriorating services. Where officials demand bribes for service, the poor may not even have access to such low-quality services.

Table 2.1 How Corruption Contributes to Poverty

Causes of poverty	How corruption contributes to problem
Lower investment and growth	Unsound economic policies
	Unpredictable processes
	Distorted public expenditures
	Extra payments, uncertainty, and negotiating time for business
	Misallocation of talent
Poor have smaller share in growth	Administrative barriers and weak property rights pose larger problem for poor
	Regressive bribery "tax" on small firms
Poor lack good health care and education	Shortage of government revenues
	Diversion of investment away from health care and education
	Leakage in the delivery of services
	Poor least able to afford bribes for service
Poor lack means of redress	Weak and uneven rule of law
	Elites able to influence judicial decisions

Source: Authors' research.

In addition to creating these disadvantages for the poor, corruption also denies the poor an effective means of redress. Where the rule of law is weak, the poor cannot depend on the judicial system to uphold their rights or the contracts into which they have entered. In particular, the poor are unlikely to prevail against the elite where money and power influence judicial decisions.

These economic, social, and political distortions increase inequity and worsen outcomes for the poor. (Table 2.1 shows the immediate causes of poverty in the first column and the different channels through which corruption contributes to the problem in the second column.)

Corruption has devastating effects on other aspects of society, too. Corruption jeopardizes efforts to protect the environment as payoffs derail the formulation or implementation of effective policies. In politics, corruption undermines the legitimacy of political leaders and leads to the public's disaffection with the regime. In addition, corruption facilitates trafficking, money laundering, and organized crime. Corruption not only contributes to weak economies, inequality, environmental damage, illegitimate leaders, and organized crime, it also increases social polarization and, in extreme cases, can trigger social and political upheaval.

Unbundling Corruption

The foregoing discussion lays out the costs of corruption in its many manifestations, but a more nuanced approach to addressing it must unbundle corruption into its distinctive forms. While the typologies vary, academics and development organizations undertake such an exercise to distinguish among the impact of—and responses to—different kinds of corruption. Johnston (1986), for example, distinguishes between corruption with high and low stakes and corruption with many and few suppliers, noting that the most unstable and disintegrative kind of corruption occurs where the stakes are high and the suppliers are many, such as in Mexico during the oil boom. Offering a different typology with reference to post-Communist countries, Karklins (2002) distinguishes between low-level administrative corruption, self-serving asset stripping by officials, and state capture by corrupt networks, noting that the political consequences are most severe where corruption is institutionalized in collusive networks (most often in connection with state capture).

In a similar vein, the U.S. Agency for International Development (USAID) and the World Bank distinguish between administrative corruption and grand corruption. "Administrative corruption" refers to distortions in *implementation* of laws, policies, and regulations, and "grand corruption" refers to distortions in their *formulation*. While earlier work on corruption tended to focus on the more visible administrative corruption, new survey methodologies have facilitated a focus on grand corruption and suggested its more substantial socioeconomic costs. The Executive Opinion Survey (carried out annually by the World Economic Forum) of firms from 102 countries shows, for example, that firms in all regions consider bribery to influence laws a greater constraint to their business than administrative bribery (Kaufmann 2005).

State capture by powerful conglomerates represents a particularly distorting kind of grand corruption that challenges traditional approaches to governance. Clearly, state capture challenges the notion that government provides a business climate to a passive enterprise sector (including some multinational corporations). The reality turns out to be more complex, with powerful elites and conglomerates playing an important role in shaping the rules of the game for business. As a result, state capture requires rethinking the traditional advice of controlling corruption as if it were solely a problem within the bureaucracy. Instead, reforms must address the broader political and economic imbalances in society that facilitate state capture by fostering both political and economic competition.

Causes of Corruption

At its root, corruption flourishes in conditions of poverty and weak public institutions. Bad incentives and systems, rather than bad ethics, induce people to act corruptly. That is why corruption tends to be more prevalent in developing and transition countries.

Poverty creates perverse incentives for public officials, businesspeople, and households. For public officials, the motivation to extract corrupt payments is high because they receive low and sometimes irregular salaries and face significant risks of illness, accidents, and unemployment.[2] For businesspeople, the motivation to pursue wealth through corruption is high because scarce capital, poorly skilled workers, a low demand for consumer goods, and other conditions decrease the prospects for advancement in the market (Johnston 1993, 198). For households, the motivation to pay a bribe is high where goods and services (such as medicine) are scarce and otherwise may not be available.

More generally, poverty weakens the mechanisms for securing government accountability. Poverty keeps people focused on survival and limits their time

---

[2] During many transitions from Communism, for example, budget shortfalls meant that public sector workers were not paid for months at a time, which made bureaucrats more vulnerable to corruption (World Bank 2000, 29).

and energy to hold leaders to account. Low levels of development also reduce education and literacy, which limits the ability of citizens to serve as watchdogs over officials' activities (Treisman 2000, 404). Within the government, low levels of development also reduce the resources to implement and maintain monitoring and oversight mechanisms (World Bank 2000, 20). Research suggests that economic development explains more of the variation in corruption levels across countries than any other variable: in Triesman's cross-country study, for example, per capita income explained between half to three-quarters of the variation in perceived corruption indexes, depending on which set of indexes he used (Treisman 2000, 429).

An inadequate framework for government accountability can also facilitate corruption. A lack of transparency, inadequate oversight, weak enforcement, and ineffective electoral systems reduce the likelihood of exposure and censure for wrongdoing and push the cost-benefit calculus in favor of corruption. Mechanisms of accountability operate to greater or lesser effect across different branches and units of government. Such mechanisms of horizontal accountability include anti-corruption legislation, ethics codes, internal reporting and whistle-blowing, audit requirements, investigative bodies, prosecutors, the judiciary, law enforcement, and legislative oversight. Evidence from a private sector survey finds, for example, that reported levels of corruption are higher where judicial predictability is weak (World Bank 1997, 104). On the other hand, mechanisms of accountability can also operate between government and the public. Such mechanisms of vertical accountability include free and fair elections, competitive political party funding, freedom of information, a free and independent media, and freedom of assembly and speech. As shown in figure 2.1, increasing evidence points to the importance of civil liberties in effectively addressing corruption.

Figure 2.1 *Corruption Is Associated with Absence of Civil Liberties*

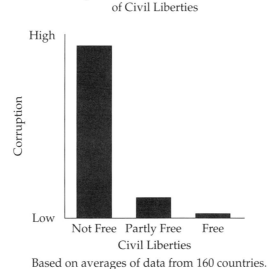

Corruption is Associated with Absence of Civil Liberties

Based on averages of data from 160 countries.

Source: Authors' research.

Alongside a weak accountability framework, an unprofessional civil service can facilitate corruption. Abuses of patronage, nepotism, and favoritism orient employees toward exchanges of personal favors and compliance with patrons' wishes rather than toward impartial and efficient performance of their jobs. In extreme cases, employees do not have an incentive to perform their official duties, but actually pay for their jobs with the understanding that they will make money through bribes. The strongest antidote to this problem is meritocracy in hiring, promoting, and firing civil servants, and government surveys confirm that meritocracy has a strong association with corruption control (World Bank 1997, 104). By contrast, the evidence on civil service pay is often ambiguous. The difference between public and private salaries may represent a "rate of temptation" and have a positive association with corruption, but simply raising public sector salaries may not reduce corruption. Instead, complementary reforms, such as improved accountability, must accompany pay reform to have any effect on corruption.

Another institutional weakness that facilitates corruption is a state's intrusive stance in the economy. Policies that create an artificial gap between demand and supply or that increase public officials' discretion create opportunities for corruption. Such policies include a high degree of state ownership and service provision, excessive business regulation and taxes, arbitrary application of regulations, and trade restrictions. In this context, officials can profit from their office through such corrupt acts as bribes, extortion, asset stripping, and selling jobs. Data confirm that corruption is more prevalent in countries with highly distorted policies (World Bank 1997, 104).

Related to this, an uncompetitive private sector can also fuel corruption. In some transition and developing countries, for example, a source of grand corruption is the concentration of economic power in monopolies that then wield political influence on the government for private benefits. The problem is particularly acute in natural-resource–rich countries, where private monopolies in oil and gas, for example, wield considerable economic and political power that leads to different forms of corruption: nonpayment of taxes, offshore accounts, purchasing licenses and permits, and purchasing votes and decrees that restrict entry and competition. The way to address this kind of corruption is to demonopolize, deregulate, and facilitate competition. Two initiatives are worthy of note: (a) the special committee in Chad that aims to provide citizen accountability checks on resource revenue and (b) the Extractive Industries Transparency Initiative, championed by British Prime Minister Tony Blair.

A Multifaceted Anti-Corruption Strategy

Fighting corruption requires tackling these underlying causes. Especially where corruption is widespread, fighting corruption through investigations and enforcement on a case-by-case basis is not enough. The effort also must reduce opportunities for corruption, increase competition in the economy, strengthen political accountability, increase civil society participation, and improve incentives for good performance. These reforms target the relationships among core state institutions, the interactions between the state and firms, the relationship between the state and civil society, the political system, and public administration. Box 2.1 and figure 2.2 illustrate the comprehensive set of reforms that aim to control corruption.[3]

---

[3] This figure and the following discussion of each block of reforms are adapted from World Bank (2000) and the World Bank's Public Sector Web site, http://www1.worldbank.org/publicsector/anticorrupt/index.cfm.

Box 2.1 *A Multifaceted Anti-Corruption Strategy*

Institutional Restraints
Corruption can be stemmed through institutional restraints. Through the separation and independence of the three branches of power, "horizontal accountability" creates a system of checks and balances within the government itself. Strengthening the judiciary's institutional capacity is essential to curbing corruption because law enforcement officials are often under the sway of powerful interest groups, which means that they are unable to enforce the existing laws. Thus, through capacity building and oversight, an independent judiciary but also the legislative branches can ensure that the executive does not abuse its power and that it is punished if and when it does. The executive branch can also exercise oversight through the agency of institutions such as the Offices of the Ombudsman or anti-corruption agencies.

Political Accountability
A multipronged approach to corruption would not be complete without a measure of political or "vertical" accountability. This form of accountability ensures that the power of public officials is circumscribed by a series of checks and balances (for example, asset declarations and conflict-of-interest rules) implemented by parties outside the government. In this context, free and fair elections (accompanied by transparent party financing) can also be a mechanism of public accountability. It follows that freedom of information and (by extension) free media are indispensable if the electorate is to make informed choices. The media can also keep the government in check through investigative journalism.

Civil Society Participation
Through advocacy, awareness raising, and monitoring of government activities (including draft legislation), civil society organizations (CSOs) have an important role to play in curbing corruption. Furthermore, CSOs, by working in concert with public officials, can encourage the mobilization of resources and protect their members from reprisals. Their effectiveness is therefore contingent on a permissive legal environment and the receptivity of public officials.

Public Sector Management and Competitive Private Sector
Corruption can also be curbed via public and private sector reforms. The former reforms include creating a meritocratic civil service, encouraging sound financial management and revenue collection, restructuring service delivery, and decentralization. Private sector reforms (that is, liberalization, deregulation, and simplification of rules, as well as privatization and restructuring of monopolies) would also significantly reduce the opportunities for corruption.

How to combine and sequence these reforms to achieve the greatest impact on corruption is a particularly daunting challenge. There is no blueprint to follow because corruption reform must respond to each country-specific reality. For instance, a country that is subject to state capture by the corporate elite will require a strategy different from that of a country where the main source of corruption originates in the political structure or in the bureaucracy. Specific questions about corruption reforms, therefore, include which types of changes are feasible under which political conditions and how reforms should be prioritized within the political, civil society, and corporate realities of each country setting.

Institutional Restraints

Institutional restraints on power can be an important mechanism in checking corruption. This mechanism of "horizontal" accountability creates checks and balances

Figure 2.2 *Reforms for Improving Governance and Combating Corruption*

Institutional Restraints on Power
- Independent and effective judiciary
- Independent prosecution, enforcement
- Legislative oversight
- Supreme audit institution

Political Accountability
- Political competition
- Transparency in party financing
- Asset declarations, conflict-of-interest rules
- Freedom of information & the press
- Investigative journalism

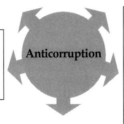

Anticorruption

Civil Society Participation
- Public hearings of draft laws
- Citizen oversight
- Role for NGOs

Competitive Private Sector
- Economic policy reform
- Competitive restructuring
  of monopolies
- Regulatory quality/simplification
- Transparency in corporate
  governance
- Collective business associations

Public Sector Management
- Meritocratic civil service with adequate pay
- Budget management (coverage, treasury, procurement, audit)
- Tax and customs
- Sectoral service delivery (health, education, energy)
- Decentralization with accountability

Source: Authors' research.

within the government by separating powers among state institutions. If given adequate independence, the judicial and legislative branches can restrain abuses of power by the executive branch and penalize abuses if they occur. Within the executive branch, separate institutions can also exercise oversight, such as the 57 Offices of Inspector General that operate within departments and agencies of the U.S. government, or the anti-corruption agencies or Offices of the Ombudsman that are common in other countries.

To varying degrees, many countries have adequate laws on the book, but are unable to effectively enforce them. Powerful politicians, elite interests, or oligarchs influence the operation of the judiciary and the police. The challenge in these countries is to promote independence of judicial and law enforcement institutions by revising procedures for appointing, assigning, remunerating, and removing judges and prosecutors. Strengthening the judiciary's institutional capacity is also important to promote swift and fair procedures and eliminate opportunities for courts to extract bribes from litigants. Capacity building can include augmenting and upgrading staffs, improving legal training, revising laws, and strengthening investigative capabilities. Where corruption of the judiciary is endemic, however, innovative approaches may be needed, such as alternative dispute resolution mechanisms, more systematic involvement for NGOs, and dissemination strategies through the media.

The legislature represents another important mechanism of horizontal accountability. Legislatures can exercise oversight of the executive through public accounts and audit committees, require disclosure of government documents, and implement sanctions. To be effective, however, legislatures need political space to operate independently of the executive, including a role for opposition parties. At the same time, political systems must orient legislators to the concerns of their constituents, rather than to those of major donors. Rules promoting legislators' representative role would include public disclosure of all legislative votes, scaling back immunity laws for legislators, and political finance reform.

Supreme audit institutions serve as another mechanism of horizontal accountability. They can curb corruption by overseeing the management of public funds and the quality and credibility of governments' reported financial data. To work effectively, they must have independence from the executive branch in their mandate, staffing, budget, and program of activities. In some countries, supreme audit institutions are an integral part of the judiciary, while in others they are independent bodies that report to parliament. In either case, supreme audit institutions are a crucial part of detecting and preventing corruption because they promote transparency and accountability in government programs and actions.

Political Accountability

Political, or "vertical," accountability refers to the constraints placed on the behavior of public officials by organizations and constituencies with the power to apply sanctions on them. As political accountability increases, the costs to public officials of making decisions that benefit their private interests at the expense of the broader public interest also increase, thus working as a deterrent to corrupt practices.

Where they are free and fair, elections can serve as an effective mechanism of political accountability. To operate with this effect, elections should be run by nonpartisan agencies, and citizens should have the right to vote, run for public office, and form political parties. In addition, political parties should receive media coverage roughly proportional to their popular support and should disclose the sources and amounts of financing.

To make informed choices, however, the public needs adequate information; therefore, freedom of information is critical for political accountability. Such information should cover the accounts of governmental, private, and multinational institutions; budgetary priorities, assumptions, and drafts; senior officials' disclosure of income, assets, and potential conflicts of interest; and the voting records of legislators. Beyond the basic availability of information, other attributes of information help curb potential abuses. These include *comprehensiveness* (ensuring inclusion of key items, such as offline financial and budgetary items), *relevance* (avoiding superfluous information overload), *quality*, and *reliability.*

Linked to freedom of information, free media are critical to inform the public and promote political accountability. The media keep information flowing from the government to the citizens and, more pointedly, help uncover abuses and raise public awareness about the costs of corruption. Efforts to make the media more effective in this role include prohibiting censorship, promoting access to information, discouraging the use of libel and defamation laws, protecting journalists from harm, encouraging a diversity of media ownership, and providing training in investigative journalism.

Civil Society Participation

Organizations that make up "civil society" (that is, citizen groups, nongovernmental organizations, trade unions, business associations, think tanks, academia, religious organizations, and the media) can also have an important role to play in constraining corruption. Civil society activists can create public awareness about corruption, pressure governments to control it, and monitor government behavior. In partnership with public officials, civil society organizations can also mobilize resources to fight corruption and protect members from reprisals (Johnston and Kpundeh 2002). Indeed, coalition building is the cornerstone of TI's approach to fighting corruption, which has fostered coalitions constituted as national chapters in approximately 90 countries.[4]

The ability of citizens to form and work within such organizations depends on a permissive legal environment and a receptivity of public officials to citizen participation. The right to form organizations, the ease of securing necessary licenses, and the safety of activists create a permissive environment for civil society activity. In addition, the willingness of officials to work with citizens and the establishment of mechanisms for consultation and monitoring facilitate effective dialogue and oversight.

Public Sector Management

Another set of anti-corruption reforms focuses on the internal management of public resources to reduce incentives and opportunities for corruption. These reforms include instilling meritocracy and adequate pay in public administration, enhancing transparency and accountability in fiscal management, restructuring service delivery, and decentralizing state functions with accountability.

Civil service reform can improve incentives within public administration and so help reduce corruption. Most notably, recruitment and promoting on merit, as opposed to political patronage or ideological affiliation, are positively associated with both government effectiveness and control of corruption. While achieving change takes time, effective reform in this area includes the introduction of a comprehensive performance management system, with pay and promotion linked to performance.

Sound financial management constitutes another pillar of good and clean government. This entails timely reporting on financial operations, a comprehensive budget with the prohibition of off-budget expenditures, transparency in the use of public expenditures, and competitive and transparent procurement procedures, including the use of outsiders in bid evaluations.

Alongside such financial management practices, sound revenue collection is another pillar of clean government. With this objective, tax and customs reform are usually the focus because they are responsible for the majority of the central government's revenues and constitute a notorious source of corrupt dealing. To address this problem, reforms must eliminate and simplify tax and trade regulations, reduce discretion in cargo and tax-return processing, and professionalize tax and customs operations with a focus on results orientation and integrity.

Restructuring service delivery can also help reduce corruption. Experience shows that exposing public administrations to pressure from their clients has a major impact on improving service delivery. Reform measures in this area include

---

[4] See Transparency International's Web site: http://www.transparency.org.

setting and publishing service standards, administering and publishing client surveys to assess agencies' performance against these standards, setting up a wide range of user groups and consultative bodies, developing Internet-based approaches to delivering services, and offering alternatives for public services such as contracting out or having both public and private provision of services.

Decentralization can also influence corruption by bringing government closer to the people. While decentralization is no panacea for corruption, it could help reduce it where the design of decentralization and the prevailing institutional arrangements are favorable. In particular, decentralization may improve local governance where there is local democracy, and local democracy may work best in socially and economically homogeneous communities.

Competitive Private Sector

Finally, limiting distortions caused by the state and fostering a competitive private sector can reduce opportunities for corruption. A number of reforms reduce the discretionary power of politicians and bureaucrats and thereby eliminate avenues for self-dealing and collusion. These include liberalization, deregulation, simplification of rules, and privatization. It should be noted, however, that privatization bears considerable risks of corruption if not administered properly.

Other economic reforms can reduce the potential for private sector elites to capture the policy-making apparatus. These reforms include competitive restructuring of monopolies, improving transparency in corporate governance, and strengthening business associations.

The Politics of Reform

Efforts to fight corruption over the past decade have shown that the dynamics of corruption are inherently political. In some settings, corruption is driven by political calculations. In patronage systems, for example, public officials use corrupt resources to maintain support and defuse political opposition (Khan 1999, 17), and under crony capitalism, public officials grant protection of property rights to privileged asset holders who have close ties to the ruling elite (Haber 2002, xiv). In other settings, corruption can shape political forces and outcomes, as in the case of state capture and illicit political funding. Under these circumstances, any analysis of the political will to fight corruption must probe the complex forces that shape and can affect such political will, rather than settle for a mechanistic assessment of whether the political leadership is committed to change.

Anti-corruption efforts therefore require a thorough understanding of the politics of corruption. Such an understanding entails identifying who wins and loses from proposed reforms and what their respective resources and interests are. It also entails examining such institutional attributes as the quality of civil and political liberties, the structures of horizontal accountability, the coherence of the state, the cohesiveness of the party system, the concentration and organization of the business sector, and the strength of civil society organizations. In addition, this kind of analysis must consider any openings for reform, such as a scandal causing pressure for change in some areas, a politician pledging specific reforms, an economic crisis, or external pressure (for example, from the International Monetary Fund or the World Bank).

Conclusions

The many failed development projects in the past did not pay enough attention to controlling corruption. Now that corruption has entered center stage on the development agenda, reforms must address several fronts: improving the bureaucracy and civil service, strengthening checks and balances in government, promoting political competition and accountability, facilitating citizen participation, and strengthening economic competition. Indeed, the evidence points to the need for a more holistic approach to development that links institutional, legal, political, and economic variables and provides a climate for successful development. This requires the active involvement of all key stakeholders for a sustained improvement in governance. In this regard, legislators can play a pivotal role. As lawmakers, financiers, overseers, and representatives, legislators can help to strengthen the accountability framework and foster political and economic competition. Through such work, they can make a notable contribution to reduced corruption in their country.

Bibliography

de Soto, Hernando. 2000. *The Mystery of Capital: Why Capitalism Triumphs in the West and Fails Everywhere Else.* New York: Basic Books.

Friedman, Eric, Simon Johnson, Daniel Kaufmann, and Pablo Zoido-Lobatón. 2000. "Dodging the Grabbing Hand: The Determinants of Unofficial Activity in 69 Countries." *Journal of Public Economics* 76 (3, June): 459–93.

Haber, Stephen. 2002. "Introduction: The Political Economy of Crony Capitalism." In *Crony Capitalism and Economic Growth in Latin America: Theory and Evidence,* ed. Stephen Haber. Stanford, CA: Hoover Institution Press.

Hellman, Joel, Geraint Jones, and Daniel Kaufmann. 2000. "Seize the State, Seize the Day: State Capture, Corruption, and Influence in Transition Economies." Policy Research Working Paper 2444, World Bank, Washington, DC.

Huntington, Samuel P. *Political Order in Changing Societies.* 1968. New Haven, CT: Yale University Press.

Johnson, Simon, Daniel Kaufmann, John McMillan, and Christopher Woodruff. 2000. "Why Do Firms Hide? Bribes and Unofficial Activity after Communism." *Journal of Public Economics* 76: 495–520.

Johnston, Michael. 1986. "The Political Consequences of Corruption: A Reassessment." *Comparative Politics* 18 (4, July): 459–77.

———. 1993. "'Micro' and 'Macro' Possibilities for Reform." *Corruption and Reform* 7 (3): 189–204.

Johnston, Michael, and Sahr J. Kpundeh. 2002. "Building a Clean Machine: Anti-Corruption Coalitions and Sustainable Reforms." Working Paper 37208, World Bank Institute, Washington, DC.

Karklins, Rasma. 2002. "Typology of Post-Communist Corruption." *Problems of Post-Communism* 49 (4, July/August): 22–32.

Kaufmann, Daniel. 1997. "Corruption: The Facts." *Foreign Policy* (107, Summer): 114–31.

———. 2000. "Governance and Anticorruption." In Vinod Thomas, Mansoor Dailami, Ashok Dhareshwar, Daniel Kaufmann, Nalin Kishor, Ramon Lopez, and Yan Wang, *The Quality of Growth.* New York: Oxford University Press.

———. 2005. "Debunking Myths on Worldwide Governance and Corruption: The Challenge of Empirics—and Implications." The David B. Goodman Lecture, University of Toronto (February 10).

Khan, Mushtaq Husain. 1999. "New Approaches to Corruption and Governance and Their Implications." Paper prepared for the conference, "Reinventing the World Bank: Opportunities and Challenges for the 21st Century," Northwestern University (May).

Kuczynski, Pedro-Pablo, and John Williamson, eds. 2003. *After the Washington Consensus: Restarting Growth and Reform in Latin America.* Washington, DC: Institute for International Economics.

Mauro, Paulo. 1997. "The Effects of Corruption on Growth, Investment, and Government Expenditure: A Cross-Country Analysis." In *Corruption and the Global Economy,* ed. Kimberly Ann Elliott. Washington, DC: Institute for International Economics.

Murphy, Kevin, Andrei Shleifer, and Robert Vishny. 1991. "The Allocation of Talent: Implications for Growth." *The Quarterly Journal of Economics* 106 (2): 503–30.

Naím, Moisés. 1994. "Latin America: The Second Stage of Reform." *Journal of Democracy* 5 (4, October): 32–48.

Neff, Nathaniel H. 1964. "Economic Development through Bureaucratic Corruption." *The American Behavioral Scientist* 8 (2, November): 8–14.

Tanzi, Vito, and Hamid Davoodi. 1997. "Corruption, Public Investment, and Growth." Working Paper 139, International Monetary Fund, Washington, DC.

Treisman, Daniel. 2000. "The Causes of Corruption: A Cross-National Study." *Journal of Public Economics* 76 (3): 433–35.

Wei, Shang-Jin. 1998. "Corruption in Economic Development: Beneficial Grease, Minor Annoyance, or Major Obstacle?" Paper presented at the Workshop on Integrity in Governance in Asia, Bangkok, Thailand (June 29–July 1).

Wolfensohn, James D. 2005. "Address to the Annual Meeting of the IMF and World Bank." In *Voice for the World's Poor: Selected Speeches and Writings of World Bank President James D. Wolfensohn, 1995–2005,* ed. Andrew Kircher. Washington, DC: World Bank.

World Bank. 1997. *World Development Report 1997: The State in a Changing World.* Washington, DC: World Bank.

———. 2000. *Anticorruption in Transition: A Contribution to the Policy Debate.* Washington, DC: World Bank.

3

On the Political Nature of Corruption

Daniel Lederman, Norman V. Loayza, and Rodrigo R. Soares

Introduction

Corruption is generally regarded as one of the most serious obstacles to development. Recent evidence shows corruption has a negative impact on important economic outcomes. Mauro (1995) and Burki and Perry (1998) claim that corruption reduces economic growth through reduced private investment; Kaufmann, Kraay, and Zoido-Lobotón (1999) find that corruption limits development, as measured by per capita income, child mortality, and literacy; and Bai and Wei (2000) argue that corruption affects the making of economic policy. Therefore, it is important to understand the determinants of corruption and the limitations that they impose on the prospects of growth and development.

In the previous chapter, Kaufmann and Dininio investigated the causes of corruption and also presented a multifaceted anti-corruption strategy. In this chapter, we explore in more detail two of the five strategies presented in chapter 2: political accountability and the structure of public sector management.

The literature in political science and economics has made numerous efforts in this direction and has stressed the importance of political institutions in shaping the patterns of government corruption; nevertheless, the corresponding empirical literature is relatively scarce.[1] This chapter summarizes our attempts to contribute to the emerging empirical literature on the determinants of government corruption across countries and over time, with particular attention devoted to the role of political institutions.[2]

We will show that political and economic institutions affect corruption through two channels: political accountability and the structure of provision of public goods. Political mechanisms that increase political accountability, either by encouraging punishment of corrupt individuals or by reducing the informational problem related to government activities, tend to reduce the incidence of corruption. Likewise, economic

---

[1] Though still scarce, the empirical literature on political institutions and corruption is growing. Some important contributions are Tanzi (1998); La Porta et al. (1999); Fisman and Gatti (2000); Treisman (2000); Persson, Tabellini, and Trebbi (2001); and Kunicova and Rose-Ackerman (2002).

[2] This case study summarizes the analyses contained in Lederman, Loayza, and Soares 2005.

institutions that generate a competitive environment in the provision of public services tend to reduce the extraction of rents, therefore reducing corruption.

Our analyses show that some specific political institutions are strongly associated with the prevalence of corruption. In short, democracies, parliamentary systems, political stability, and freedom of the press are all associated with lower corruption. Conversely, a country's legal tradition and "openness" are not important factors in explaining the prevalence of corruption, once political variables are taken into account.

This chapter is organized as follows. Part One discusses the nature of corruption, by distinguishing corruption from other types of crimes and characterizing it as a political phenomenon. Part Two outlines the indicators of corruption used and identifies the variables whose role will be studied. Part Three discusses the results and findings on the role of political institutions in curbing or increasing corruption.

Part One: The Nature of Corruption

There is no question that corruption is a type of crime. Therefore, factors leading to common crimes could also play an important role in determining the incidence of corruption, thus linking the occurrence of corruption with other types of crimes. Surprisingly enough, this is not the case. Whereas different types of "common" crimes often go hand in hand, none of them significantly influences the frequency of corruption.

This suggests that factors distinguishing corruption from other crimes, related precisely to its connections to government activities and authority, play an important role. Corruption is a different phenomenon with its own characteristics and determinants, as noted almost a century ago by Francis McGovern (1907, 266):

> [Corruption's] advent in any community is marked by the commission of bribery, extortion, and criminal conspiracies to defraud the public, without a corresponding increase in other unrelated crimes. Its going, likewise, is accompanied by no abatement in the usual grist of larcenies, burglaries, and murder. It is, indeed, a unique and highly complex thing; an institution, if you please, rather than a condition of society or a temper or tendency of any class of individuals.

The analysis of the determinants of corruption must consequently focus on its "institutional" features. From this perspective, political institutions would seem to be important determinants of corruption because by shaping the rules of the interaction between citizens and politicians, political institutions can affect its incidence. Ultimately, the political macrostructure—related to the political system, balance of powers, electoral competition, and so on—determines the incentives for those in office to be honest and to police and punish misbehavior.

The Political Determinants of Corruption

A large part of the growing literature on the determinants of corruption has focused on the political nature of corruption and how different institutional designs affect its extent.

The problem of corruption in the public sector is almost a direct consequence of the nature of government interventions. Governments get involved in the provision of public goods that the private sector is unable or unwilling to provide. In addition, these transactions between the government and the citizens imply an unequal access to, and distribution of, information (Banerjee 1997). In this context, corruption arises spontaneously because of the existence of corrupt opportunities resulting from discretionary powers and monitoring failures. The institutional design largely influences the occurrence and nature of such opportunities.

The specific design of political institutions affects corruption mainly through two channels. The first relates to political accountability: any mechanism that increases political accountability, either by encouraging the punishment of corrupt individuals or by reducing the informational problem related to government activities, tends to reduce the incidence of corruption. The second relates to the structure of provision of public goods: institutions generating competition in the provision of the same public service tend to reduce corruption. The following discussion further explores these two points.

POLITICAL ACCOUNTABILITY AND CORRUPTION.   It has long been recognized that enhanced political accountability that allows for the punishment of politicians that adopt "bad policies" will result in lower levels of corruption because politicians align their preferences with those of their citizens. Three main characteristics can be identified in this respect: the degree of competition in the political system, the existence of checks-and-balances mechanisms across different branches of government, and the transparency of the system.

The first feature—political competition—has long been recognized as an important factor determining the efficiency of political outcomes (Downs 1957). In brief, the existence of free and fair elections guarantees that politicians can, to some extent, be held liable for the actions taken while in public office (Linz and Stepan 1996; Rose-Ackerman 1999). Any institution or rule that provides a punishment mechanism for politicians, such as the loss of elections or the possibility of being forced out of office, can induce politicians to improve their behavior by aligning their own interests with those of their constituents. The more the system forces politicians to face the electorate and the risk of losing office, the higher are their incentives to stick to good governance. This would imply, for example, that political systems allowing for clean and fair executive reelections would have less myopic and more electoral-conscious politicians and, therefore, less corruption (Linz 1990; Linz and Stepan 1996; Bailey and Valenzuela 1997; and Rose-Ackerman 1999).

The second point relates to the existence of checks-and-balances mechanisms across different branches of power. Generally, separation of powers—together with checks and balances—helps prevent abuses of authority, with different government bodies disciplining each other in the citizens' favor (McGovern 1907; Persson, Roland, and Tabellini 1997; Rose-Ackerman 1999; and Laffont and Meleu 2001). This is true in regard to the relations among the executive, legislative, and judiciary powers and also the relations among different levels of the executive power. For example, parliamentary systems allow for a stronger and more immediate monitoring of the executive by the legislature because in this case, parliaments have the power to remove politicians from executive office (Linz 1990; Linz and Stepan 1996; and Bailey and Valenzuela 1997). This oversight capacity in parliamentary systems might be weakened when a single party dominates the legislature. As long as it is not in the interest of one of the government branches to collude with the other branches, separation of powers creates mechanisms to police and punish government officials that misbehave, thus reducing the level of corruption. Moreover, developing adequate checks and balances for particular contexts may take time, either as a result of an institutional learning process or because of some inertial feature of corruption (Tirole 1996; Bailey and Valenzuela 1997; Treisman 2000). Political stability under a democratic regime, in this case, is also an important factor determining the efficacy of the checks-and-balances mechanisms and the level of corruption.

Another feature of institutional accountability is related to transparency. Transparency depends crucially on freedom of the press and expression and on the degree of decentralization in the system. Freedom of the press, so that right- and wrongdoings on the part of the government can be publicized, tends to reduce the informational problem between citizens and governments, thus improving governance (Peters and Welch 1980; Fackler and Lin 1995; Giglioli 1996; Rose-Ackerman 1999; and Djankov et al. 2001). Transparency can also be improved by decentralization: on a local level, monitoring of the performance of elected representatives and public officials is easier and therefore the informational problem less severe. Thus, in this sense, decentralized political systems tend to have stronger accountability mechanisms and lower corruption (Nas, Price, and Weber 1986; Rose-Ackerman 1999).

STRUCTURE OF PROVISION OF PUBLIC GOODS.   Corruption usually entails the extraction of bribes by someone who is vested with some form of public power. Besides determining the incentives for politicians to fight corruption, the political structure determines the "market structure" of the provision of public goods. This in turn determines the capacity of public officials to extract such graft. When several government agencies provide exactly the same service and citizens can freely choose where to purchase it, competition among agencies will reduce corruption. Competition can drive corruption to zero, just as perfect competition among firms drives prices to cover just the costs (Shleifer and Vishny 1993; Weingast 1995).

Conversely, when different government agencies provide complementary services—as, for example, when several licenses are required for a particular activity or different levels of government legislate in regard to the same activity—power is shared among different bureaucracies and each can extract illicit payments from the same source. This institutional setup increases corruption and the inefficiency of the system (Shleifer and Vishny 1993).

Decentralization will thus reduce corruption as long as power is decentralized into units that can substitute (or compete with) one another and that do not have overlapping responsibilities. In practice, however, political decentralization, in the sense of enhancing the autonomy of local (or provincial) governments, tends to bring together both of these effects. On the one hand, it increases the ability of states to compete against each other; on the other hand, it allows states to increase regulation over areas already covered by the central government. Which of these effects predominates over the incidence of corruption varies from case to case.

EXISTING EMPIRICAL EVIDENCE.   The goal of this case study is to analyze how important political institutions are in determining perceived corruption.

This specific issue has not received much attention, although a growing body of work has tried to link various dimensions of institutional development to the incidence of corruption. Some found a link between corruption and legal traditions: countries with French or socialist legal traditions are more prone to corruption; countries that had to undergo British colonization, less so (La Porta et al. 1999; Treisman 2000). Others draw a connection between corruption and the transparency of bureaucratic rules and processes (Tanzi 1998) or find a definite negative effect of fiscal decentralization on corruption (Fisman and Gatti 2000).

Another part of research relates corruption directly to specific features of the political system. Some researchers examined the connection between electoral systems and corruption—reinforcing the point about electoral competition made above (Persson, Tabellini, and Trebbi 2001). Others analyzed the effect of electoral rules on corruption—showing that a system featuring proportional representation is more prone to corruption then majoritarian ones and that the effect of proportional representation was worsened under presidential systems (Kunicova and Rose-Ackerman 2002).

Finally, some researchers have argued that corruption is directly related to some policy variables, such as relative public wages (Van Rijckeghem and Weder 2001) and openness (Ades and di Tella 1999; Laffont and N'Guessan 1999).

Part Two: Empirical Study

Indicators of Corruption

The greatest obstacle in the empirical analysis of corruption is that, for obvious reasons, there is no directly observable indicator. It is necessary, therefore, to rely on some sort of survey. Typically, studies of corruption are derived from some subjective evaluation surveys, based on opinions of international businessmen, countries' citizens themselves, or experts on country risk analysis.

There are a couple of such indicators, such as the International Country Risk Guide (ICRG), which measures corruption as the likelihood that government officials (both high- and low-ranking) would demand or accept bribes (or both) in exchange for special licenses, policy protection, biased judicial sentences, or avoidance of taxes and regulations or simply to expedite government procedures. The index is based on the analysis of a worldwide network of experts and treats corruption mainly as a threat to foreign investment. The *World Development Report (WDR)* uses a similar definition and treats corruption as an obstacle to business in general. The index, calculated by Gallup International, uses a survey of citizens to measure the frequency of cases of corruption among public officials. The Global Competitiveness Survey (GCS) indexes measure the frequency of irregular payments connected with imports, exports, business licenses, police protection, loan applications, and so forth, as well as the frequency of irregular payments to government officials (including the judiciary). They are based on surveys of business executives. Finally, the Country Risk Review (CRR-DRI) index is part of Standard & Poor's credit rating system for emerging markets. It uses analysts' opinions to measure the prevalence of corruption among public officials and the effectiveness of anti-corruption initiatives.

Although such surveys have their own limitations, the fact that they have similar results is an indication that they are a relevant measure of corruption.

Estimation Strategy

In our view, the institutional design of the political system is the ultimate determinant of corruption because it shapes the incentives facing government officials. Our research has taken into account the possibility (and popularly held view) that certain people and cultures are intrinsically more corrupt then others. In addition, we considered the role of public wages, trade policies, and competitiveness. We also studied other variables, including the size of government and the distribution of resources across different levels of government, allowing us to identify the effect of electoral decentralization. Finally, we examined whether corruption naturally falls with economic development.

Variables

What we sought to identify was the role played by each of the following political variables:

- **Democracy.** Free and fair elections. We expect democracy to reduce corruption.
- **Presidential Democracy.** Because the legislatures in parliamentary systems can remove the leaders of the executive branch more readily than in presidential systems, we expect this variable to have a positive impact on corruption, especially after accounting for the control of the legislature by the political party of the executive.
- **Reelection.** Whether the head of the executive can run for multiple terms. As mentioned, we expect that reelection in presidential systems will be associated with lower corruption because politicians have an incentive to behave according to their citizens' interests if they wish to be reelected.
- **Democratic Stability.** The time of an uninterrupted democratic regime since 1930. Such stability permits institutional learning and the development of checks and balances adequate to the particular culture and political tradition. This increases accountability and gives time for other political institutions to materialize their effects (Linz 1990; Linz and Stepan 1996; Tirole 1996; Bailey and Valenzuela 1997; Rose-Ackerman 1999; and Garman, Haggard, and Willis 2001). Consequently, we expect democratic stability to reduce corruption.
- **Closed Lists.** A democratic country that features closed lists in the elections of the legislature. On one hand, the use of closed lists in legislative elections creates incentives for individual politicians to worry about the reputation of the party as a whole, which could help reduce corruption (Linz 1990; Linz and Stepan 1996; Bailey and Valenzuela 1997; Rose-Ackerman 1999; and Garman, Haggard, and Willis 2001). On the other hand, the potential oversight of individual politicians by opposition parties is hampered by closed lists, which could thus raise the incidence of corruption (Kunicova and Rose-Ackerman 2002).
- **State Government.** Whether there are multiple levels of subnational government. As mentioned, decentralization affects several different aspects of the political system. First, decentralization tends to increase accountability through easier monitoring of governments at the local level. Through this channel, decentralization would reduce corruption. Second, decentraliza-

tion affects the structure of provision of public goods, possibly simultaneously increasing the competition among states and establishing overlapping
bureaucracies from local and central governments. These two forces have
opposite effects on corruption. Therefore, the effect of decentralization on
corruption is, in principle, ambiguous (Shleifer and Vishny 1993; Weingast
1995; Nas, Price, and Weber 1986; Rose-Ackerman 1999; and Ahlin 2000).

- **Executive Control.** Whether the executive's party has control of all relevant
chambers of the legislature. Because the oversight of the executive is weaker
when the same party controls the legislature, we expect that this variable
will have a positive effect on the incidence of corruption.
- **Freedom of the Press.** Freedom of the press captures the transparency of the
system. By increasing transparency, freedom of the press reduces the informational problem in the political system and increases accountability (Peters
and Welch 1980; Fackler and Lin 1995; Giglioli 1996; and Djankov et al. 2001).

Some of these variables are subgroups of others. For example, a presidential system is a type of democratic system, and reelections are permitted in certain presidential democracies. Thus, the effects of these variables must be interpreted as con-
ditional on the preceding one, as in "given that the country is democratic, this is the
effect of the presidential system on corruption," and so on. (This view is illustrated
in the decision tree in figure 3.1.)

Figure 3.1 *The Political Tree*

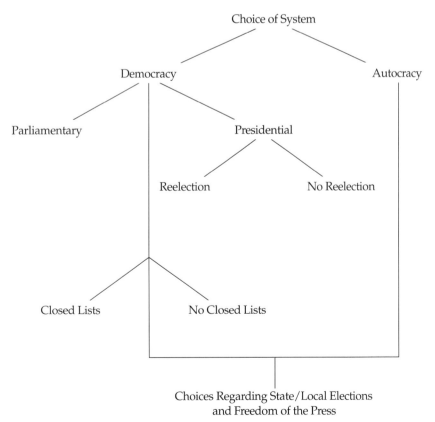

Source: Lederman, Loayza, and Soares 2005.

Figure 3.2 Evolution of Corruption by Regions of the World, 1984–99

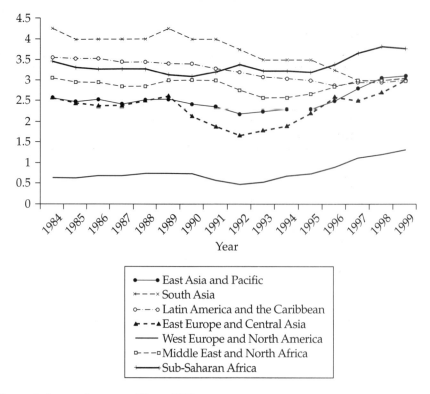

Source: Lederman, Loayza, and Soares 2005.

An interesting aspect then is to consider the evolution over time and space. Figure 3.2 illustrates this point by plotting the evolution of the corruption index through time by regions of the world (using simple averages for the countries belonging to the respective region). Although there seem to be some comovements of the series across the different regions, there are also some independent patterns. For example, as Latin America and South Asia have experienced a decline in corruption since the late 1980s, Western Europe and North America have experienced a slight increase during the same period.

Part Three: The Results

Our statistical study of variables on political institutions basically confirms the assumptions made above: democracy, time of democratic stability, and freedom of the press can most strongly be associated with the reduction of corruption. (Table 3.1 presents the results of the regressions.)

Transition from authoritarianism to democracy reduces the prevalence of corruption considerably. Similarly, each additional 20 years of uninterrupted democracy or an increase in press freedom (for example, from the level of Turkey to that of the United Kingdom) lowers the probability of a high level of corruption significantly. On the other hand, within democracies, presidential systems—as opposed to parliamentary systems—raise the probability of high levels of corruption.

Table 3.1 *Results: Corruption Regressions*

	Ordered Probit				Ordinary Least Squares (OLS)			
	(1)	*(2)*	*(3)*	*(4)*	*(5)*	*(6)*	*(7)*	*(8)*
Democ	−0.1580	−0.5238	−1.8054	−0.7097	−0.2078	−0.4598	−1.2111	−0.6140
	0.1302	0.1547	0.3149	0.2368	0.1195	0.1227	0.2009	0.1870
	0.2250	0.0010	0.0000	0.0030	0.0820	0.0000	0.0000	0.0010
Presid	1.0367	0.4324	1.2732	1.1194	0.9261	0.3591	0.7589	0.8403
	0.1030	0.2028	0.3340	0.2710	0.0907	0.1679	0.2237	0.2150
	0.0000	0.0330	0.0000	0.0000	0.0000	0.0330	0.0010	0.0000
Reelect	−0.2244	0.0429	−0.3354	−0.3062	−0.2329	0.0385	−0.1668	−0.2676
	0.1375	0.1810	0.2929	0.2609	0.1254	0.1477	0.2153	0.2149
	0.1030	0.8130	0.2520	0.2410	0.0630	0.7940	0.4390	0.2140
Dstab	−0.0340	−0.0423	−0.0410	−0.0453	−0.0272	−0.0307	−0.0234	−0.0284
	0.0024	0.0032	0.0055	0.0049	0.0019	0.0022	0.0033	0.0035
	0.0000	0.0000	0.0000	0.0000	0.0000	0.0000	0.0000	0.0000
State	−0.0968	0.1525	0.4359	0.1625	−0.1039	0.0828	0.1693	0.0759
	0.0425	0.0543	0.1015	0.0768	0.0370	0.0407	0.0618	0.0557
	0.0230	0.0050	0.0000	0.0340	0.0050	0.0420	0.0060	0.1730
List	−0.1654	0.0426	−0.0817	0.3171	−0.1553	−0.0018	−0.0501	0.1937
	0.0860	0.1035	0.1733	0.1472	0.0683	0.0689	0.0904	0.0909
	0.0550	0.6810	0.6370	0.0310	0.0230	0.9790	0.5800	0.0330
Control	0.1628	−0.0574	−0.4270	−0.1001	0.1419	−0.0413	−0.3092	−0.0667
	0.0955	0.1068	0.1864	0.1429	0.0825	0.0808	0.1112	0.1028
	0.0880	0.5910	0.0220	0.4830	0.0860	0.6090	0.0060	0.5170
Press	−0.0113	−0.0056	−0.0210	−0.0014	−0.0099	−0.0043	−0.0152	−0.0006
	0.0022	0.0031	0.0061	0.0043	0.0020	0.0024	0.0042	0.0033
	0.0000	0.0690	0.0010	0.7500	0.0000	0.0740	0.0000	0.8500
Govrev			0.0389				0.0239	
			0.0098				0.0065	
			0.0000				0.0000	
Transf			−0.0632				−0.0184	
			0.0221				0.0110	
			0.0040				0.0950	
Open			0.0000				−0.0015	
			0.0030				0.0019	
			0.9930				0.4510	
Lngdp				−0.1826				−0.1940
				0.1412				0.1056
				0.1960				0.0670
Tyr15				−0.1090				−0.0469
				0.0443				0.0304
				0.0140				0.1230
Leg_brit		0.2598	0.3293	0.6279		0.1518	0.1735	0.3470
		0.1122	0.2510	0.1672		0.0844	0.1485	0.1216
		0.0210	0.1900	0.0000		0.0730	0.2430	0.0040
Elf		0.0123	0.0210	0.0109		0.0100	0.0132	0.0103
		0.0021	0.0040	0.0029		0.0016	0.0024	0.0020
		0.0000	0.0000	0.0000		0.0000	0.0000	0.0000
Period dummies	Yes	Yes	Yes	Yes	Yes	Yes	Yes	Yes
Reg/nature vars	No	Yes	Yes	Yes	No	Yes	Yes	Yes
N Obs	1158	1010	490	605	1158	1010	490	605
Pseudo R/R2	0.24	0.33	0.45	0.38	0.57	0.70	0.79	0.74

Source: Lederman, Loayza, and Soares 2005.
Note: Obs.: Std. errors and p-values below coefficients. Dep var. is ICRG corruption index (0 to 6; higher values = more corruption). Ind. vars. are (*d* for dummy): democracy *d*, presidential *d*, possibility of reelection *d*, time of democratic stability, indicator of local elections for state govs., gov. control of legislative *d*, freedom of press index, gov. revenues (% GDP), transfer from central government to other levels (% GDP), openness to trade (imports as % GDP), ln of per capita GDP, avg. schooling in the pop. above 15, British legal tradition *d*, index of ethno linguistic fractionalization, period *d*'s, region *d*'s (E. Asia and Pacif., E. Eur. and C. Asia, M. East and N. Afr., S. Asia, Sub-Saharan Afr., and L. Am. and Carib.), and nature variables (landlock *d*, area, tropical *d*, long., and lat.). *Govrev, transf, open, lngdp,* and *tyr15* lagged. Regressions include all obs. available between 1984 and 1997. Robust std. errors used.

Furthermore, it seems that cultural and historical factors determine simultaneously democracy and corruption, but democracy alone reduces corruption once these factors are accounted for. With freedom of the press, the case is the opposite. Freedom of the press is significantly related to less corruption, but once the level of development is taken into account, its effect falls to zero.

The possibility of reelection, the existence of local elections, relative wages in the public sector, economic openness, financial transfers from central to other levels of government, income levels, and education are also associated with lower corruption. Additional research suggests that the congestion of different bureaucracies regulating the same activities dominates the potentially beneficial effects of decentralization.

On the other hand, especially the presidential system, but also government control of all houses, is associated with higher corruption. Closed lists, however, do not appear to have a significant impact on the incidence of corruption.

As for the cultural, policy, and development variables, it seems that as expected, the size of the government increases corruption, while the distribution of resources from the central government to other levels of national government reduces corruption. Although as mentioned, decentralization increases corruption through the possibility of local states interfering on spheres already being partly legislated at the federal level, when it comes to distribution of resources, monitoring at the local level is easier than at the central level. Therefore, more resources used by local government translate into more resources falling under closer control by citizens.

The effects of economic openness and the British legal tradition that we find do not agree with the previous literature. Openness has no significant effect here.[3] These results should not be interpreted as evidence that trade competition is ineffective in reducing corruption, but rather as an indication of the supremacy of political institutions as determinants of both trade policies and corruption. The negative effect of the British legal tradition on corruption, which is one of the main results in Treisman (2000), is also absent here. In our view, the differences in relation to the previous literature come from our focus on the importance of political mechanisms. Political institutions are the main outside force shaping the incentive structure that determines both corruption and the implementation of specific policies. Thus, in our case study, openness is correlated with democracy, parliamentary systems, freedom of the press, and absence of corruption, but the political variables seem to be determining openness and corruption.[4] Also, rather than having a direct negative effect on corruption, the British legal tradition is strongly associated with democracy, stability, freedom of the press, and parliamentary systems, and these political variables tend to diminish corruption. Thus, once the political system is taken into account, the norms associated with the British legal tradition by itself may in fact increase corruption. Analyzed alone, the informality of the British law, in which practices are strongly based on unwritten rules, seems to be more subject to corrup-

---

[3] Although it was found to reduce corruption in Ades and di Tella (1999), Dutt (1999), and Laffont and N'Guessan (1999).

[4] This result is also in line with the literature on institutions and development, which finds that the effect of institutions dominates that of policies in shaping long-term phenomena; see Easterly and Levine (2002) and Rodrik, Subramanian, and Trebbi (2002).

tion than other traditions, where rules are explicitly defined. In this light, our result would not be surprising.

Finally, considering regional differences, both the East Europe and Central Asia and the Latin America and the Caribbean regions have higher levels of perceived corruption than would be expected from our variables. There seems to be some truth to the popular belief that these places of the world are particularly prone to the problem of corruption, although their recent transitions to democracy bode well for the future of governance in these regions.

Conclusion

This paper explores the link between political institutions and corruption. We show that the behavior of corruption is very distinct from the behavior of common crimes, and we argue that this indicates the relevance of explanations that are unique to corruption. These factors are mainly associated with the environment in which relations between individuals and the state take place. We argue that political institutions, by determining this environment, are crucially important in determining the incidence of corruption. Ultimately, the political macrostructure—related to the political system, balance of powers, electoral competitiveness, and so on—determines the incentives for those in office to be honest and to police and punish misbehavior of people inside and outside the government bureaucracy. Our results show that corruption tends to decrease systematically with democracy, parliamentary systems, democratic stability, and freedom of the press.

Another interesting result is related to decentralization. According to the theoretical literature, different types of decentralization may have different effects on corruption. Political decentralization, in the sense that states are more autonomous (potentially being able to legislate over areas already covered by the central government), seems to increase corruption, while decentralization (in the sense that expenditures are more decentralized through the different levels of national government) seems to reduce corruption. The inclusion of political institutions in the analysis of the determinants of corruption turns out to be refreshing. Justifying all the attention given by the theoretical literature to the institutional determinants of corruption, our results indicate that political variables are indeed among the most important determinants of corruption across countries and over time. After political institutions are accounted for, other factors usually found to be important—such as openness, wages in the public sector, and legal tradition—lose virtually all their independent relevance.

Generally, this study should raise the attention given to formal accountability mechanisms. Future research could explore whether agencies subject to different accountability mechanisms within a given country (such as transparency standards) also differ in terms of the corruption they engender. Discussion on the actual mechanisms of political decentralization should also be encouraged. Efforts should be targeted at creating competition in all levels of the political structure, avoiding regulations in which different agencies—or levels of power—have overlapping jurisdictions. Finally, the results of this study should help in designing and assessing the impact of anti-corruption efforts. Political institutions do matter for corruption, and they should be centerpieces in the preparation and evaluation of anti-corruption reforms.

Bibliography

Acemoglu, D., S. Johnson, and J. Robinson. 2001. "The Colonial Origins of Comparative Development: An Empirical Investigation." *American Economic Review* 91 (5): 1369–1401.

———. 2002. "Reversal of Fortune: Geography and Institutions in the Making of the Modern World Income Distribution." *Quarterly Journal of Economics* 117 (4): 1231–94.

Ades, A., and R. di Tella. 1999. "Rents, Competition, and Corruption." *American Economic Review* 89 (4): 982–93.

Ahlin, C. 2000. "Corruption: Political Determinants and Macroeconomic Effects." Unpublished manuscript, University of Chicago, Chicago.

Bai, C. E., and S. J. Wei. 2000. "Quality of Bureaucracy and Open-Economy Macro Policies." Working Paper 7766, NBER, Cambridge, MA.

Bailey, J., and A. Valenzuela. 1997. "The Shape of the Future." *Journal of Democracy* 8 (4, October): 43–57. http://muse.jhu.edu/cgi-bin/access.cgi?uri=/journals/journal_of_democracy/v008/8.4bailey.html.

Banerjee, A. 1997. "A Theory of Misgovernance." *Quarterly Journal of Economics* 112 (4): 1289–1332.

Bardhan, P. 1997. "Corruption and Development: A Review of Issues." *Journal of Economic Literature* 35 (3): 1320–46.

Beck, T., G. Clark, A. Groff, P. Keefer, and P. Walsh. 2001. "New Tools in Comparative Political Economy." *World Bank Economic Review* 15 (1): 165–76.

Burki, S., and G. Perry. 1998. *Beyond the Washington Consensus: Institutions Matter.* Washington, DC: World Bank.

Collier, P., and A. Hoeffler. 1998. "On Economic Causes of Civil War." *Oxford Economic Papers* 50 (4): 563–73.

Djankov, S., C. McLiesh, T. Nenova, and A. Shleifer. 2001. "Who Owns the Media?" Policy Research Working Paper 2620, World Bank, Washington, DC.

Downs, A. 1957. "An Economic Theory of Political Action in a Democracy." *Journal of Political Economy* 65 (2): 135–50.

Dutt, P. 1999. "The Consequences of Trade and Industrial Policies for Corruption." Doctoral dissertation, Department of Economics, New York University, New York.

Easterly, W., and R. Levine. 2002. "Tropics, Germs, and Crops: How Endowments Influence Economic Development." Working Paper 9106, NBER, Cambridge, MA.

Fackler, T., and T. Lin. 1995. "Political Corruption and Presidential Elections, 1929–1992." *Journal of Politics* 57 (4): 971–93.

Fisman, R., and R. Gatti. 2000. "Decentralization and Corruption: Evidence across Countries." Policy Research Working Paper 2290, World Bank, Washington, DC.

Garman, C., S. Haggard, and E. Willis. 2001. "Fiscal Decentralization: A Political Theory with Latin American Cases." *World Politics* 53 (2): 205–36.

Giglioli, P. P. 1996. "Political Corruption and the Media: The Tangentopoli Affair." *International Social Science Journal* 48 (3): 381–94.

ICRG (International Country Risk Guide). 1999. *Brief Guide to the Rating System.* http://www.icrgonline.com.

Kaufmann, Daniel, and Aart Kraay. 2002. "Growth without Governance." *Economia* 3 (Fall): 169–230.

Kaufmann, Daniel, Aart Kraay, and Pablo Zoido-Lobatón. 1999. "Governance Matters." Policy Research Working Paper 2196, World Bank, Washington, DC.

Kunicova, J., and S. Rose-Ackerman. 2002. "Electoral Rules as Constraints on Corruption." Unpublished manuscript, Yale University, New Haven, CT.

La Porta, R., F. Lopez-de-Silanes, A. Shleifer, and R. Vishny. 1999. "The Quality of Government." *Journal of Law, Economics, and Organization* 15 (1): 229–79.

Laffont, J. I., and M. Meleu. 2001. "Separation of Powers and Development." *Journal of Development Economics* 64 (1): 129–45.

Laffont, J. I., and T. N'Guessan. 1999. "Competition and Corruption in an Agency Relationship." *Journal of Development Economics* 60 (2): 271–95.

Lederman, D., N. Loayza, and R. Soares. 2005. "Accountability and Corruption: Political Institutions Matter." *Economic and Politics* 17 (March): 1–35.

Linz, J. 1990. "The Virtues of Parliamentarism." *Journal of Democracy* 1 (Fall): 84–92.

Linz, J., and A. Stepan. 1996. "Toward Consolidated Democracies." *Journal of Democracy* 7 (2): 14–33.

Maddala, G. S. 1983. *Limited-Dependent and Qualitative Variables in Econometrics.* Cambridge, U.K.: Cambridge University Press.

Mauro, P. 1995. "Corruption and Growth. *Quarterly Journal of Economics* 110 (3): 681–712.

McGovern, F. 1907. "Legal Repression of Political Corruption." *Proceedings of the American Political Science Association* 4: 266–76.

Nas, T., A. Price, and C. Weber. 1986. "A Policy-Oriented Theory of Corruption." *American Political Science Review* 80 (1): 107–19.

Persson, T., G. Roland, and G. Tabellini. 1997. "Separation of Powers and Political Accountability." *Quarterly Journal of Economics* 112 (4): 1163–1202.

Persson, T., G. Tabellini, and F. Trebbi. 2001. "Electoral Rules and Corruption." Working Paper 8154, NBER, Cambridge, MA.

Peters, J., and S. Welch. 1980. "The Effect of Charges of Corruption on Voting Behavior in Congressional Elections." *American Political Science Review* 74 (3): 697–708.

Rodrik, D., A. Subramanian, and F. Trebbi. 2002. "Institutions Rule: The Primacy of Institutions over Geography and Integration in Economic Development." Unpublished manuscript, Harvard University, Cambridge, MA.

Rose-Ackerman, S. 1999. *Corruption and Government: Causes, Consequences, and Reform.* Cambridge, U.K., and New York: Cambridge University Press.

Shleifer, A., and R. Vishny. 1993. "Corruption." *Quarterly Journal of Economics* 108 (3): 599–617.

Soares, R. R. 2004. "Crime Reporting as a Measure of Institutional Development." *Economic Development and Cultural Change* 52 (4): 851–71.

Tanzi, V. 1998. "Corruption around the World: Causes, Consequences, Scope, and Cures." Working Paper 98/63, IMF, Washington, DC.

Tirole, J. 1996. "A Theory of Collective Reputations (with Applications to the Persistence of Corruption and to Firm Quality)." *Review of Economic Studies* 63 (1): 1–22.

Treisman, D. 2000. "The Causes of Corruption: A Cross-National Study." *Journal of Public Economics* 76 (3): 399–457.

Van Rijckeghem, C., and B. Weder. 2001. "Bureaucratic Corruption and the Rate of Temptation: Do Wages in the Civil Service Affect Corruption, and by How Much?" *Journal of Development Economics* 65 (2): 307–31.

Weingast, B. 1995. "The Economic Role of Political Institutions: Market-Preserving Federalism and Economic Growth." *Journal of Law, Economics, and Organization* 11 (1): 1–31.

4

Political Will

Sahr Kpundeh and Phyllis Dininio

Introduction

As chapters 5–11 will show, legislators can play a powerful role in curbing corruption. Through their legislative, financial, oversight, and representative roles, legislators can help to strengthen systems of accountability, reduce opportunities for corruption, improve incentives for official probity, and channel popular demand for integrity. Their efforts can complement anti-corruption efforts that may be under way in other branches of government or in civil society and can serve as a check on corruption in the executive branch. Their ability to check executive abuse may be strongest in parliamentary systems and in regimes where the executive's party does not control all chambers of the legislature.

These abilities, however, do not necessarily translate into action. The political will of legislators to fight corruption may be weak, dormant, or nonexistent. Some legislators may not perceive fighting corruption to be in their best interest. Indeed, political will is the reflection of complex circumstances that incorporate the aspirations of individual leaders, a calculation of the benefits and costs that would result from changes in rules and behaviors, and belief in the ability to muster adequate support to overcome resistance to reforms. Political will neither originates nor becomes manifest in a vacuum.

While the desire to fight corruption can reside in many locations,[1] this chapter focuses on political will located in the legislative branch. For clarity, we define the concept of political will as the demonstrated credible intent of political actors (elected or appointed leaders, civil society watchdogs, stakeholder groups, and so forth) to attack perceived causes or effects of corruption at a systemic level. The focus is on the motives and actions of political actors in support of anti-corruption reforms.

Identifying Political Will

Identifying political will to fight corruption is not always straightforward. Anti-corruption rhetoric can represent a desire to defuse opposition, bolster support, or

---

[1] Examples abound of reform efforts that have arisen from each branch of government, the political opposition, civil society, international organizations, and private sector institutions.

placate external agencies, rather than to undertake significant reform. Some politicians publicize allegations and evidence of corruption in an effort to demonstrate opponents' and former administrations' hypocrisies and (supposedly) their own virtue. In extreme cases, they use anti-corruption campaigns to get rid of their opponents. As such, anti-corruption campaigns are tactical responses to political challenges, rather than sincere attempts at reform (Riley 1983; Gillespie and Okruhlik 1991).

The rhetoric in countries like Nigeria and the Russian Federation underscores the cosmetic nature of many reform strategies. As characterized by Olowu (1993), in Nigeria, "Political actors often talk of accountability and integrity, but this by itself does not translate into a genuine commitment to detect and penalize unethical behavior. Even when anti-corruption agencies are created, they are usually denied the resources needed to achieve their stated purpose." Similarly, in Russia, anti-corruption legislation was promulgated in 1997 that required government officials to make public statements of personal net worth. However, the legislation was not accompanied by provisions for verifying information or sanctioning the submission of false statements. As a result, public cynicism intensified when some of the nation's wealthiest individuals reported absurdly low net worth statements, contradicted by their extravagant lifestyles and possessions.

Even where anti-corruption commitment is real, political will can unravel. Among government officials and politicians, political will is usually strongest at the outset of new administrations, which would explain why, in chapter 3, Lederman, Loayza, and Soares show that elections lead to reduced corruption. However, such political will can wane as opposition to reform solidifies and new opportunities for corruption emerge. Fatigue, fear, resignation, and opportunism may diminish the commitment of reformers and attenuate political will. As a result, anti-corruption reforms may break down, and corruption may reemerge (Dininio 2005).

Given the prevalence of anti-corruption rhetoric and the propensity of political will to unravel, assessing political will becomes an important undertaking. Such assessments must distinguish between reform approaches that are intentionally superficial and those that are serious. They also must distinguish between public officials' motivation at the outset of well-intended campaigns and their motivation once opposition or fatigue sets in. Examples abound of exploitative rulers who have hidden their motives behind a facade of cosmetic measures or well-intended reformers who have engineered their own destruction through ineffective strategies. In light of these traps, supporters of the reform process can look at several indicators that can serve as demonstrations of political will.

A first indicator of political will is the *domestic origin of the initiative*. This indicator examines whether the principal advocates for change really perceive corruption as an issue requiring attention or whether an external group has induced or coerced the advocates to endorse the anti-corruption issue. Homegrown initiatives involve reformers who themselves perceive corruption as a salient issue and are willing to champion the efforts necessary to fight it. Imported or imposed initiatives, by contrast, face the challenge of building commitment and ownership (Brinkerhoff and Kulibaba 1999).

A second indicator is *a high degree of analysis* that a regime has applied to understanding the context and causes of corruption. Has the regime sought to recognize the complexities that give rise to aberrant behavior? Has it identified and developed measures to deal with those institutions, mandates, and behaviors that either impede or promote integrity in government?

A third indicator is *a high level of participation* in the reform process. Has the regime adopted a strategy that is participative, incorporating and mobilizing the interests of many stakeholders? Effective reform management recognizes that stakeholders act on the basis of their own interests and that dialogue and participation enhance opportunities for success. Although leadership is crucial to the policy-making phase, shared ownership is equally essential to ensuring sustainability. Effective implementation requires educated officials who are responsible for enforcing or adopting reforms. It also hinges on the support of citizens.

A fourth indicator is the *inclusion of prevention, education, and sanctions* in reform strategies. The record of failure is exceedingly high for anti-corruption efforts that use the blunt instrument of prosecution (or the fear of prosecution) as their principal tool for compliance. Serious reformers recognize that effective strategies must stress prevention and education, as well as prosecution. These strategies might restructure the principal-agent relationship, provide positive incentives for compliance, publicize positive outcomes, and establish effective sanctions for compromised individuals and institutions.

A fifth indicator is *the dedication of adequate resources* for anti-corruption reforms. As the examples of superficial reforms in Nigeria and Russia demonstrate, an easy way for regimes to enjoy the appearance of fighting corruption without really doing so is to establish new procedures and offices without providing adequate funding for them to function properly.

A sixth indicator of political will is the *objective monitoring and evaluation* of reform efforts to allow for course corrections and to ensure that policy goals and objectives are ultimately met. The willingness to publicly report the findings of policy evaluations, whether they are positive or negative, can encourage public support and strengthen reformers against their critics.

Challenges to Political Will

The demands of their job present a fundamental challenge to legislators' commitment to fight corruption. In their position, legislators face a tension between public-serving and private-serving actions. As representatives of the people, they are expected to use their office for the public good. Yet as elected politicians, they are forced to consider their own prospects in the next election and are oriented to foster the good will of their constituents and campaign contributors (Thompson 1995). The politics of "pork," vote buying, and the access afforded big donors are common responses to electoral exigencies. Securing such benefits for constituents and campaign contributors may entail legitimate favors or may entail corruption. The line between the two is often not clear and is by no means fixed across time and cultures.

At the same time, legislators' role in policy making, authorizing budgets, and providing oversight gives them extensive opportunities for political or financial gain. Authorizing activities such as drilling, altering regulations, disbursing subsidies, or funding bailouts, as well as influencing appointments to positions in executive agencies, create opportunities for legislators to profit from a quid pro quo or to further their own financial interests. These exchanges may strengthen legislators' campaigns for reelection or may line their own pockets. To the extent that legislators are themselves resorting to corruption, their political will to fight it may be compromised.

Certain features of the political environment can intensify the tension that legislators face between public- and private-serving actions. Where corruption is driven by political calculations in the first place, securing legislators' commitment to reform may be problematic. In patronage systems, for example, public officials use corrupt resources to maintain support and defuse political opposition (Khan 1999, 17), and with state capture, public officials allocate laws, rules, regulations, and judicial decisions to those with the greatest ability to pay (Hellman and Kaufmann 2001). When an exchange of resources—rather than an appeal to ideology—characterize the means of winning office, legislators may be less inclined to back an anti-corruption agenda.

Apart from these political calculations, fear may undermine legislators' commitment to reform. Dominant executives and strong vested interests (such as those connected to organized crime) may buttress corrupt networks and make attempts to dismantle them politically and personally dangerous. Too many reformist legislators have been victims of attacks and assassination (*Corruption Notebooks* 2004).

Short time horizons can also orient legislators to private-serving actions. Political instability, term limits, certain electoral defeat, and decisions to retire all reduce the time horizons of legislators. Politicians with short time horizons cannot count on future employment or the future returns from good governance (Jin 2005). Rather than pursuing the public good, therefore, they have an incentive to seek self-enrichment while in office and "get it while they can" (Manzetti and Blake 1996, 665). Such an orientation clearly works against their commitment to fight corruption.

Strengthening Political Will

Given the many challenges to political will, serious anti-corruption reforms must consider strategies for strengthening it. A range of options is available for strategists, including elite, societal, institutional, and international approaches (Johnston 1998). While corruption reforms must respond to each country's particular array of political, economic, and corruption problems, they also must rest on a political foundation that affords the space for action. Fostering opportunities for anti-corruption forces to gather strength and credibility creates this foundation.

Elite Approaches

Elite approaches to strengthening political will focus on the legislators themselves. They involve efforts to increase legislators' understanding of the issue and opportunities for them to address it. Elite approaches can support corruption diagnostic surveys, service delivery surveys, and assessments to collect and disseminate information about the costs and potential responses to corruption. They can also provide occasions (and possibly the protection) for legislative reformers to take action through workshops, task forces, and other forums (examples of such action include the recent training of Thai and Sri Lankan legislators by WBI on corruption).

Another elite-focused option for strengthening political will among legislators is to facilitate their participation in parliamentary networks, such as the Global Organization of Parliamentarians Against Corruption (GOPAC) and the Parliamentary Network on the World Bank (PNoWB) (as John Williams describes in chapter 14). Their participation in such networks can simplify the task of seeking reliable information and advice and can help them develop new insights through the interaction of different perspectives. As he explains, parliamentary networks can also give participants a shared voice and association with like-minded colleagues, which can be comforting when carrying out the "often lonely fight against corruption."

Societal Approaches

Societal approaches to strengthening political will among legislators focus instead on citizens and aim to foster better-informed voters and advocates. Corruption is a sensitive subject with few witnesses. Public awareness helps remove the taboo and veil of secrecy that engulf corrupt activities. The citizenry is empowered if it understands its own stake in the abuse of public funds. Money diverted from its intended use into corrupt activities results in fewer schools, higher taxes and school fees, lower salaries, fewer jobs, and so forth. Debates on malfeasance and its remedies that are broadcast via radio and television and conducted in classrooms, at community activities, and through formal workshops begin to personalize corruption—explaining clearly and explicitly how individuals are affected. Once people feel that they personally have a stake in the elimination or control of corruption and that they have the power to do something about it, they can demand action from the leadership. Their support is crucial in forming constituencies and galvanizing the political will to pursue reform.

Related to the aim of informing voters is the promotion of a free press. As Macdonell and Pesic point out in chapter 8, independent media can play a significant role in raising public awareness and mobilizing public opinion against corruption. They can also help to investigate and report incidents of corruption, especially when journalists are able to expose wrongdoing without fear or reprisals. The media, hence, can stimulate citizen demands for integrity and provide an independent source of oversight. Through both these channels, they can help to strengthen legislators' political will to fight corruption.

A public constituency against corruption can go beyond voting and develop an organized form of expression and response. Through civic associations, NGOs, and social movements, citizens can expose wrongdoing and advocate change. For example, in the 1980s, the citizens' Vetting Committees in Ghana and the People's Revolutionary Tribunals in Burkina Faso organized rank-and-file political activists and ordinary citizens to expose profiteering, smuggling, and other exploitative practices by private merchants. More recently in Latin America, NGOs like Núcleo de Estudos da Violência da Universidade de São Paulo (NEV/USP) and Viva Rio in Brazil, Centro de Estudios Legales y Sociales (CELS) and Coordinadora contra la Represión Policial e Institucional (CORREPI) in Argentina, Alianza Cívica in Mexico, and many others have documented police abuses, corruption of public officials, and electoral fraud and have mobilized intense public support (Smulovitz and Peruzzotti 2000). Such mobilization can activate horizontal mechanisms of accountability, such as special commissions, investigations, and impeachment, and can trigger electoral fallout. This kind of activity can bolster the willingness of legislators to pursue reforms.

The link between anti-corruption organizations and legislators and the effect on legislators' political will can intensify in the context of parliament–civil society coalitions. As described by Johnston in chapter 10, coalitions with social groups opposed to corruption minimize the risks of, and increase the incentives for, legislators to confront corruption. Such coalitions provide legislators with electoral support and punishments, political funding and organization, legitimacy, policy mandates, grievances, and feedback on the effects of reform. The organizing and educating functions of a coalition make these sorts of political rewards and sanctions more effective.

In addition to their involvement in such organized efforts, private firms can act independently to fight corruption and thereby strengthen legislators' political will. Large multinational firms, in particular, can take a stand against corruption and refuse to invest in countries where corruption levels are high. Some, like Merck & Co., not only orient corporate policies to high ethical standards, but also support seminars, ethics institutes, and industry codes of conduct to improve the business environment where they operate. The criminalization of foreign bribery by firms based in Organisation for Economic Co-operation and Development (OECD) countries and efforts by the International Chamber of Commerce, Transparency International (TI), and other organizations to denounce corruption and develop self-regulatory measures have fueled the international movement among private sector firms to resist corruption (Brinkerhoff and Kulibaba 1999).

Institutional Approaches

Institutional approaches to strengthening legislators' political will focus on reforms of political and economic institutions. Principal among these is a variety of reforms to strengthen the legislatures themselves. Such reforms include establishing effective committees, promoting access to information and research, improving bill-drafting capabilities, and opening channels of communication to citizens. Legislators' effectiveness in these areas can position them to check a dominant executive and fortify their resolve to do so.

Transparency reforms can also help to strengthen legislators' political will. Transparency diminishes opportunities for corrupt exchanges and exposes legislators' votes on key issues. Published or broadcast proceedings of legislative bodies, as well as public information on budgets, revenue collection, statutes, and rules, help to curb abuses and to more directly apportion credit or blame for legislators' actions. In this way, they can buttress legislators' resolve to refrain from corruption and to help fight it.

The likelihood of success can also bolster the resolve of legislators to fight corruption. Effective investigative bodies, prosecutors, judiciaries, law enforcement, audit infrastructures, and ethics frameworks can lead to the successful enforcement of anti-corruption laws passed by legislators and the application of sanctions for misdeeds identified by legislators. In a virtuous circle, this kind of success encourages further efforts in this vein. By contrast, weak or corrupt accountability institutions are likely to derail such legislation and legislative oversight.

In a similar way, the success of initial anti-corruption measures can bolster legislators' resolve. Reforms that generate quick and demonstrative results, such as cost reductions, can generate enthusiasm, mobilize support, and defuse opposition. While other reforms may require longer time horizons, they will only be possible where political will is sustained. Securing these easy wins initially and periodically thereafter will be an important aspect of sustaining political will.

On this topic, longer time horizons themselves may bolster reformers' political will to take on the protracted challenge of fighting corruption. Security in office encourages a long-term perspective on societal issues. Leaders whose positions are tentative, by contrast, may be more inclined to concentrate on short-term issues and leave aside the long-term and politically complex issue of corruption. There is a danger, however, that increasing political security may cause political leaders to feel immune to criticism and more willing to loot (for example, former Philippine leader Ferdinand Marcos and former Zairian leader Mobutu Sese Seko). As mentioned in chapter 3 by Lederman, Loayza, and Soares and as shown by others such as Rose-Ackerman (1999), democratic politics that combines free and fair elections with effective systems of accountability may provide the desired stability without excessive political security.

International Approaches

At the international level, donors and financial institutions can reinforce legislators' political will. Corruption has emerged as a priority for the international community as part of a general rethinking of aid in the post–Cold War era. Western benefactors no longer feel the need to support corrupt regimes; rather, as it becomes clear that aid programs are effective only if fiscally responsible leaders manage them, donors are demanding accountability and transparency in business and government practices. To the extent that donors tie aid to demonstrable commitment or progress toward fighting corruption, they can bolster domestic political will. Donors can also provide the financial resources and technical assistance that allow for continued attention to anti-corruption efforts.

International conventions can also strengthen legislators' commitment to fighting corruption. Signatories to regional and international anti-corruption conventions face peer pressure to introduce reforms and show progress in fighting corruption. Monitoring of progress is part of most conventions' requirements. The chief conventions that are working in this regard are the United Nations Convention against Corruption, the Organisation for Economic Co-operation and Development (OECD) Convention on Combating Bribery of Foreign Public Officials, the Organization of American States' Inter-American Convention against Corruption, the Council of Europe's Groups of States against Corruption, the Stability Pact Anti-Corruption Initiative for South Eastern Europe, the African Union Convention on Preventing and Combating Corruption, and the Asian Development Bank/OECD Anti-Corruption Initiative for Asia-Pacific.

Conclusion

This discussion of political will suggests that fighting corruption is a long-term process—shifting the frame of reference from weeks and months to years. It also is a process that unleashes opposition to reform. Historical accounts document well-intentioned reformers who, unable to mobilize supportive constituencies, faltered because they could not neutralize the resistance.

To sustain an effective anti-corruption campaign, political will must be broadly based. Broadening political participation popularizes the mandate for accountability and enhances the array of tools and strategies that can be utilized to deal with corruption. Political will is most effective when it is inclusive—incorporating the interests of a wide range of constituencies.

At the same time, political will is most enduring when it is institutionalized and not dependent on the personality and intentions of particular persons. Reformers can promote institutionalization by establishing and equipping political institutions with adequate autonomy, authority, resources, and qualified personnel. Such institutionalization develops a forum of mutually reinforcing accountability. The will to fight corruption has much in common with the will to pursue any other goal. It must be given space to grow from within a political system and eventually become an integral part of political, social, and economic processes.

Bibliography

Brinkerhoff, Derick W., and Nicolas P. Kulibaba. 1999. "Identifying and Assessing Political Will for Anti-Corruption Efforts." Working Paper 13, Implementing Policy Change Project, USAID Center for Democracy and Governance, Washington, DC (January).

Corruption Notebooks, The. 2004. Washington, DC: Center for Public Integrity.

Dininio, Phyllis. 2005. "Averting the Risks of Recorruption." In *Fighting Corruption in Developing Countries: Strategies and Analysis,* ed. Bert Spector. West Hartford, CT: Kumarian Press.

Gillespie, Kate, and Gwen Okruhlik. 1991. "The Political Dimensions of Corruption

Cleanups: A Framework for Analysis." *Comparative Politics* 24 (1, Winter): 77–95.

Hellman, Joel, and Daniel Kaufmann. 2001. "Confronting the Challenge of State Capture in Transition Economies." *Finance and Development* 38 (3, September): 31–36.

Jin, Jongsoon. 2005. "Corruption and the Time Horizons of Politicians." Doctoral dissertation, American University, Washington, DC.

Johnston, Michael. 1998. "What Can Be Done about Entrenched Corruption?" In *Annual World Bank Conference on Development Economics 1997,* ed. Boris Pleskovic, 149–80. Washington, DC: World Bank.

Khan, Mushtaq Husain. 1999. "New Approaches to Corruption and Governance and Their Implications." Paper prepared for the conference, "Reinventing the World Bank: Opportunities and Challenges for the 21st Century," Northwestern University (May).

Manzetti, Luigi, and Charles H. Blake. 1996. "Market Reforms and Corruption in Latin America: New Means for Old Ways." *Review of International Political Economy* 3 (4, Winter): 662–97.

Olowu, Dele. 1993. "Corruption in Nigeria: Causes, Consequences and Remedies." In *Ethics and Accountability in African Public Services,* ed. S. Rasheed and Dele Olowu. Nairobi: African Association for Public Administration and Management.

Riley, Stephen. 1983. "The Land of Waving Palms: Corruption Inquiries, Political Economy, and Politics in Sierra Leone." In *Corruption: Causes, Consequences, and Controls,* ed. M. Clarke, 190–206. London: Frances Pinter.

Rose-Ackerman, Susan. 1999. *Corruption and Government: Causes, Consequences, and Reform.* Cambridge, U.K., and New York: Cambridge University Press.

Smulovitz, Catalina, and Enrique Peruzzotti. 2000. "Societal Accountability in Latin America." *Journal of Democracy* 11 (4, October): 147–58.

Thompson, Dennis F. 1995. *Ethics in Congress: From Individual to Institutional Corruption.* Washington, DC: The Brookings Institution.

Part II
Legislation

5

Parliament and Anti-Corruption Legislation

Jeremy Pope

Introduction

Parliament has a critical role to play in fighting corruption, both in enacting appropriate laws to counter corruption and in seeing, through its committees, that these laws are enforced. Relevant laws cover a wide field, as the United Nations Convention against Corruption (ratified in 2003) aptly demonstrates. Indeed, many of the laws that parliaments will be considering over the months ahead will be intended to implement countries' obligations arising from their being party to that convention.

A principal focus is the criminal law. However, the criminal law can act as a deterrent to corruption only up to a point. If the laws are not enforced or enforceable, then those who breach them have little to fear and the laws themselves can become meaningless.

Indeed, the first question a lawmaker must ask is whether a new law is needed at all. A classic case occurred in Geneva when it was found that the official who licensed the opening of new restaurants had been extorting large sums from would-be restaurateurs. Only then was it asked whether the post was needed at all. It was not, and it was abolished. Another example concerns the inspection of motor vehicles in a transition country where virtually all the cars were substandard and bribing the inspectors was near universal. The answer was not to try to enforce a clearly unenforceable law, but to address the question in some other way. In the meantime, the law was repealed and the inspectors dismissed.

Some see the passing of new anti-corruption laws as a necessary first step toward countering corruption (even in countries that already have an adequate range of laws that could counter corruption—if only they were enforced). As a result, laws to punish bribery and other forms of corruption have proliferated around the world—and frequently at the expense of paying attention to ensuring that the laws can and will be enforced or to see that preventive measures are also taken. Passing a new law can seem to be a cost-free way of appearing to take action while in reality changing little.

Three categories of laws are discussed here:

- Laws that punish the corrupt (for example, criminal laws and conflict-of-interest laws) and so deter possible offenders

- Laws that contribute to an administrative and social environment in which corrupt acts are less likely to take place (for example, freedom-of-information laws and disclosures of assets by officials)
- Laws on areas in which corrupt actions would be likely to occur if the legislation is not "corruption-proofed" (for example, laws on procurement and laws providing for welfare payments to citizens)

Laws to Punish and Deter the Corrupt

The criminal law is relevant to the fight against corruption only where there is likelihood that it will be enforced. Thus the first point to note is that there is little point in enacting new laws if the existing ones are not being enforced.

Once concluding that a new criminal law is necessary, parliamentarians should observe nine general principles:

- Complying with international human rights standards (to ensure constitutionality at home and an absence of criticism abroad)
- Not being unduly repressive (in some countries, laws are not enforced because the relevant authorities regard them as being far too severe and so to be inherently "unfair")
- Giving clear guidelines on sentencing (so that sentences are more or less consistent between one case and another)
- Providing penalties proportionate to the degree of seriousness of the offense (to provide for mandatory draconian penalties can prove counterproductive; for example, if a court considers that the facts of an offense do not warrant such a penalty, it may well temper justice with mercy, and some prosecutors may decline to prosecute when they consider the likely penalties to be unjust)
- Combining the various criminal laws dealing with corruption so that they are all in one place (thus making access to these laws as easy as possible for civil servants and others)
- Conducting regular reviews of the criminal law framework (to ensure that things are working as intended and that the relevant laws are achieving their objectives)
- Making any necessary special provisions for corruption cases concerning "proof" (for example, requiring individuals to establish the origins of "unexplained" wealth to the satisfaction of the court, or at the very least to raise a credible explanation of legitimate acquisition)
- Providing for the proceeds of corruption to be subject to recovery by the state (as we will note, this can be done through civil—that is, noncriminal—proceedings)
- Seeing the crime of corruption as including both the payment and the receipt of bribes (while recognizing that there can be a fine line between the payment of a "bribe" and a payment that has been effectively "extorted" under duress by an official)

Drafting the Laws

Anti-corruption legislation generally targets bribery, nepotism, conflicts of interest, and favoritism in the award of contracts or of government benefits. In doing so, some law drafters try to list every imaginable activity and try to make each illegal. However, the corrupt are nothing if not imaginative, and quickly find ways around narrow-based prohibitions. It is therefore generally more effective to draft quite general prohibitions—such as the "abuse of public office for private gain."

General language can capture everything, but its disadvantage is that it can also be used by rivals within the system to challenge actions that are completely innocent, particularly if investigators and judges are subject to political or other pressures. In these ways, an anti-corruption law can, itself, become a source of corruption.

Those enacting the laws should first ask themselves a series of questions:

- Has there been appropriate consultation with the public generally and, in particular, with groups whose interests are particularly affected? (This is not to give either of them a "veto" on a proposed new law, but rather to ensure that there are not unexpected consequences should it be enacted.)
- What is the capacity of the institutions that will have to enforce the law? (If they lack capacity, is there a need for other institutions to be involved? Is there scope for reducing the burden that the law will place on them by making the provisions "self-enforcing"—an extreme example being to give citizens the private right to enforce a criminal law for themselves and without the state being involved?)
- Can the law under consideration be framed in ways that make it simple for the prosecution to prove its case without diminishing from the fairness of the trial itself? (In many countries, a forest of unjustifiable technicalities stands between a prosecutor and a final conviction. A parliament that is serious in confronting corruption will want to feel confident that its laws will be enforced.)
- Are the police, prosecutors, courts, and other enforcement agencies staffed by honest, technically competent professionals? (Surveys in many parts of the world show the citizenry believing that the police and the judicial system are among the most corrupt of their countries' institutions—in which case, is there any point in passing laws that will then be exploited by the corrupt? Should not the police and the judicial system be reformed first?)
- Are the enforcers independent of the executive, both in theory and in practice? If they are not, should parliament be creating additional means by which political opponents can be victimized while friends of the system flourish illegally?
- To whom, and in what ways, are the enforcers themselves accountable? (If this is inadequate, should not the system of accountability be addressed as the priority issue?)

Even with favorable answers to all of the above, it may still take time to build the essential capacity and structures for the fair and professional administration and enforcement of the law, and during this strengthening process, the law drafters must take into account the weaknesses of the agencies that will be responsible for enforcing the laws they prepare.

Laws in Clear Language Can Minimize Areas of Discretion

The World Bank has suggested that in countries where those with discretion commonly abuse it, parliaments should enact "bright-line" rules—rules that are easily understood, simple to apply, and demand little or no judgment to determine their applicability. Such laws contrast with those containing standards that are open to interpretation by enforcement agencies.

Bright-line rules eliminate an enforcer's discretion, but in some circumstances, they do so at some cost. For instance, if nepotism and favoritism in government recruitment are serious problems, legislation could prohibit government employees from hiring a friend or relative unless he or she was "qualified" for the position. With this legislation, the prosecutors and courts would be left to determine whether a particular relative was qualified and so would have considerable discretion in enforcing the law, creating a fertile field for corruption.

Where bright-line rules are employed, the legislation could absolutely prohibit the appointment of any friend or relative outright, with no exceptions or qualifications. In this case, the enforcers would have no discretion. If an official's relative appeared on the payroll, the breach would be obvious. (If the law contained an exception for "qualified" individuals, arguments about the nephew's qualifications would be used to justify—and obscure—the appointment.) Without the exception, the breach is clear for all to see, and citizens, the media, and watchdog groups can readily determine whether their government is serious about enforcing anti-corruption laws.

However, such bright-line laws are absolutist, inflexible, and allow no exceptions. They are simplified (sometimes oversimplified) to the point of being arbitrary. In the case of an anti-nepotism law, a government may well lose the person best qualified for the job. On one hand, weak courts are generally ill equipped to try to develop and impose standards when they are working from more general principles. On the other hand, where public officials are working in the fear of being considered corrupt, the provision of bright-line rules provides them with the confidence to take decisions.

The World Bank (2001) has recommended that countries with weak enforcement institutions should consider including the following bright-line rules in their anti-corruption laws:

- No government employee may receive any gift, payment, or anything of value in excess of a small sum from anyone who is not a member of that person's immediate family.
- No employee may hold, directly or indirectly (that is, through family or other agents), an interest in a corporation or other entity affected by that employee's decisions.
- Every year, all employees above a certain pay level must publicly disclose all assets they hold directly or indirectly.
- No employee may hire a relative (with a precise specification on how distant a relation must be before he or she is not a "relative").
- All employees must disclose any relationship with people hired and with firms or entities to whom they award a contact or concession.

Advance Rulings Can Avoid Problems

Where general provisions in an anti-corruption law create broad discretions, there is much to be said for enabling those in doubt to be able to obtain advice and guidance from the relevant enforcement agency. If, based on the facts disclosed, the enforcement authority concludes that the action proposed would not constitute a violation, the employee would be free from any later prosecution. To prevent the process from unduly slowing government action, agency representatives can be required to rule on the request within a set period. If they do not, the law can provide that the proposed action is lawful. In many countries, there would need to be legislation to provide for such a procedure to be effective.

Some Particular Types of Laws

CONFLICTS OF INTEREST, NEPOTISM, AND CRONYISM. In most countries where corruption is a serious problem, it is fed by conflicts of interest, nepotism, and cronyism; thus, these are often the immediate targets of a national anti-corruption strategy.

A *conflict of interest* arises when a person, as a public sector employee or official, is influenced by personal considerations when carrying out his or her job. In such cases, decisions are made for the wrong reasons. Moreover, a perceived conflict of interest, even when the right decisions are being made, can be as damaging to the reputation of an organization and erode public trust as much as an actual conflict of interest.

Most countries consider the matter so important—and so fundamental to good administration—that they enact a specific conflict-of-interest law. This can provide, for example, that "a State officer or employee shall not act in his official capacity in any matter wherein he has a direct or indirect personal financial interest that might be expected to impair his objectivity or independence of judgment."[1]

The drafters of Thailand's 1997 Constitution saw conflicts of interest as being so important as to require provisions not only in the ordinary law but also in the Constitution itself. Specific provisions require government officials to be politically impartial, and others prohibit a parliamentarian from placing him- or herself in a conflict-of-interest situation. Section 110 clearly states that a Member of the House of Representatives shall not

- "hold any position or have any duty in any State agency or State enterprise, or hold a position of member of a local assembly, local administrator or local government official except other political official other than Minister;
- "receive any concession from the State, a State agency or State enterprise, or become a party to a contract of the nature of economic monopoly with the State, a State agency or State enterprise, or become a partner or shareholder in a partnership or company receiving such concession or becoming a party to the contract of that nature; or
- "receive any special money or benefit from any State agency or State enterprise apart from that given by the State agency or State enterprise to other persons in the ordinary course of business."[2]

Section 111 provides the following:

"A Member of the House of Representatives shall not, through the status or position of Member of the House of Representatives, interfere or intervene in the recruitment, appointment, reshuffle, transfer, promotion and elevation of the salary scale of a Government official holding a permanent position or

---

[1] For a detailed discussion of the issue at senior levels of government, see Carney (1998).
[2] See http://www.ect.go.th/english/laws/constitutioneng.html#6-2.

receiving salary and not being a political official, an official or employee of a State agency, State enterprise or local government organization, or cause such persons to be removed from office."[3]

Nepotism is a particular type of conflict of interest. Although the expression tends to be used more widely, it strictly applies to a situation in which a person uses his or her public power to obtain a favor—very often a job—for a member of his or her family. A number of countries do not yet have a law outlawing the practice.

Where they do, it is generally desirable that the prohibition against nepotism should not be a total ban on all relatives. Indeed, a blanket ban on employing relatives of existing staff (as opposed to a ban on the hiring of relatives of staff to positions where one relative will be exercising supervision over another) can be held to be in breach of human rights guarantees against discrimination; however, as discussed above, it does prohibit a public servant from using (or abusing) his or her public position to get public jobs for family members. The objective should not be to prevent families from working together, but to prevent the possibility that a public servant may show favoritism toward family members in the exercise of discretionary authority on behalf of the public to hire qualified public employees.

Nepotism frequently occurs in the private sector, particularly in the context of promoting family members within family-owned corporations (where it is seen as legitimate), and this is probably an area of private sector conduct that lawmakers should leave alone. The impact of any preference is ultimately on the bottom line (profit) of the corporation, and the bottom line is family "property." Nepotism may cause ill feeling in the workplace in the private sector, but there seems to be no "public interest" reason why the state should intervene and legislate against it.

In the public sector, however, nepotism is damaging to the public interest. It means that the most suitable candidate fails to get a post or a promotion and that the public as a whole suffers as a consequence—in addition to the person who, had there been no nepotism, would have won the position. In other settings, it can mean that a less competitive bid wins a government contract at the cost of the taxpayers' money.

Nepotism can also cause conflicts in loyalty within any organization, particularly where one relative is placed in a direct supervisory position over another. Fellow employees are unlikely to feel comfortable with such a situation, and it is one that should be avoided. An example of a legal prohibition reads:

"No persons related as father, mother, brother, sister, uncle, aunt, husband, wife, son, daughter, son-in-law, daughter-in-law, niece, or nephew may be placed in a direct supervisory-subordinate relationship."[4]

Even worse, of course, would be a judge sitting in a case in which he or she had a financial interest or in which a relative or good friend was involved. In a civil case, the parties might be asked whether they were content for the judge to hear the case, after he or she has explained the potential conflict to them. In a criminal case, however, the judge should simply declare his or her ineligibility and decline to sit. Any failure to do so would generally be considered to be in violation of conflict-of-interest laws.

---

[3] Ibid.
[4] Ibid.

More marginal, perhaps, is the question that arises when the sons and daughters of judges appear as advocates in court before their parents. In some court systems, this has caused no complications, but in others, it has aroused fierce controversy and given rise to serious allegations of collusion and corruption.

Cronyism is a broader term than nepotism and covers situations in which preferences are given to friends and colleagues. In Britain, cronyism is captured in such expressions as the "old school tie" or the "old boys' club."

It is essential that government agencies have clearly stated and well-understood policies and procedures, as well as written codes of conduct, to deal with actual, potential, and perceived conflicts of interest, including nepotism and cronyism. Some countries are starting to impose a legal requirement to do this on their various ministries and agencies. One model is a law that sets out clearly the fundamental values of the public service and then requires agencies to draft their own vision statements and codes of conduct to reflect these values in the particular circumstances of their operations. In the implementation of these policies, a large measure of common sense is called for on the part of managers, and in this, the services of an Ethics Office can be particularly valuable.

POSSESSION OF UNEXPLAINED WEALTH Frequently, it is most apparent that public officials are enriching themselves at the public's expense. Sometimes one need go no further than a customs office car park to see the evidence. But, in the absence of evidence of bribes actually being demanded or received, how can an enforcement agency obtain the proof it needs to gain a criminal conviction?

Where resources are scarce, enforcement agencies often do not have the capacity to take on many cases, and this can mean that much—perhaps all—administrative corruption goes virtually unpunished.

In Hong Kong (whose legislation has attracted considerable interest and emulation around the world), a way forward was found that not only means that it is relatively simple to prosecute cases of repeated administrative corruption but also serves as a strong disincentive to be corrupt. It was made a criminal offense for a public servant to possess wealth in excess of his or her official salary unless the public servant can give a satisfactory explanation for his or her possession of such wealth. The illicit enrichment concept has also been adopted and incorporated into the Inter-American Convention against Corruption (OAS 1996), which requires state parties to establish the offense of the accumulation of a "significant increase" in assets by a government official where that official cannot reasonably explain the increase in relation to his or her lawful functions and earnings.

The value of such an offense in controlling the conduct of public servants, especially senior public servants, is being increasingly realized. The question is whether the human rights and fundamental freedoms of a public servant charged with such an offense are infringed. There are two aspects to be considered: first, whether an offense of merely possessing unexplained wealth in excess of an official salary infringes on his or her right to a fair trial; and second, whether placing on the accused the onus of having to establish the defense of "satisfactory explanation" infringes on the right to be presumed innocent until proved guilty according to law.

The Hong Kong Bill of Rights Ordinance, in article 11(1), provides in the exact words of the International Covenant for Civil and Political Rights that "Everyone charged with a criminal offense shall have the right to be presumed innocent until proved guilty according to law." Not long after the Bill of Rights came into force in

Hong Kong, senior public servants, charged with possessing excessive wealth, challenged the validity of the law, claiming that it infringed on their right to be presumed innocent until proved guilty.

The highest appeals courts in both Hong Kong and the United Kingdom rejected this assertion. They acknowledged that in this sort of offense the primary responsibility for proving matters of substance against the accused, beyond reasonable doubt, rests with the prosecution. Only when it has shown that the accused's wealth could not reasonably have come from the official salary does the accused have to provide a satisfactory explanation. A "satisfactory explanation" would be one that might reasonably account for the wealth in excess of the salary. It is a matter peculiarly within the knowledge of the accused. However, the requirement that he or she provide a satisfactory explanation needs strong justification if this departure from the fundamental principle of the Rule of Law (that the prosecution has the onus of proving every element of the case against the accused) is to be compatible with the protection of human rights.

What is such "strong justification?" As the British Privy Council has said, "Bribery is an evil practice which threatens the foundations of any civilized society." It has also said that there is "notorious evidential difficulty" in proving that a public servant has solicited or accepted a bribe. But there is, the Privy Council said, "a pressing social need to stamp out the evil of corruption in Hong Kong."

The Court of Final Appeal of Hong Kong has echoed that view: "Nobody . . . should be in any doubt as to the deadly and insidious nature of corruption" (Fung 1997). In another case, the British Privy Council said that the offense of possessing excessive unexplained wealth was "manifestly designed to meet cases where, while it might be difficult or even impossible for the prosecution to establish that a particular public servant had received any bribe or bribes, nevertheless his material possessions were of an amount or value so disproportionate to his official salary as to create a prima facie case that he had been corrupted" (de Speville 1997).

In summary, the right to a fair trial and the right to be presumed innocent until proved guilty according to law require that the onus of proof must fall on the prosecution, but may be transferred to the accused when he or she is seeking to establish a defense. Provisions that enshrine the right to be presumed innocent do not prohibit presumptions of fact or law against the accused, although such presumptions must be confined within reasonable limits that take into account the importance of what is at stake and maintain the rights of the defense. Nor do they prohibit offenses of strict liability (that is, offenses that do not require a criminal intent on the part of the accused). They do, however, impose certain evidential and procedural requirements that bear on the pursuit of the corrupt.[5]

REMEDIES THROUGH CIVIL LAW. There are several good reasons for having strong recovery mechanisms against corruption in the civil law, as opposed to the criminal law. Civil courts provide a less onerous atmosphere than the criminal courts for dealing with the consequences of corruption. In the civil court, the burden of proof is not as demanding, and in appropriate cases, the burden of disproving assertions can be more effectively and, at the same time, more fairly placed on the suspect.

---

[5] For details of the cases and a more technical description of the issues, see de Speville (1997), on which this section and the following section are based.

Evidence obtained through civil law need establish guilt through only a "balance of probabilities" rather than "beyond a reasonable doubt."

The corrupt official may be able to create enough dust to enable him or her to evade the criminal law, but the civil law has a broader reach. Judgments obtained in civil courts can usually be enforced in a large number of foreign countries to obtain the contents of foreign bank accounts and other assets. This increases the deterrent factor because the corrupt official must think long and hard about where to hide the gains of his or her corrupt activities.

However, corrupt officials increasingly hide their wealth in family trusts and in other ways to enable them to claim, should the time come, that they have no control over the property. In many countries, this form of evasion is causing acute problems. The public at large boils with rage as corrupt officials are seen to do a short spell in prison and then simply pick up the benefits of their illicitly acquired assets, all safely packaged in the names of their spouses or lawyers.

There are several civil law solutions, including the following:

- Undoing "trusts" and "gifts" and treating them as being ineffective
- Declaring "matrimonial property" claims brought by spouses against assets suspected as having been illicitly acquired to be null and void and based on a nonexistent "ownership"
- Creating a presumption of "continuing control" of property by an accused arising from the circumstances in which the property was transferred to someone else

Remedies through Civil Law for the State. The state is also considered to be a victim of corruption when its officials are involved because technically the moneys taken by a corrupt public official legally belong to the state. The bribes taken are held, technically, in trust for the state; therefore, the state can sue the official for the full amount of the value of the bribes that he or she has received, even if the official (or ex-official) has spent most of the money. It can also make an equitable claim for compensation for breach of fiduciary duty.

It is arguable that the person who actually gave the bribe is also liable for the resulting theft from the state's coffers. Although in some countries existing legal traditions can be invoked, it would generally be preferable to place the matter beyond all argument by passing legislation. It would be a marked disincentive to bribers if they knew that they might be sued by the state and must pay an amount equivalent to the original bribe. In terms of corrupt public procurement, this "repayment" would logically cancel out an element of the price distortion generated by the original bribe, given that this is inevitably reflected in the final price or quality (or both) of delivery.

The extent of liability for corruption in a systemic situation should also be such that if a group of persons received bribes within the one corrupt arrangement, each individual would become personally liable, not only for the amount that he or she took out of the common arrangement but also as " constructive trustees" in respect of bribes received by the others.

The civil law should also clearly state that contracts that are obtained through corrupt means are enforceable only at the discretion of the state. This would enable the state to decide for itself, and in the public interest, whether to be bound by a contract tainted by corruption. To avoid the arbitrary treatment of such contracts on the part of the state, a superior court could be empowered by the state to inquire into the circumstances in which a contract was obtained and to declare it void if corruption was clearly an element in its award. A bidder's knowledge that such contracts rest on shaky ground may be a further inducement against corrupt conduct.

Remedies through Civil Law for the Private Citizen. There are several reasons why private citizens, too, should be able to sue in cases of corruption. The first involves the potential liability of the state for the losses incurred by a citizen or group of citizens because of the actions of a corrupt official. For example, if the state can be shown to have been negligent in its administration, then those who suffer a loss because of a corrupt public procurement exercise may well have a substantial claim for compensation.

If the private sector has little confidence in the anti-corruption efforts of the police and prosecution arms of government, one way of building support would be to empower the private sector to police itself by being able to sue through the civil courts. But whom should they sue? It is surely desirable, on the part of the state, to direct claims away from itself and in the direction of the corrupt public official—the wrongdoer. A court can quite simply establish that the responsibility for the loss lies with the person or entity (or both) that gave or accepted the bribe. For example, where a public procurement exercise has been rigged, the private interests that have been harmed by the corruption could be empowered or encouraged to sue the perpetrators.

In cases in which the state is not in a position to pay adequate compensation, it should consider empowering its citizens to take court action against corrupt officials when they have reason to believe that there may be sufficient assets to make such action worthwhile.

The Council of Europe's 1999 Civil Law Convention on Corruption, to which many European countries are signatories, provides in article 3 that "[e]ach Party shall provide in its internal law for persons who have suffered damage as a result of corruption to have the right to initiate an action in order to obtain full compensation for such damage."

PRESUMPTIONS THAT ASSETS ARE CONTROLLED BY AN ACCUSED PERSON. Corrupt officials can conceal the proceeds of their corruption by transferring them to friends or relatives, but retaining control over them. In response to this, national laws sometimes provide (in relation to the offenses of bribery and unexplained excessive wealth) that where there is reason to believe that any person was holding assets on behalf of the accused or acquired the assets as a gift from the accused, those assets shall be presumed to have been in the control of the accused. This presumption applies where there is no evidence to the contrary—with the onus of providing that evidence resting with the accused.

Again the question arises: does such a so-called "reverse onus" infringe on the right of the accused to be presumed innocent? And again, the Hong Kong Court of Final Appeal has shown a sensible way forward, one that balances the interests involved:

> Before the prosecution can rely on the presumption that pecuniary resources or property were in the accused's control, it has of course to prove beyond reasonable doubt the facts which give rise to it. The presumption must receive a restrictive construction, so that those facts must make it more likely than not that the pecuniary resources or property were held . . . on behalf of

the accused or were acquired as a gift from him. And construed restrictively in that way, the presumption is consistent with the accused's fundamental right, being a measured response to devices by which the unscrupulous could all too easily make a mockery of the offences.

CONTAINING CORRUPTION IN THE PRIVATE SECTOR. In an age of privatization—when many important services, previously provided by the state, are now entrusted to the private sector—governments increasingly seek to maintain an honest environment in the private sector. Frequently, the state cannot opt out of the "risk." If, for example, a privatized railway system effectively collapses, the state may have no alternative but to intervene and pick up the pieces.

Typically, countries are adopting the model of the "market economy," whose functioning is undermined when corrupt practices flourish, denying the public the benefits that should flow from competitive (and not corrupt) market practices. This means that the state has a legitimate interest in intervening to ensure the "health" of the private sector. This can assist the business sector to establish and maintain a commercial environment conducive to fair competition and efficiency. Moreover, it can protect employers from unscrupulous employees who abuse their powers for personal gain. A good example of such a law provides that

* an agent (normally an employee) cannot solicit or accept an advantage without the permission of his or her principal (normally the employer) when in the course of conducting his or her principal's affairs or business; *and*
* the person who offers the advantage also commits an offense[6]

Immunity and Statutes of Limitation

There are two major potential roadblocks to the implementation of the criminal law—provisions that confer forms of immunity on officials and statutes of limitation (by which criminal proceedings must be brought within a set time limit).

Any discussion of *immunity* raises four questions:

* Who is given the protection?
* What acts are covered by the protection?
* For how long does the protection continue?
* To what institutions does the protection extend (for example, to debates in the legislature and to proceedings in the courts)?

The immunities and privileges refer to instances whereby selected officials are specifically shielded from public prosecution or from civil action. The category of official who is granted this immunity and the level of the immunity can be defined either in a country's constitution or in its legislation.

Such protection is not designed to bestow a personal favor on the officeholder; rather, it seeks to facilitate the officeholder in performing the functions of his or her office. It is certainly not designed to enable a senior public official to conduct

---

[6] Section 9 of the Prevention of Bribery Ordinance (Hong Kong). Similar provisions are in the Secret Commissions Act (New Zealand).

private business without having to pay rent, pay his or her creditors, or honor contractual obligations.

Rather it should be designed

- to ensure that the elected representatives of the people can speak in the legislature without fear of criminal or civil sanctions and a host of claims for defamation,
- to protect elected representatives from being arbitrarily detained and so prevented from attending the legislature,
- to act as a shield against malicious and politically motivated prosecutions being brought against them, and
- to be no wider than is absolutely necessary

Immunities, in respect of politicians, should therefore be viewed as contributing to the protection of the democratic process—not as establishing a class of individuals who are above and beyond the reach of the law.

Statutes of limitation rightly require that criminal proceedings be commenced within a given time frame, except in particularly serious cases (such as murder and major fraud). However, in some countries, the law requires that proceedings must not only be started but also be concluded within a set time frame—thus opening the door to the corrupt and their unethical lawyers to deliberately obstruct the proceedings so as to enable the accused to escape conviction and punishment. Clearly, no parliament serious in its work would ever enact such a law. This also provides an example of why legislators should look very carefully at drafts of laws that are based on laws of other countries.

Enforcing the Laws

The most well-thought-out laws will not of themselves control corruption. The present crises in many countries to a large degree stem from the fact that laws are simply not being enforced (see box 5.1). Legal institutions are often failing because of the weaknesses in the judicial systems themselves, coupled with a lack of political will to strengthen the institutions. When an administration is reluctant to combat corruption, it frequently ensures that the enforcement agencies are kept short of

---

Box 5.1 *Unenforceable Laws*

Laws can be unenforceable in practice because the procedures are so obstructive to a prosecutor (a good example are the corruption prosecutions in Italy, where the procedural law requires that a prosecution be heard to finality within a time period that makes it possible for a defendant to delay proceedings to the point of rendering them a nullity). Other instances can be cited of evidential laws that are so restrictive as to render it difficult, if not impossible, to prove a case. Laws may also be unenforced for a variety of reasons, good and bad. In the "good" category are prosecutors who are unwilling to bring cases under laws that they believe to be draconian and to invoke penalties out of all proportion to the offenses alleged. In the "bad" category are prosecutors who leak information to defendants (as did a former public prosecutor in Hong Kong) or otherwise accept bribes and favors in exchange for deliberately making procedural errors that result in acquittals. An alert parliamentarian is on the lookout for instances in both categories.

the resources they need to do their jobs. When considering budget allocations, parliamentarians should insist that these agencies be provided with at least the minimum they require to enable them to do their jobs. If not, the enforcement agencies are simply rendered paper tigers.

Laws Contributing to an Administrative and Social Environment in Which Corrupt Acts Are Less Likely to Take Place

The inevitable failure of laws designed solely to punish the corrupt and so bring levels of corruption under control moves the focus toward laws with a preventive role. Corruption experts see a range of both types of law as being required. Among the latter are laws providing for the following:

- Access to information (including official secrets legislation)
- Disclosure of assets by public officials
- Freedom of expression
- Freedom of the press
- Protection of "whistleblowers" and complainants
- Enabling civil society to mobilize
- Democratic elections
- Banning those convicted of offenses of moral turpitude from holding or running for election to public office or from holding directorships
- Managing gifts and hospitality
- Creating the Office of the Ombudsman
- Providing for judges to be able to review the legality of administrative actions

Skillfully drafted, these can create an environment in which corrupt acts are less likely to occur, without adding to the list of punitive measures. Particularly is this so when there is a broad and effective Freedom of Information Act, entitling the citizens (and journalists) to access official information. Ordinary citizens need information for many purposes in the course of their lives, and in some countries, access to information has been shown to be an effective weapon with which to fight poverty. Legislators may well find themselves caught between a public that demands greater access to information and an executive (and government officials) who want to keep the public out. The balance is not always easy to strike, but there are now numerous examples of good and effective legislation in other countries to which legislators can refer.[7]

In many parts of the world, the argument is advanced that one of the key instruments for maintaining integrity in the public service should be the periodic completion, by all those in positions of influence, of declarations of their own incomes, assets, and liabilities and those of their immediate families. It is a thesis that is winning support from international agencies, and it is an approach that would seem to offer a corruption "quick fix" if it is as effective as its sponsors believe it to be. Some countries—predominantly in the industrialized world—already have these arrangements. Some also require senior officeholders to divest themselves of their major investments, and others permit the establishment of "blind trusts" (Pulle 1996).

---

[7] For examples from around the world, see http://www.privacyinternational.org.

It goes without saying that disclosures of assets and income will not be accurately completed by those who are taking bribes or who intend to do so. However, it is generally believed that the requirement that they formally record their financial positions can lay an important building block for any subsequent prosecution based on unexplained wealth. It would, for example, preclude them from suggesting that any later wealth that had not been disclosed had, in fact, been acquired legitimately.

Disclosure, the argument runs, should also extend to a certain postservice period as a deterrent to the receipt of corrupt payments after retirement. (Studies have suggested that it is unlikely that corrupt payments are made more than three years after a person has retired.)

But does disclosure work? Experience has been patchy. Initially, in some countries with corruption problems, politicians legislated for disclosure, but then ignored requirements completely. Some others established an agency merely to receive declarations that were not made available to the media or the public and gave the agency no power (or no resources) with which to check their accuracy. More recently, however, in several countries, the process has claimed some scalps—though whether through carelessness rather than corrupt intent is at least arguable. The transgressions have generally been because the first declarations had not been completed accurately, rather than failures to notify significant changes in wealth thereafter. What the declarations do achieve, however, is to provide a record of a person's interests, a record that can be invaluable later when it comes to dealing with questions of alleged conflicts of interest.

Having accepted the argument in favor of disclosure, several questions follow: To whom should disclosure be made? What matters should be included? How wide should coverage of members of the household be? How often should disclosures be made? What access should the media and members of the public have to these declarations? And, in the case of career public servants, what levels of seniority must be required to submit to this process? There are no obvious answers to any of these questions.

The tricky part of this process is not so much deciding on the categories of assets to be disclosed or on the categories of the officials who should be making disclosure, but rather determining the extent to which there should be public access to the declarations. The litmus test must be whatever is needed to achieve public peace of mind—not whatever is conceded by the most determined opponents of disclosure. Nor are matters always as simple as they may seem. A Minister of Finance from Colombia has been quoted as suggesting that for a politician in his country to make his or her wealth known to the public would be to give an open invitation to kidnappers to move in and claim the sums disclosed as a ransom.

In Nigeria, the Code of Conduct Commission was empowered, from 1979 onward, to require the filing of returns by all public officials. However, it had neither the resources nor the legal powers to actually check the contents of any of these. As a consequence, throughout a prolonged period of looting by public officials, the only prosecutions ever mounted were against public officials who failed to file an annual return—not for filing a false one.

In Tanzania, the legislation was a fraud on the public: it appeared to require the declaration of all property held by a public official, but after all the exceptions to this requirement had been listed, there was virtually nothing left. The legislation, enacted in the dying days of a particularly corrupt presidency, was clearly for public consumption only.

During Boris Yeltsin's presidency in Russia, there was a proposal that every public official, from the President to the street cleaners, should make written declarations to the tax police, arguably the most corrupt arm of the Russian administration. The whole proposal was a logistical impossibility—and not surprisingly came to nothing. On the other hand, more meaningful public disclosure requirements have been introduced in some transition and developing countries (for example, Bulgaria and Thailand).

In Australia, a system whereby officials make written disclosures to the head of their department annually has been seen as being effective in that country, but these are not made public. Similar disclosures are managed by ethics counselors in Canada, and there *are* rights of public access. Such systems seem to work in environments where there is a relative absence of systemic corruption. Where corruption is a major problem, other approaches are generally necessary.

The most contested area for disclosures is generally that of the interests of parliamentarians themselves. When enacting laws providing for disclosures, parliamentarians are in a classic position of conflict of interest because they are, in effect, legislating for, and about, themselves, their families, and those in the political leadership of the executive. A cynical public, however unfairly, will view claims by parliamentarians to be entitled to protect their own privacy and that of their families as little more than a pretext behind which to hide obscure and corrupt dealing.

South Africa has introduced a scheme for the monitoring of all parliamentarians (including ministers) designed to cut the Gordian knot. A compromise has been reached in an effort to meet legitimate claims to privacy. Certain disclosures are made openly and publicly; some are made as to the substance of the interest, but the actual value is disclosed privately; and the interests of family members are disclosed, but in confidence. The argument for the last is that members of a parliamentarian's family have a right to privacy, and it should be sufficient for the disclosure to be made on the record, but not on the *public* record.

The development of effective and fair regimes for the monitoring of the incomes, assets, and liabilities of senior public officials is followed closely by anti-corruption activists, for if they can be made to work—and there are obvious difficulties—then they should be able to serve as a valuable tool in restraining abuses of office.

No discussion of creating such an environment is complete without mentioning the centrality of a sound official records management system. The keepers of the archives need sound legislation (and the necessary resources) to place them in a position to create sound records management policies and to collect and archive documents as and when ministries cease to need them. In many ways, the archivists underwrite the effectiveness of freedom-of-information laws. Legislation to provide for the proper management and preservation of official papers is of the highest importance.

Laws on Subjects in Which Corrupt Actions Would Be Likely to Occur If the Legislation Is Not "Corruption-Proofed"

Corruption can occur in myriad places, and every piece of proposed legislation should be scrutinized to ensure that it is not creating circumstances that lend themselves to corruption. In other words, every draft law should be corruption-proofed.

Corruption should not be left to be dealt with after the event and after the damage has been done. Ideally, it should be nipped in the bud and without the need to rely on punitive measures.

For example, a law must be clearly stated and unambiguous to limit the ability of public servants to provide "interpretations" that they can then exploit. A law must be examined to ensure that needlessly broad discretions are not given and that where it is necessary to provide for the exercise of discretion, there are clear guidelines as to how decisions are to be made. If the intention is to provide benefits for the public (or for a section of the public), legislators should ensure that the intended beneficiaries will be made aware of the new rights they are acquiring, thus reducing the chances that the funds involved will be exploited. Complaints systems, too, should be made available (either in the particular legislation or more generally).

A classic example of a law that must be corruption-proofed is provided in the field of public procurement. This is a major challenge for many parliaments, charged as they are with providing an appropriate legal framework to protect the public interest. A carefully framed procurement law can provide for a large degree of transparency, access to information, reasonable time limits, public scrutiny of the opening of bid envelopes, and the like—each a factor that can add to the integrity of the process.

The "blacklisting" (or debarment) of companies and individuals who bribe public servants to win public tenders has received a great deal of publicity as an anticorruption strategy.

However, its success in contributing to good governance is limited if it is relied on as the main policy for ensuring that public procurement is "clean." Like any sanction, its power relies on the idea that rule breakers will be caught so that potential wrongdoers are deterred. It alters the risk-versus-profit ratios that are understood to govern premeditated acts of corruption.

If the procurement process as a whole cannot prevent corrupt companies or individuals from winning contracts, debarment by itself will not be an effective remedy. One of the important lessons of the experiences of Singapore, the World Bank, and New York State, among others, is that debarment is only one part—albeit an important part—of a properly organized procurement process.

Other existing procurement processes also must be risk assessed and refined to prevent fraud. This includes eliminating opportunities for corrupt bidding by way of qualification for bidding and providing for disclosure, transparency in the bidding process, standards of transparency, and controls over the extent of postcontractual variations of price or specifications.

Two questions must be asked by policy makers and parliamentarians before a law for a blacklisting process is considered: What are the strengths or weaknesses of the existing procurement process? What is blacklisting expected to achieve for the agency in question?

Conclusion

Parliamentarians, in their law-making phase, can play a major part in creating a social as well as a legal environment in which corruption is less likely to occur and detected when it does. (Please see the case study that follows this chapter.) The control of corruption is not a moral crusade, and it is not achieved through appeals to the better side of people's nature. Rather it is gained, at least in part, through carefully thought out and carefully crafted legislation.

Bibliography

Carney, Gerard. 1998. "Conflict of Interest: Legislators, Ministers, and Public Officials." Working Paper, Transparency International (TI), Berlin. http://ww1.transparency.org/working_papers/carney/index.html.

de Speville, Bertrand. 1997. *Reversing the Onus of Proof: Is It Compatible with Respect for Human Rights Norms?* Paper presented to the 8th International Anti-Corruption Conference (IACC), Lima, Peru (September 7–11).

Fung, Daniel R. 1997. *Anti-Corruption and Human Rights Protection: Hong Kong's Jurisprudential Experience.* Paper presented to the 8th International Anti-Corruption Conference (IACC), Lima, Peru (September 7–11).

OAS (Organization of American States). 1996. "Inter-American Convention against Corruption." General Assembly Resolution (AG/RES.) 1398 (XXVI-O/96) (June 7). www.oas.org/juridico/english/ga-res97/Eres1398.html.

Pulle, Bernard. 1996. "Conflicts of Interest Avoidance: Is There a Role for Blind Trusts?" *Current Issues Brief* 1996–97 (14, December). http://www.aph.gov.au/library/pubs/CIB/1996-97/97cib14.htm.

World Bank. 2001. "Writing an Effective Anticorruption Law." PREMnote 58, Poverty Reduction and Economic Management, World Bank, Washington, DC (October). www1.worldbank.org/publicsector/legal/PREMnote58.pdf.

Case Study on the Role of Parliament in the Fight against Corruption: The Case of the Kenyan Parliament

Fred Matiangi

Introduction

Corruption is one of the socioeconomic and political challenges of independent Kenya. When in 1996, Kenya was ranked the third most corrupt country in the world in Transparency International's (TI's) corruption perception index, local and international governance agencies developed a more sustained interest in the country's governance. Since then, discourse on the governance situation in Kenya has frequently revolved around the government's efforts to deal with graft and establishing an integrity system in the public service. Corruption is pervasive in Kenya, and it affects the country's public and private life. Many institutions of its government, including Parliament, the judiciary, and especially the executive arm, have been affected by corruption.[1]

This case study examines the role that the Kenyan Parliament has played over the years in the war against corruption. It focuses on its role from all three key functions of parliament, namely legislation, representation, and oversight.

Any parliament is a creature of the constitutional framework that defines the society within which it exists. The Kenyan Parliament is no exception. In addition, parliaments are often influenced by the sociopolitical and economic dynamics of their societies. In the political and historical context of the Kenyan Parliament, four major experiences have shaped its institutional and political character: the economics of transition and the challenge of conflict of interest, the political events of the 1960s and the tensions of postindependence politics, one-party state politics, and the constitutional position of parliament. The impact of these experiences is evident in the institutional profile of the Kenyan Parliament to date and its contribution to the war against corruption. These experiences are briefly appraised below.

---

[1] There have been widespread complaints in the Kenyan media about corruption in Parliament, especially in the handling of mileage claims by Members of Parliament (MPs) and the possibility of vested interests outside Parliament affecting parliamentary business. The much-publicized example is that of "cash for questions" allegations, whereby MPs are alleged to be induced by cash rewards to ask particular questions in Parliament.

The Economics of Transition and the Challenge of Conflict of Interest

The history of corruption in Kenya dates back to colonial times. Although some researchers and investigators have noted that the colonial government rarely understood the traditional African cultural practice of leaders' entitlement to gifts and favors from their subjects, the measures it took in Kenya, as in many African communities, smacked of abuse of power.

The colonial government therefore advised its collaborators to adopt moderation. Many chiefs did not adhere to the caution, however, and took advantage of colonial practices like the livestock tax to unduly enrich themselves.

The colonial government thus enacted in 1956 the Prevention of Corruption Act (Cap 65).[2] At this time, the colonial government was mainly concerned about the way public officials often used their positions to accumulate wealth, and the Legislative Council of Kenya (LEGCO) addressed itself to the issue of graft. Instructively, however, the 1956 Prevention of Corruption Act did not define corruption succinctly, and most of the concepts it outlined reflected the general worries of the time, especially the aspect of public officials taking advantage of their positions to enrich themselves.

The debate in the LEGCO reflected neither knowledge nor broader understanding of corruption. Rather, it mainly dwelt on the issue of gifts and bribery to public officials. It was important, however, because for the first time in Kenya, corruption became an issue in legislative affairs (albeit, in a superficial way).

The Kenyan public's awareness about corruption was not pronounced at that time, although there is evidence that by the time Kenya became independent in the early 1960s, corruption had become a key feature of the emerging public service.

At independence, the government's focus was mainly on the economics of transition. Thus, the emphasis was on the economic empowerment of the African people and the associated political desire to transfer wealth from the hands of colonialists and foreigners to the hands of the indigenous people. These efforts would lead to many unintended activities that in turn would affect the integrity of public service: the emerging Kenyan elite, in the Parliament and in the executive alike, sought advantages to acquire wealth.

The government soon appointed a commission[3] to inquire into the public service structure and remuneration. The commission made a number of far-reaching recommendations, some of which have led to profound conflicts of interest in the public service in Kenya. Notably, it recommended that public servants[4] could also engage in private business, thereby planting the original seed for conflicts of interest.

Hardly surprisingly, less attention was paid to integrity. Parliament played no role at all in opposing the emerging conflict-of-interest trend nor did it legislate on any aspects of the impending doubling of the number of public servants working in the private sector.

---

[2] Between 1956 and 1991 (when it was significantly amended), the Prevention of Corruption Act of 1965 had been amended eight times; however, in 1991, it was amended to create the defunct Kenya Anti-Corruption Authority.

[3] The Commission of Inquiry into the Public Service Structure and Remuneration, 1971 (also referred to as the "Ndegwa Commission" after its chairman, former Head of the Civil Service and later Governor of the Central Bank of Kenya, Duncan Ndegwa).

[4] For all intents and purposes, "public servants" include parliamentarians.

An incestuous relationship would thus emerge between public service and private interests that would undermine any interest in integrity issues. Studies have shown, for instance, that there is a correlation between wealth and politics in Kenya.[5] Those who play active and influential roles in politics are the well-to-do, or they become well-to-do by virtue of office.

With the systematic decline of professionalism in the public service, there entered instead a culture of deliberate interference with the public service for personal gain. Parliament's legislative and oversight role was effectively compromised again, largely for personal gain.

The Political Events of the 1960s and Tensions of Postindependence Politics

Kenya's constitution at independence envisioned a multiparty parliamentary democracy. Two dominant political parties, the Kenya African National Union (KANU) and the Kenya African Democratic Union (KADU), shaped the politics of the day.

In 1964, when Kenya became a republic, the constitutional changes that came with this development created a very strong executive under an "imperial" presidency. The president wielded immense powers, which explains the manipulative master-servant relationship that developed between the executive and the Parliament.

This relationship would deteriorate in the wake of a falling-out between the late President Jomo Kenyatta and his Vice President, Jaramogi Oginga Odinga. The latter's formation of the Kenya People's Union (KPU) and its consequent strong opposition to the government gave President Kenyatta an excuse to further strengthen his constitutional stranglehold on Parliament.

When in 1969 (after a fracas in Kisumu), Kenyatta banned KPU, Kenya became a de facto one-party state. Parliament became even weaker and more dependent on the executive, which dictated the constitutional changes that took place, like the Ngei amendment after the 1974 general elections[6] and the use by the president of his executive powers to detain outspoken Members of Parliament without trial.

Even in these circumstances, however, some individual MPs took up the cause of anti-corruption. Some MPs, notably the late J. M. Kariuki and George Anyona,

---

[5] See, for example, Frank Holmquist, "Business and Politics in Kenya in the 90s," a paper presented at the African Seminar Centre for African Studies, University of Copenhagen.

[6] Muigai Githu, "Amendment Lessons from History," The Advocate 2, no. 3 (February 1993). This amendment of the constitution was specifically "ordered" by the president to facilitate his forgiving of the late Paul Ngei. Ngei, a close friend of President Jomo Kenyatta, a coaccused at the Kapenguria trial, and formerly a Minister of Local Government, had less than a month before the amendment been found guilty of an election offense by an election court and had been barred from contesting any elections for five years, as was then provided for in the relevant election law. President Kenyatta intervened to save Ngei from political oblivion. The result was this amendment, which extended the prerogative of mercy, enjoyed by the president under section 27 of the constitution, to the removal of disqualification arising out of the report of an election court once an election offense has been proved against an election candidate. The substance and the procedure of this amendment put the bona fides of the government at issue and greatly compromised the government's alleged commitment to the rule of law.

questioned the allocation of public resources and the management of public institutions. They both paid a price; the latter was detained, while the former was assassinated in 1975. This culture of intimidation and dictatorship greatly limited Parliament's role against graft.

One-Party State Politics

Kenya's presidential transition in 1978, from Jomo Kenyatta to Daniel arap Moi, saw the relationship between the executive and the Parliament worsen. In the aftermath of the 1982 coup attempt, the government amended Section 2 of the constitution, making Kenya a de jure one-party state. This ushered in unprecedented erosion of basic democratic practices and further eroded Parliament's powers.

KANU presided over a "reign of political terror," with the whims of the party holding sway in national affairs. Numerous amendments to the constitution were choreographed by KANU, all resulting in the strengthening of the executive at the expense of Parliament and the judiciary.

This situation was ripe for rampant corruption as the executive used state resources to strengthen its hold on power. Parliament had been transformed into a toothless watchdog that could do nothing, and even its basic institutional structures like the committee system were inoperable.

A classic case of the impact of one-party state politics on parliament's capacity to fight graft was best demonstrated in 1985 when the then-President Daniel arap Moi and senior officials, including the then-Head of the Civil Service, Simeon Nyachae, demanded an amendment to the Exchequer and Audit Act to take away the security of tenure of the Office of the Controller and Auditor General (CAG).

The State Corporations Act was equally affected through an amendment that empowered the president to exempt some state corporations from audit. All these efforts were intended to facilitate pilferage from state corporations without any of the watchdog institutions raising questions.

What ensued was plunder of state resources while Parliament watched helplessly. The Public Investments Committee (PIC) of the Parliament, which had been created by Standing Orders of Parliament in 1979, was for all intents and purposes moribund. Its very first chairman, Kenneth Matiba, an astute businessman and private sector insider who had been elected MP for Kiharu in the 1979 general elections, was held in very high suspicion by the ruling elite.

When the business of the PIC commenced with the summoning of chief executives of state corporations, the Office of the President interrupted its work, knowing that the PIC intended to contest the president's powers to appoint and supervise the chief executive officers (CEOs) of state corporations. The PIC was consistently sabotaged, and some of its members were intimidated by the executive. In any case, the party was stronger, and those who did not toe the KANU party line of having nothing to do with the PIC knew they would soon be out of Parliament. The Committee remained moribund until after the multiparty elections of 1992.

The Constitutional Position of Parliament

The Constitution of Kenya vests the legislation, representation, and oversight of the executive responsibilities in Parliament. Parliament executes the oversight responsibilities through the watchdog committees created by Standing Orders, particularly Standing Orders 147 and 148, which created the Public Accounts Committee (PAC) and the PIC, respectively.

In many Commonwealth countries, the powers of parliament to intervene in integrity-related matters reside more with the watchdog committees of the PAC and its equivalents (such as the PIC). However, in Kenya, the effectiveness of the parliamentary committees has been overly weak, thanks to a history of an overbearing executive.

The executive's effectiveness often influences that of Parliament. Parliamentary watchdog committees' work is often based on reports generated by the Office of the Controller and Auditor General. The KANU regime did everything to ensure that this Office would be inefficient.

Although the Controller and Auditor General's security of tenure was reinstated, the executive essentially deprived the Office of professional staff, who were poorly compensated compared with their counterparts in the private sector, while the budget of the Office was cash-starved. The Office was therefore routinely behind in filing its reports, which in turn adversely affected the work of the PAC and PIC, which depended on the Auditor General's reports for their own work.

Under the constitution, Parliament has no direct powers to sanction corruption; rather, it recommends sanctions that it is the responsibility of the Attorney General's office to implement. However, this office often rationalizes its inability to take action with a litany of excuses ranging from lack of compelling evidence to inability to investigate further the recommendations of the PAC and PIC.

Despite the constitutional handicaps, the Kenyan Parliament has raised the issue of graft in the executive and has legislated against corruption in the recent past. It has investigated and prepared reports on corruption, thereby sensitizing the public on the vice. In recent years, the most significant such cases include the Goldenberg Scandal, the debate and enactment of anti-graft legislation, and the recent special audit conducted by the PAC on the procurement by the Office of the Vice President of passport-issuing equipment by the Anglo Leasing and Finance company.

The Goldenberg Scandal

The Goldenberg Scandal is perhaps the largest case of official corruption in Sub-Saharan Africa; it was a fraudulent export compensation scheme put in place by the government, ostensibly to help earn Kenya foreign exchange through the export of gold and diamonds. It turned out later that it was a government-sanctioned scheme to siphon funds from the Central Bank of Kenya.

The scandal came to light when the whistle was blown in Parliament by the opposition MPs Anyang Nyongo and Paul Muite, who had gained information from junior officials in the Central Bank. They tabled papers in the House demonstrating that about 24 billion[7] Kenyan shillings (K Sh) had been transferred to Exchange Bank, which was owned by Goldenberg International, a phony company set up by Kamlesh Pattni.

---

[7] The British billion (a million million) is different from the American billion (a thousand million). The author is using the British meaning here.

The public's awareness of the Goldenberg Scandal then began. In this case, Parliament (using its privilege under the Powers and Privileges Act) was most effective in exposing the scandal and thus preventing further looting.

Parliamentary Anti-Corruption Select Committee

The most significant contribution of Parliament in curbing corruption was through the Anti-Corruption Select Committee (or the "Kombo Committee," as it is commonly referred to, after its Chairman, Musikari Kombo).

Rampant corruption was a much-talked-about issue in the media. Parliament took a bold initiative, and after an acrimonious debate, an increasingly assertive back bench succeeded in pushing through a private Member's motion for the establishment of a Parliamentary Anti-Corruption Committee to, among other things, study and investigate the causes, nature, extent, and impact of corruption in Kenya; identify the key perpetrators and beneficiaries of corruption; recommend effective and immediate measures to be taken against such individuals in corruption; and recover public property appropriated by them.

The Committee advertised and made announcements in the press, inviting the public to submit oral and written evidence of corruption to it. The Committee received more than 1,000 written memoranda, at times summoned authors of such memoranda to appear before it to explain some claims, and visited sites of alleged corrupt deals and activities.

Two years after its formation, the Committee submitted its report to Parliament. Although weak on tangible evidence, the report was damning in its findings and recommendations. It found out that corruption was so extensive and deep rooted that almost 56 percent of tax revenue was misappropriated corruptly.

With regard to the causes of corruption, the Committee noted the following:

> Poverty, authoritarian rule, erosion of accountability in the process of government, misuse of political power, unsatisfactory civil service wages, and weak law enforcement institutions aid and abet corruption in society in general and in the public service in particular. Those causes have been reinforced by a growing national culture that seems to tolerate corruption provided it is beneficial to the immediate family or kin-group. Blind political loyalties also lead to high tolerance of corrupt practices.[8]

The Committee recommended a number of actions, including the introduction in Parliament of an Anti-Corruption and Economic Crimes Bill, the outlawing of *harambee* (public collections or fund raising) in public offices, and major reforms in the judicial system in the country.[8]

In addition, the Committee drew up a list of people in public life considered to be most corrupt. This stirred up the hornet's nest. Debate on the report in Parliament was intense and acrimonious because the "list of shame" read like a Who's Who in the corridors of power. The government responded by intimidating most of its backbenchers into voting to expunge the infamous list, but not before it found its way into the hands of the press. Although the press did not publish the list (because of the stiff libel laws), it based extensive commentaries on it.

---

[8] Kenya National Assembly—"Report of the Parliamentary Anti-Corruption Committee," p. 4.

Although it put on a brave face throughout this episode, the government was considerably shamed. The Kombo Committee also succeeded in doing two other things: it raised the public's awareness of corruption in high places, and it brought realization to Parliament about its constitutional capacity to address graft. It also gave Parliament a chance to come to terms with its institutional weakness to decisively deal with graft.

Parliament's role in the war against graft was enhanced by the formation in 2001 of the African Parliamentarians' Network Against Corruption (APNAC) (see chapter 14). This network of Members of Parliament from the whole of Africa forged a closer working relationship with TI to agitate for legislation against corruption. In Kenya, the Kombo Committee immediately formed the Kenyan chapter of APNAC upon its formation.

The government in 2001 drafted and tabled in Parliament the Anti-Corruption and Economic Crimes Bill, 2001, which was a clear case of the executive trying to manipulate the war against corruption. It made very controversial proposals, including a general amnesty for all economic crimes committed prior to December 1, 1997.

In addition to a vigorous public debate sparked off by this bill, most parliamentarians saw it as an attempt by the government to manipulate the legislative process to give itself immunity from economic crimes it had committed. The opposition in Parliament, largely led by Musikari Kombo and the then-leader of the official opposition, Mwai Kibaki, opposed the bill.

The general elections of 2002 resulted in the transfer of power from KANU to the newly formed National Alliance Rainbow Coalition (NARC). The new government was elected to power on an anti-corruption platform. Some of the very first bills it brought to Parliament were anti-graft pieces of legislation: the Anti-Corruption and Economic Crimes Bill, 2003, and the Public Officer Ethics Bill, 2003.

The Anti-Corruption and Economic Crimes Bill sought, among other things, to define corruption broadly. In addition, the bill was aimed at creating a constitutionally entrenched Kenya Anti-Corruption Commission (KACC) with express powers to investigate graft, conduct civic education and preventive services, check on practices and procedures in public institutions, and even audit the electoral process in the country to ensure avoidance of corruption in the process of election to public office.

The Public Officer Ethics Bill was intended to promote ethics and accountability among public officers. It introduced a code of conduct for public servants and introduced mandatory disclosures of assets and liabilities by public servants.

The enactment of the two bills into law after a vigorous debate in Parliament saw Parliament make a very significant contribution to the war against graft: first, Parliament effectively played its constitutional role by legislating against graft, and second, through the very vigorous and candid debate on the bills, the general public's awareness of the need to continue fighting corruption was enhanced.

The Anglo Leasing Scandal is the most recent case of Parliament using its constitutional responsibility of oversight to fight graft. On April 20, 2004, the opposition MP for Ntonyiri, Maoka Maore, tabled in Parliament documents showing that the Offices of the President, the Vice President, the Ministry of Home Affairs, and the Treasury were in the process of illegally procuring passport-issuing equipment, in which the country stood to lose about K Sh 7 billion.

The matter raised a furor in Parliament, and a ministerial statement was demanded from the Office of the Vice President and Minister of Home Affairs. The

Vice President, who is also the Leader of Government Business in Parliament, gave a ministerial statement in the House denying any wrongdoing on the part of the government. MPs did not accept the statement and questioned the transaction. Instructively, a few days later, the Ministry of Finance (through the Central Bank) announced that the money the government had paid as down payment for the procurement of the passport-issuing equipment had been returned to the Central Bank.

In the meantime, a more skeptical and increasingly assertive Parliament demanded more explanations from the executive. When it was not forthcoming, the PAC, in a rare exercise of powers, ordered the National Audit Office to conduct a special audit of the passport-issuing equipment contract.

In conducting the special audit, the PAC received evidence from senior public officials whom it summoned, including the Permanent Secretaries in the Offices of the Vice President and the Treasury. It found out that on August 1, 2003, a firm by the name of Anglo Leasing and Finance, Ltd., of the United Kingdom submitted to the Office of the Vice President and Ministry of Home Affairs an unsolicited technical proposal for the supply and installation of an Immigration Security and Document Control System (ISDCS). The firm indicated in its proposal that it could supply and install the equipment through its officially designated systems subcontractor, Francois-Charles Oberthur Fiduciare of Paris, France.

The PAC submitted a damning report to Parliament. It noted first that the government received much less money in refund than what it had paid to Anglo Leasing and Finance and second that the Office of the Vice President and Ministry of Home Affairs had not demanded full compensation and the interest accrued.

The PAC noted that this was contrary to what the Minister of Finance had told the House (that is, that he actually had been "well briefed and was satisfied with the way the relevant officers handled the transactions." The PAC therefore recommended that the Finance Minister be held personally responsible for allowing his Ministry to involve the government in a very expensive project with Anglo Leasing and Finance, whose physical location, directors, and shareholders were unknown.

The debate that followed the tabling of the report in the House was again acrimonious, with the NARC members introducing amendments to expunge paragraphs that indicted the Finance Minister. The government side succeeded in deleting the paragraphs recommending sanctioning of the Finance Minister. However, on the day of taking the final vote on the report, the House rejected the report on the basis that it had been diluted by the removal of the clauses on the Finance Minister's culpability.

Conclusion

Since the reintroduction of multiparty democracy in 1991, the Kenyan Parliament has increasingly asserted itself, at least in the context of the current constitutional framework. In so doing, its voice against corruption continues to grow, and the public, too, is developing greater interest in the integrity of Parliament. Recently, the Kenyan Parliament has been a target of lobbyists, as witnessed in the case of debate on the Tobacco Control Bill, 2004 (see box 1). A group of parliamentarians were feted at an exclusive resort on the coast of Kenya (ostensibly to discuss the bill). The truth emerged later that industrialists with vested interests had played host to the gathering of MPs in a matter that generated public debate in the media about the ethics of lobbying and conflict of interest.

Box 1. *The Perception of Corruption within the Parliament*

Though the parliament plays a critical role in challenging government corruption in Kenya, some citizens see it not as part of the solution but as part of the problem. A September 2005 nationwide survey revealed that a growing number of Kenyans consider Members of Parliament (MPs) to be corrupt. According to the survey, 6 percent of Kenyans queried believe that none of their MPs are corrupt, 43 percent believe that some MPs are corrupt, and 40 percent that most or all are corrupt. The extent of perceived corruption of MPs rose from 15 percent in 2003 to 40 percent in 2005, making the MPs second only to the police in perceptions about public corruption (Afrobarometer 2006).

In what ways are MPs vulnerable to corruption? For one, in systems such as Kenya's, MPs who become ministers gain access to resources far beyond those of backbenchers, and the enticement to use them for personal and party purposes can be very great. In the Anglo Leasing Case described in this chapter, both the finance minister and justice minister resigned in response to corruption charges.

Second, the Kenya Parliament's control over its own staffing and resources, critical to its independence from the executive, also provides greater opportunities for corruption. Although parliament members can legally vote to give themselves significant pay increases and perks, many Kenyans consider those rewards to be excessive and therefore a type of corruption (that is, using state resources for private gain). The parliament now has authority over its own management and budget, sets its own salaries, and manages a very large constituent development fund (2.5 percent of the national budget). The increased parliamentary budget, plus the funds being distributed to constituencies, increases the possibilities of corruption.

And third, the parliament's greater ability to amend, pass, or kill legislation, and its greater influence in amending the national budget, make it important to individuals and organizations wishing to influence policies. This is a healthy development, but it also increases the likelihood that they will attempt to influence public policy by providing MPs with private benefits. No one lobbies a weak legislature, but as legislators' authority over policies increases, so will attempts to influence them. The concern generated by the tobacco lobby's bringing MPs to a Kenya beach resort to influence the Tobacco Control Bill illustrates this.

What can be done to help limit corruption in legislatures? Open meetings, clear and rigorous ethics codes, and ethics committees can help. Most of the world's legislatures hold their plenary sessions before the press and public, but many still conduct committee meetings behind closed doors. Opening them to the press and public brings more light into the decision-making process. Sunshine is the best antiseptic. Ethics committees, which exist in several legislatures, make determinations regarding legislative misconduct. Clear and well-enforced ethics codes for public officials, including MPs and staff, help remove the ambiguity about what is and what is not corruption—and make clear the consequences of corrupt behavior.

Source: Johnson 2006.

References

Afrobarometer 2006. "Corruption in Kenya, 2005: Is NARC Fulfilling Its Campaign Promise?" Afrobarometer Briefing Paper No. 26, January 2006. http://www.afrobarometer.org/papers/AfrobriefNo26.pdf.

Johnson, J. 2006. Unpublished report. World Bank Institute. Washington DC: World Bank.

Part III
Oversight and Financial Control

6

Effective Financial Scrutiny

Joachim Wehner

Introduction

Fiscal transparency has become a major theme in the international debate on good governance. This debate has focused mainly on deriving standards for the provision of relevant budgetary and audit information by the government (IMF 2001; OECD 2002). There is less of a consensus to date on how parliaments can contribute to fiscal transparency. Some view parliaments as spendthrift and part of the problem of poor budgetary practices (for example, Bagehot 1963). From this perspective, it is the executive that is the true guardian of public money and guarantor of sound administration. However, recent case studies strongly suggest that budgeting without effective checks and balances can provide an open door to corruption and poor fiscal performance (Santiso and Belgrano 2004; Burnell 2001). Proponents of the latter perspective emphasize the budget's function as a tool for holding the executive to account. A lack of accountability is widely regarded as a precondition for corruption (Klitgaard 1998).

Framing the debate over financial scrutiny as a struggle of executive versus legislature can be misleading, however, because sound budgeting requires both a competent executive and a legislature that has the capacity for effective scrutiny. In democratic countries, ultimate accountability of the executive is to the electorate; however, several years can pass between elections. During this interval, "horizontal accountability" (O'Donnell 1998) in the form of independent checks and balances plays an essential role in safeguarding government integrity. In a general sense, accountability can be thought of as an obligation to answer for the execution of one's assigned responsibilities (Murray and Nijzink 2002). In practice, accountability has quite often proven a "notoriously elusive idea" (White and Hollingsworth 1999).

The budget process is a principal mechanism used by legislatures to hold the executive to account. Other practices for legislative oversight include, for example, question time and commissions of inquiry (Pelizzo and Stapenhurst 2004). The budget process is a fundamental accountability mechanism because of its periodic nature and because it encompasses all government activities. In modern democracies, the approval of the budget is typically required on an annual basis and follows an explicit timetable. This means that the legislature has a regular and predictable opportunity to scrutinize the policy and administration of the government.

Refusal to approve the budget can shut down even the most powerful administrations (Williams and Jubb 1996). The centrality of supply for the ability to govern means that the executive has an incentive to take legislative scrutiny seriously, if it is effective.

The purpose of this chapter is to give an overview of how legislatures in different countries exercise financial scrutiny. Institutional arrangements are influenced by country-specific factors, so there is no single best approach. Nonetheless, it is possible to draw inspiration from comparative experience about the effectiveness of different institutional arrangements. The following analysis uses comparative data as much as possible. The chapter comprises three main sections. The first section gives a brief overview of the budget process, with particular reference to the role of legislative bodies. The following two sections deepen this discussion by looking at particularly important aspects of legislative financial scrutiny: dealing with the draft budget and audit findings, respectively.

The Budget Cycle

This section gives an outline of an annual budget process. Budgets must be passed regularly, usually on an annual basis, to ensure that government continues to operate. A typical government budget process follows a timeline that can be separated into four different stages: drafting, legislative approval, implementation, and audit and evaluation (Stourm 1917; Lee and Johnson 1998). (This basic sequence is represented in figure 6.1.) The stages heuristic is useful for studying budget processes, but there are many differences across countries (for instance, with regard to the influence of various actors and the timing of the process). For this reason, the following paragraphs give a necessarily generalized overview.[1]

The drafting stage is concerned with compiling a budget proposal that can be submitted to the legislature. Realistic macroeconomic projections are the basis for crafting a sound budget because revenues, as well as expenditures, are sensitive to economic performance (Crippen 2003). The fiscal policy of a government sets overall limits within which tax and spending choices must be made. These choices are increasingly made on the basis of a medium-term fiscal framework (Boex, Martinez-Vazquez, and McNab 2000). In most countries, the drafting stage involves extensive negotiations between spending departments and the central budget office about the allocation of funds across different functions. A consolidated draft is typically approved at the highest political level, which is also appropriate for final decisions on contentious issues that could not be resolved at the administrative level.

During the legislative stage, parliament scrutinizes the expenditure and revenue proposals of the executive. Most democratic constitutions enshrine the "power of the purse" so that no financial measures can be imposed without parliamentary consent. Therefore, once a comprehensive budget has been drafted, it must be approved by the legislature to become effective. Arguably only the U.S. Congress retains the technical capacity, in the form of an extensive legislative budget office, to draft an alternative budget on its own (Anderson 2005). In most countries, the legislature has the option to approve, reject, or amend the budget as tabled by the

---

[1] Readers are referred to the series of national budget system reviews that are carried out by the OECD and published in its OECD Journal on Budgeting.

Figure 6.1 *The Basic Sequence of an Annual Budget Cycle*

Drafting ⟩	Legislating ⟩	Implementation ⟩	Audit ⟩
Before the beginning of the relevant fiscal year		Fiscal year starts and ends	After the fiscal year

Source: Author.

executive. The exact form of legislative approval is less important than the fact that it must be comprehensive. In some cases, the legislature passes separate legislation for appropriations and changes to the tax code; in others, it considers a unified budget bill. The principle of legislative authorization of all public spending and taxation ensures the rule of law in public finance.

Implementation of the budget commences with the beginning of the fiscal year (Tarschys 2002). This stage of the budget process is mainly in the hands of the executive. Funds are apportioned to spending departments in line with the approved budget. Sometimes, however, in particular in developing countries, cash availability constraints lead to certain expenditures being cut below voted amounts and other adjustments to approved spending (for example, Stasavage and Moyo 2000). Frequent adjustments may reflect uncertainties in the economic environment, but "continuous" budgeting is also a symptom of a poorly functioning budget system. Some countries use contingency reserves to cover unforeseeable spending needs; however, such reserves must be clearly accounted for and should not be excessive in size. Any significant adjustments to the budget should be captured in adjustment or supplemental appropriations that are tabled in the legislature for approval. In-year monitoring provides an opportunity to pick up problems before they result in significant deviations between the approved budget and actual spending.

The audit and evaluation stage follows the end of the fiscal year. A supreme audit institution, such as an auditor general or audit court, is tasked with assessing government accounts and financial statements (Stapenhurst and Titsworth 2001; White and Hollingsworth 1999). In addition, the role of internal audit has received increasing attention (Diamond 2002). In many countries, external audit findings are considered by the legislature, and how exactly this is done will be discussed further below. If the audit process is effective, recommendations based on audit findings are reflected in future budgets. The timely submission of audit reports requires that departments produce their financial statements in time for the audit institution to meet the prescribed deadline.

These four stages provide a useful framework for understanding budget systems, but it is important to remember that their exact nature and timing differ across countries. Moreover, budget cycles overlap. At any one time, a number of budgets are at different stages of the process. For example, while one budget is being drafted, a second budget might be awaiting legislative approval, a third is in the process of being implemented, and a fourth (which has already been implemented) might be subject to audit and evaluation. This overlapping nature of budgeting means that the maintenance of fiscal oversight can be a complex challenge. The following two sections extend the discussion of two particularly important components of legislative financial scrutiny.

Ex Ante Scrutiny

The role of parliament in approving the budget differs sharply across different countries. Some are powerful players in the budget process and significantly shape budgets. Others generally approve the budget as tabled by the executive without any changes. This section will discuss some important institutional requirements for effective ex ante scrutiny. These include sufficient time, strong parliamentary committees, access to high-quality budgetary information and analysis capacity, and sufficient constitutional powers over the budget. The role of party political dynamics is also discussed.

A first requirement is that the budget must be tabled sufficiently in advance of the fiscal year to which it relates to allow for proper legislative scrutiny. Even well-resourced legislatures would find it difficult to scrutinize budget documents without sufficient time. International experience suggests that a minimum of three to four months is required for the approval of the budget by the legislature on the basis of meaningful analysis (OECD 2002). Table 6.1 shows that the majority of parliaments have between two and four months before the beginning of the fiscal year to scrutinize the draft budget. Only the U.S. Congress has substantially more time to formulate budget policy.

Second, a developed committee system enables a legislature to divide its labor in a way that generates expertise across different policy areas (Mezey 1979). Debates on the floor of the legislature tend to be about the broad strokes of the budget and to have a publicity function for both the government and the opposition. Detailed discussions of budget figures usually become possible in a smaller forum provided at committee level, away from the political limelight. There are different ways to involve legislative committees in the budget approval process. Most national legislatures have a specialized finance or budget committee. Input from sectoral committees can contribute expertise in particular policy areas during the scrutiny of relevant expenditures. In Sweden, for instance, the Finance Committee approves total spending and aggregate ceilings for various expenditure areas, whereas sectoral committees have the power to shape the budget of departments under their jurisdiction (Blöndal 2001). In short, legislative committees are the engine room of the legislature and "at least a necessary condition for effective parliamentary influence in the policy-making process" (Mattson and Strøm 1995).

Third, legislative decision making must be based on comprehensive, accurate, appropriate, and timely information supplied by the executive. The amount of supporting documentation that accompanies the budget figures is crucial. Often the only source of narrative information is the budget speech. This makes it difficult for parliamentarians and their staff, as well as the public, to understand the policy

Table 6.1 *Tabling of the Budget in Advance of the Fiscal Year*

	Number of legislatures
Up to two months	10
Two to four months	23
Four to six months	5
More than six months	1
Total	**39**

Source: OECD and World Bank 2003.

Box 6.1 *What Types of Budget Documentation Should Be Available?*

The OECD has developed Best Practices for Budget Transparency that deal with the availability of budget information and specific disclosure requirements. The OECD recommends the following documents:

- A comprehensive budget that includes performance data and medium-term projections
- A prebudget report that states explicitly the government's long-term economic and fiscal policy objectives, and its economic assumptions and fiscal policy intentions for the medium term
- Monthly reports that show progress in implementing the budget, including explanations of any differences between actual and forecast amounts
- A midyear report that provides a comprehensive update on the implementation of the budget, including an updated forecast of the budget outcome for the medium term
- A year-end report that should be audited by the supreme audit institution and released within six months of the end of the fiscal year
- A preelection report that illuminates the general state of government finances immediately before an election
- A long-term report that assesses the long-term sustainability of current government policies

Source: OECD 2002.

---

basis of the budget and to evaluate whether the budget adequately reflects government policy. Many budgets do not sufficiently relate expenditures to budget objectives. The "OECD Best Practices for Budget Transparency" gives an overview of the types of budget documentation that ideally should be available (see box 6.1).

Legislative research capacity can support legislators in dealing with large volumes of information. Several more-active legislatures, in budgetary terms, have access to independent budget research capacity. The U.S. Congressional Budget Office (CBO) is by far the most comprehensive legislative budget office (Anderson 2005). CBO has about 230 highly trained staff. Some legislatures have smaller research units that specialize in budget analysis, and yet others have general research units that can deliver some budget analysis when needed. However, table 6.2 shows that in many legislatures access to independent research capacity is negligible or nonexistent. Building such capacity, even on a modest scale, can be an important component of efforts to strengthen the role of the legislature. Parliamentary research capacity can be complemented with analyses by independent think tanks, private sector economists, and academics. In some countries, political parties represented in the legislature employ specialized budget researchers.

Without a minimum of constitutionally guaranteed powers over the budget, the legislature is unlikely to play a meaningful role in the approval of the budget. Ultimately, there must be a credible threat that should the executive not address any of the concerns raised by the legislature, this will have consequences. Persistent breach of regulations and misuse of funds may be a matter for independent anticorruption agencies and the courts. However, a key power that parliaments should have is the power to cut budgets in response to poor financial management. In some countries, legislative amendment powers are counterbalanced with an executive veto, and the government may also have powers to adjust spending during

Table 6.2 *Legislative Budget Research Offices*

	Number of legislatures
None	28
With less than 9 professional staff	7
With 10 to 25 professional staff	1
With 26 or more professional staff	3
Total	**39**

Sources: OECD and World Bank 2003.

Table 6.3 *Parliamentary Budget Amendment Powers*

	Number of legislatures
Reduce and increase expenditure and revenue	32
Reduce expenditure, but not increase it	17
Reduce expenditure, but only increase it with the permission of the government	4
Reduce and increase expenditure if alternative provisions are made elsewhere	13
Rights not specified	15
Total	**81**

Source: Adapted from Inter-Parliamentary Union 1986: table 38A.

budget execution.[2] Table 6.3 indicates that most parliaments have at the very least the power to reduce existing expenditure items and that many have more permissive powers of amendment.

Finally, the crucial impact of party political dynamics must be acknowledged. The existence of clear political majorities in the legislature enhances the predictability of voting outcomes. By contrast, if the legislature comprises several parties without one of them having an outright majority of seats, the executive may have to assemble support of a number of parties to have its budget passed. It is likely to have to bargain and make concessions during this process. However, clear party majorities enhance the predictability of legislative voting behavior only when they are matched with tight party discipline, which partly depends on the incentives created by the electoral system (Carey and Shugart 1995). For instance, in countries with a closed-party-list system of proportional representation, the electorate votes for political parties rather than individual parliamentarians. The list of candidates is compiled internally by the parties, which works against more independently minded members. The overall political environment can also be decisive. When democratic fundamentals such as freedom of speech are impaired, it is highly unlikely that the legislature can act as an effective check on the government.

To sum up, a number of institutional prerequisites can help to facilitate financial scrutiny, in particular access to high-quality information and analytical capacity,

---

[2] Executive flexibility during implementation is often limited. For instance, South Africa's Public Finance Management Act (section 43) allows an accounting officer to shift a "saving" up to a limit of 8 percent of the amount appropriated under a main division to another main division within the same vote.

sufficient constitutional powers over the budget, and a well-developed legislative infrastructure that gives a strong role to committees and allows sufficient time for scrutiny. While these institutional prerequisites are important, they cannot be considered sufficient to ensure effective financial scrutiny. A modicum of political independence of the legislature from the executive is also required.

Ex Post Scrutiny

Parliamentary control of public finance would not be complete without an assurance that the budget was implemented as authorized. Effective parliamentary audit requires access to audit information that is timely and of the highest professional standard, supplied by an independent supreme audit institution.[3] Traditionally, supreme auditors have focused on compliance and financial audit, but more recently, performance or "value-for-money" audit has gained in importance. Audit reports must be produced and tabled in the legislature as speedily as possible to ensure their relevance. Long delays undermine accountability, because officials who are responsible for a loss of public money may have moved on or retired, which makes it more difficult to pursue disciplinary measures. The interest of the public is also likely to focus on more current matters.

The relationship between parliament and the audit institution can take a number of forms. In the court model tradition, in which the audit institution has judicial status, parliamentary engagement leads to a formal vote on public financial management. The French National Assembly in 1819 adopted the practice of passing an annual law approving the execution of each budget. Accounting officers were held personally responsible for any misspent funds until the passing of a formal vote by parliament for granting discharge. To this day, a formal vote on budget execution closes the cycle of financial control in public finance systems that were influenced by the Napoleonic tradition. Refusal to grant discharge can be a serious political threat. For instance, when the European Parliament rejected the discharge motion for the 1996 budget, this eventually led to the resignation of the entire European Commission in March 1999.

By contrast, the purpose of parliamentary audit in the Westminster tradition is primarily to generate recommendations on how to improve public spending. In this model, parliament is the principal audience of the auditor general. While parliament depends on high-quality audit reporting to exercise effective scrutiny, the auditor general in turn requires an effective parliament to ensure that departments take audit outcomes seriously. The power of the auditor general is to issue independent reports. Parliament is the forum in which these reports receive public attention, which creates pressure on government to respond to issues of concern. The mutual dependency of parliament and the audit institution is underlined where the auditor general has been made, by statute, an officer of parliament (for example, in the United Kingdom).

A few legislatures do not consider audit findings in detail, but to ensure effective scrutiny, most parliaments use committees to examine the reports of the public auditor (SIGMA 2002). There are different options for establishing committee capacity to consider audit findings. In some legislatures, the same committee that is

---

[3] For an overview of the different types of supreme audit institutions, see chapter 7.

responsible for approving the budget is also tasked with considering audit reports. Another option that is closely linked to the auditor general model of public audit is to use a dedicated public accounts committee (PAC) for the scrutiny of audit findings. Other parliaments involve departmentally related committees, such as those responsible for health, education, or defense, to scrutinize audit findings in their respective policy areas.

Germany is an example of a country that uses the first option of tasking the budget committee with the scrutiny of audit findings. In Germany, audit reports are considered in the Audit Subcommittee of the Budget Committee, where membership is proportionately distributed according to party representation in Parliament. Each Member is assigned the role of rapporteur for a specific ministry and must scrutinize the remarks on this entity in the audit report. The relevant ministers, or at least high-ranking bureaucrats, Finance Ministry officials, and auditors take part in the discussions (Bajohr 2000).

A more elaborate option for parliamentary audit is a dedicated audit committee. The U.K. House of Commons created its PAC in 1861 as part of the Gladstonian reforms. The Committee acquired full functionality when the first complete set of accounts was presented and examined in 1870. These reforms established an audit model predicated on close interaction between a specialized audit committee of the legislature and the auditor general, which has been adopted in most Commonwealth countries. In most Commonwealth countries that have adopted the PAC model, it is tradition that the chairperson of the committee must be a member of the opposition. This supports the nonpartisan tradition of these committees and indicates the government's willingness to promote transparency (Wehner 2003). The nonpartisan tradition of PACs has been identified as an important success factor in recent studies (see box 6.2 and annex by Ulrich and Williams).

The PAC process tends to share some essential features across countries. After parliament receives an audit report from the auditor general, hearings are the principal mechanism by which officials from departments, agencies, or other relevant bodies answer to the committee. The summoned officials appear in front of the PAC during the hearing. In most PACs, the interrogation focuses on the accounting officer, rather than on the relevant minister. The accounting officer is the civil servant in a department who is accountable to the legislature for financial management,

---

Box 6.2 *What Makes Public Accounts Committees Effective?*

In a recent survey of 35 public accounts committees in the Commonwealth carried out by the World Bank Institute, respondents were asked to identify which factors are important for ensuring the effectiveness of the committee. Frequently mentioned success factors include the following:

- A broad scope to investigate all expenditures of government
- The power to choose subjects for examination without government direction
- The power to make recommendations and publish conclusions
- Solid technical support from the auditor and research staff
- The maintenance of a nonpartisan climate
- Involving the public and encouraging media coverage

Source: Stapenhurst et al. 2005.

usually the administrative head of a department. A draft report on the hearing is prepared and debated in the committee. While it is not normally required that reports must be adopted unanimously, most PACs strongly favor consensus decisions (McGee 2002).

Not all legislatures use a single dedicated committee to consider audit findings. Some have found it useful, where appropriate, to devolve the consideration of audit reports to departmental committees (for instance, in New Zealand). This can inject subject-relevant expertise into the audit process in the legislature. In turn, sectoral committees can benefit from the more intimate knowledge of audit outcomes relating to the relevant department. Skeptics of this approach doubt that the strong and in-depth relationship that can be developed between auditors and legislators when interaction is focused on one dedicated committee can be replicable for a larger number of committees. This would seem to require additional resources to extend the liaison capacity of the auditor, but it may not be possible to duplicate many of the conventions and well-rehearsed interactions that are part of the PAC model.

The finalization of a report on audit findings by a legislative committee should not be the end of the ex post scrutiny process. In some countries, committee reports must be followed by a formal response from the government. In practice, this is not always sufficient for ensuring that committee recommendations are acted on. To monitor government responsiveness more comprehensively, some auditors use a regular tracking report to assess departmental action in response to audit findings and recommendations. In the case of the German Federal Court of Audit, a Results Report is produced two years after each Annual Report to systematically monitor the implementation of each recommendation that was made. The Status Reports published by the Canadian Auditor General since 2002 have a similar function, focusing on the most significant issues. When there is no such regular mechanism, particularly important issues may be followed up with a separate report. For example, the U.K. National Audit Office recently published a report on the government's response to PAC recommendations relating to a 2001 outbreak of foot-and-mouth disease (NAO 2005). It is perhaps not the specific form that matters, but rather that follow-up mechanisms are sufficient to motivate the executive to take audit recommendations seriously.

The discussion shows that parliamentary audit is arguably as important as ex ante scrutiny. Without a mechanism to assure itself of the proper implementation of the budget, the legislature has no guarantee that public funds were spent efficiently and effectively, as well as in compliance with the budget and relevant regulations. Effective parliamentary audit is heavily reliant on committees and sound interaction between the auditor and the legislature. These may appear to be basic points, but it is astonishing how frequently there is a mismatch between the ideal and practice of legislative audit.

Conclusion

The annual budget process is one of the most important tools that legislatures have to hold the executive to account. To use this opportunity effectively requires a number of institutional prerequisites. In particular, specialized legislative committees and access to all relevant and high-quality information are essential. In practice, however, financial scrutiny can be a daunting challenge. In terms of access to resources, many legislatures are poorly equipped to independently assess budgetary data, lacking (for instance) the backup and support of professional economists and budget researchers that the executive has access to. Moreover, the political environments in which legislative bodies function are extremely varied and not always conducive to oversight. For instance, where democracy is poorly entrenched, there may be no tradition of independent scrutiny. In developing countries, the imperative of economic development may vitiate against parliamentary oversight. Scrutiny can raise difficult questions that may be inconvenient for the executive; hence, it may try to resist disclosure. Yet, in the long run, the development of effective scrutiny is likely to yield dividends. Legislative oversight can help to keep public sector managers on their toes. The transparency it generates puts poor management in the spotlight and hence can help to boost performance. Most important, however, effective legislative scrutiny provides an assurance of government integrity.

Bibliography

Anderson, B. 2005. "The Value of a Nonpartisan, Independent, Objective Analytic Unit to the Legislative Role in Budget Preparation." Paper presented at the Southern Political Science Association Annual Meeting, New Orleans.

Bagehot, W. 1963 [1867]. *The English Constitution.* London: Collins.

Bajohr, S. 2000. "Perspektiven der Finanzkontrolle: Parlamentarische Prüfungsaufträge an Rechnungshöfe." *Verwaltungsarchiv* 91 (4): 507–39.

Blöndal, J. R. 2001. "Budgeting in Sweden." *OECD Journal on Budgeting* 1 (1): 27–57.

Boex, L. F. J., J. Martinez-Vazquez, and R. M. McNab. 2000. "Multi-Year Budgeting: A Review of International Practices and Lessons for Developing and Transitional Economies." *Public Budgeting and Finance* 20 (2, Summer): 91–112.

Burnell, P. 2001. "Financial Indiscipline in Zambia's Third Republic: The Role of Parliamentary Scrutiny." *Journal of Legislative Studies* 7 (3): 34–64.

Carey, J. M., and M. S. Shugart. 1995. "Incentives to Cultivate a Personal Vote: A Rank Ordering of Electoral Formulas." *Electoral Studies* 14 (4): 417–39.

Crippen, D. 2003. "Countering Uncertainty in Budget Forecasts." Paper presented at the 24th Annual Meeting of OECD Senior Budget Officials, OECD, Rome.

Diamond, J. 2002. "The Role of Internal Audit in Government Financial Management: An International Perspective." Working Paper WP/02/94, IMF, Washington, DC.

IMF (International Monetary Fund). 2001. *Revised Code of Good Practices on Fiscal Transparency.* Washington, DC: IMF.

Inter-Parliamentary Union. 1986. *Parliaments of the World: A Comparative Reference Compendium.* Aldershot, U.K.: Gower.

Klitgaard, R. 1998. "International Cooperation against Corruption." *Finance and Development* 35 (1): 3–6.

Lee, R. D., and R. W. Johnson. 1998. *Public Budgeting Systems*. Gaithersburg, MD: Aspen Publishers.

Mattson, I., and K. Strøm. 1995. "Parliamentary Committees." In *Parliaments and Majority Rule in Western Europe*, ed. H. Döring, 249–307. New York: St. Martin's Press.

McGee, D. G. 2002. *The Overseers: Public Accounts Committees and Public Spending*. London: Commonwealth Parliamentary Association and Pluto Press.

Mezey, M. L. 1979. *Comparative Legislatures*. Durham: Duke University Press.

Murray, C., and L. Nijzink. 2002. *Building Representative Democracy: South Africa's Legislatures and the Constitution*. Cape Town: European Union Parliamentary Support Program.

NAO (National Audit Office). 2005. "Foot and Mouth Disease: Applying the Lessons." Report by the Comptroller and Auditor General, Stationery Office, London.

O'Donnell, G. 1998. "Horizontal Accountability in New Democracies." *Journal of Democracy* 9 (3): 112–26.

OECD (Organisation for Economic Co-operation and Development). 2002. "OECD Best Practices for Budget Transparency." *OECD Journal on Budgeting* 1 (3): 7–14.

OECD and World Bank. 2003. *Results of the Survey on Budget Practices and Procedures*. Paris: OECD. http://ocde.dyndns.org/.

Pelizzo, R., and F. C. Stapenhurst. 2004. "Tools for Legislative Oversight: An Empirical Investigation." Policy Research Working Paper 3388, World Bank, Washington, DC.

Santiso, C., and A. G. Belgrano. 2004. "Politics of Budgeting in Peru: Legislative Budget Oversight and Public Finance Accountability in Presidential Systems." Working Paper Series WP/01/04, Paul H. Nitze School of Advanced International Studies (SAIS), Washington, DC.

SIGMA (Support for Improvement in Governance and Management in Transition Countries). 2002. *Relations between Supreme Audit Institutions and Parliamentary Committees*. Paris: OECD.

Stapenhurst, R., and J. Titsworth. 2001. "Features and Functions of Supreme Audit Institutions." PREMnote 59, World Bank, Washington, DC.

Stapenhurst, R., W. Woodley, V. Sahgal, and R. Pelizzo. 2005. "Scrutinizing Public Expenditures: Assessing the Performance of Public Accounts Committees." Policy Research Working Paper 3613, World Bank, Washington, DC.

Stasavage, D., and D. Moyo. 2000. "Are Cash Budgets a Cure for Excessive Fiscal Deficits (and at What Cost)?" *World Development* 28 (12): 2105–22.

Stourm, R. 1917. *The Budget*. New York: D. Appleton (for the Institute for Government Research).

Tarschys, D. 2002. "Time Horizons in Budgeting." *OECD Journal on Budgeting* 2 (2): 77–103.

Wehner, J. 2003. "Principles and Patterns of Financial Scrutiny: Public Accounts Committees in the Commonwealth." *Commonwealth and Comparative Politics* 41 (3): 21–36.

White, F., and K. Hollingsworth. 1999. *Audit, Accountability, and Government.* Oxford: Clarendon Press.

Williams, R., and E. Jubb. 1996. "Shutting Down Government: Budget Crises in the American Political System." *Parliamentary Affairs* 49 (3): 471–84.

Case Study on the Performance
of Public Accounts Committees:
A Review of the Canadian PAC, 37th Parliament

Martin Ulrich

Introduction

The following case study of the activity and results of one Westminster model public accounts committee (PAC) is an interesting reflection on points posited by the previous chapter. It is particularly illustrative of the importance of ex post scrutiny and transparency.

The Parliamentary Centre of Canada was invited by the Public Accounts Committee of the Canadian Parliament to review its practices and results at a time when it was intensely engaged in studying the Sponsorship Scandal.[1] During this period, the usual collegial atmosphere of the Committee was increasingly being challenged by partisanship, likely in response to the enormous publicity the committee study was receiving and the growing belief that it would have a substantial impact on the anticipated election. There is no way of knowing with certainty the reasons that individual members of the Committee asked for the review, but the Parliamentary Centre interpreted it as a desire by experienced members on the Committee to provide a balanced and thoughtful description of the full range of Committee activity. Such a report would balance the more fractious public image during its study of the Sponsorship Program, and (as we found out during the interviews) members— although quite happy with the Committee's performance—felt that some modest changes could enhance its value.

As it turned out, the Committee study of the Sponsorship Program likely did contribute to the governing party losing its majority status in the subsequent election, leading to a substantial change in the membership on the Committee and a short-lived 38th Parliament. Although the review was provided to the newly formed Committee, it did not formally address the study findings.

In addition to gathering and organizing information on the activities and outputs of the Committee, we interviewed active Committee members and other

---

[1] The Sponsorship Program provided funding for community events. It was a Canadian unity initiative in response to a separation referendum in the province of Quebec. An audit report of the auditor general pointed out significant problems in its management, as well as expenditures for no documented results. A subsequent commission of inquiry, led by Judge Gomery, determined that certain of the Sponsorship Program funds found their way to supporting candidates of the governing party.

knowledgeable parliamentarians and Committee staff. This annex provides a snap-
shot of the activities and outputs of one PAC at a particular time and outlines how
the members saw their roles on the Committee. It also provides suggestions on how
performance might be improved.

The report itself does not highlight the impact of the work of the Committee on
the major investigation during the final months. To help address this gap, the then
chair of the Committee provides a personal assessment of its impact.

Part One: Committee Roles

Committees generally assist the House of Commons by advising on decisions to be
made in the Chamber or by government and by engaging citizens on matters of
public interest. The PAC, although best known for its review of reports of the auditor general on particular programs or departments, also addresses broader matters.
It studies public expectations for good public administration and recommends
financial administration standards to government. Also, as was illustrated in the
case of the Sponsorship Program study, it undertakes occasional in-depth investigations that add to public transparency.

Members likely can best sort out their views of Committee priorities by developing a clear and shared understanding of each of these "lines of committee business." Based on interviews with PAC members of the 37th Parliament and a review
of their meetings and reports, the following labels and descriptions are suggested
as a starting articulation:

(a) *Exacting accountability,* by confirming the findings and recommendations
of the auditor general's reports with the responsible public officials. Because
public officials dislike the negative public exposure implicit in this process,
the PAC serves as an important incentive for the public service and ministers to manage public resources in line with public expectations. Public officials, as representatives of their ministers at PAC hearings, are not formally
accountable to the Committee, yet it is evident that the exposure to the
Committee can have an important impact. Exacting accountability can also
have a positive side. It is an opportunity for the Committee to showcase and
recognize exemplary public service practices.

(b) *Public transparency,* by undertaking investigations of programs in open—
and often televised—hearings. This contributes importantly to public
knowledge and understanding. In the opinion of some members and many
observers, transparency is a key benefit of the Committee's work. In addition to exposing incidents of mismanagement, it also informs the public on
normal standards and procedures of public administration.

(c) *Improving financial and accountability policy,* by studying and reporting
on recurring issues and reviewing findings of studies of governance practices. This is interpreted by its advocates as solving problems before they
occur—a result they consider to be particularly valuable. Standards reflect-
ing professional and public input that are debated and proposed by the PAC
will have greater credibility with the public than those imposed directly by
the government. Although such Committee studies are less frequent than
the activities associated with exacting accountability, they have been a part
of PAC activity for many years.

It is interesting to note that each of these three lines of business was described as the PAC's most important activity by at least one of its members in the 37th Parliament. Finding consensus around priorities, accordingly, is likely to require a balanced program including all three activities and creatively aligning work within each area to complement work in other areas.

Part Two: PAC Activity and Products: 37th Parliament

The intent of this section is to provide a sense as to the actual priorities of the PAC during the 37th Parliament by sorting out the Committee reports and Committee meetings as they relate to the three lines of business. The chart below provides a summary. It also includes for completeness two other areas of Committee activity: the first is that related to the consideration of the estimates and performance reports of the Office of the Auditor General, and the second is that related to Committee administrative matters.

It is important to note that the classification among the three lines of business does involve a degree of judgment about the principal purpose and impact of each study. Other observers, in some cases, might allocate studies somewhat differently. Yet Committee members felt quite comfortable distinguishing among these three different purposes. Moreover, a single study can serve more than one purpose, and it would not be surprising that different members and parties might well be pursuing different ends. Nonetheless, the classification provides new members with an impression of previous priorities and those familiar with the PAC's work an opportunity to challenge or adjust these impressions.

The 76 meetings focusing on exacting accountability included hearings on programs with officials from more than 20 different departments and agencies. Also included are meetings to review the annual *Public Accounts of Canada*. As noted in the chart, these hearings and discussions produced 34 reports—almost two-thirds of the total. Exacting accountability clearly was the dominant Committee activity during the 37th Parliament.

Most of the 52 meetings allocated to public transparency took place during the third sitting and focused on the study of the Sponsorship Program. However, the

Measures of Committee Priorities

Lines of business	Meetings[a]	Reports
Exacting accountability	76	34
Public transparency	52	2
Improving financial and accountability policy	14	10
Supply	4	6
PAC administration	14	3
Total	160	55

Source: Author's calculations based on documentation on Parliament of Canada Web site http://www.parl.qc.ca/.

a. The information in the chart regarding the allocation of meeting time should be interpreted carefully. For example, it does not include subcommittee meetings, nor does it include the considerable time devoted to informal discussions of Committee matters. Committee meetings were assigned to a line of business, based on the predominant meeting agenda item. Accordingly, the statistics on meetings should be seen as only a general indication of time allocation. Moreover, this approach almost certainly underestimates time devoted to administrative matters.

Observations of the PAC Chair on the Study of the Sponsorship Program

In February 2004, the auditor general tabled her report on government's spending regarding advertising and sponsorship—primarily in the Province of Quebec during a period of more than seven or eight years in the amount of $250 million—and discovered $100 million left unaccounted for. The event detailed below, now referred to as the "Sponsorship Scandal," is considered one of the largest corruption scandals in Canada's history.

The auditor general's report was automatically referred to the Public Accounts Committee of the Parliament of Canada, of which I had been the chair since 1997. In response to the referral, the Committee expanded its normal hearings from two meetings of two hours each week to meeting virtually five full days per week, subsequently requiring the Parliament of Canada to marshal resources in support of the dramatic increase in the workload.

Politically charged events also erupted as a result. The Liberal Party split into two parts; the Chrétien (the former leader and prime minister) Liberals, and the Martin (the then leader and prime minister) Liberals, thereby reducing their majority within the Committee. There were now five parties at the table: the Chrétien Liberals, the Martin Liberals, the Conservatives, the Bloc Quebecois, and the NDP, instead of the usual four, changing the dynamic of the Committee considerably. The Martin Liberals were initially quite open to an in-depth investigation of the scandal by the Committee, and the Chrétien Liberals under whose mandate the problem had occurred did not have sufficient votes to stop the Committee's investigation, even though the two Liberal camps had a combined majority within the Committee.

The opposition parties, supported by the Martin Liberals, called for Cabinet documents to be delivered to Parliament to determine the extent to which there had been Cabinet or ministerial involvement. I believe that this was the first time in Canadian history that Parliament had voted to call for Cabinet documents and actually received them. The Committee also reinvigorated its powers to subpoena witnesses (a prerogative last used in 1912). It was so intent on moving forward, the Committee delegated to the chair the power to subpoena witnesses without reference to the Committee. If a witness did not accept within 24 hours an invitation to appear before the Committee, a subpoena was issued by the chair. The reinvigoration of subpoena powers reiterated Parliament's supremacy as a court with powers of investigation.

Committee also looked at the Human Resources and Social Development Department's management of contributions, a follow-up on a study initiated in the 36th Parliament.

Advising on financial and accountability policy and its management attracted the least Committee attention during the 37th Parliament. Yet it did address important and diverse matters, such as international financial reporting, human resources management in the public service, governance of Crown corporations, and creation of foundations. Some of these Committee reviews were in response to reports by the auditor general, but other reviews were in response to reports of other bodies.

Although public transparency played a large role, particularly during the third sitting, the time and resources allocated to the inquiry into the Sponsorship Program were highly unusual. Opportunities for engaging in high-interest public transparency initiatives will arise only occasionally. Therefore, priority setting among the three lines of business might well focus on two issues: (a) the value of continuing work on a major transparency issue (and remaining open to other

The prime minister at the time, Paul Martin, truncated the investigation by dissolving Parliament in May 2004, three months after the investigation commenced. The Committee still had well over 100 witnesses to testify, but the dissolution of Parliament and the automatic dissolution of the Public Accounts Committee brought the Parliamentary investigation to an immediate standstill.

The political consequences of the investigation and the political price exacted on the government were high. The Liberal Party, which had enjoyed three successive majority mandates, was reduced to the barest working minority in the election of June 2004, and in the subsequent election in January 2006, they were defeated and replaced by a Conservative minority government.

The truncated political investigation by the Public Accounts Committee was followed by a judicial enquiry chaired by Mr. Justice Gomery. Several questions were raised regarding witnesses' possible perjury under oath while appearing before the Public Accounts Committee and the judicial enquiry. Lawyers at the judicial enquiry, representing some of the senior political advisers allegedly implicated in the Sponsorship Scandal, wanted to introduce testimony from the Public Accounts Committee to the judicial enquiry to demonstrate the inconsistencies of statements by the witnesses. The Parliament of Canada, exercising its rights under the Bill of Rights of 1689 of the United Kingdom, refused to allow the testimony of Parliament to be used in a court of law.

While the proceedings of Parliament are beyond the reach of the courts, Parliament can review proceedings of the judicial enquiry. Following the conclusion of the judicial enquiry, the Public Accounts Committee adopted the issue of potentially inconsistent statements by witnesses under oath at the two investigations and, through the Parliament of Canada, directed the Library of Parliament to analyze the testimony before both bodies and report inconsistencies to the Public Accounts Committee in the spring of 2006.

At the time of writing, we are still awaiting the report by the Library of Canada. Should the Public Accounts Committee and the Parliament of Canada find that there may be acts of perjury requiring further investigation, it may refer the matter to the proper authorities for prosecution.

The Sponsorship Scandal is a classic case study of the political price exacted by Parliament over government for illegal and improper behavior. It is Parliament's integral responsibility to uphold honesty and integrity in government.

Source: John Williams, Member of Parliament and Chair of the PAC, 35th, 37th and 38th Parliaments

---

opportunities that might arise) and (b) whether relatively more time should be allocated to broader issues of financial and accountability policy, compared with time devoted to exacting accountability for individual programs.

Part Three: Investing in Results

While Committee members interviewed uniformly felt that the work of the Committee was important and that the Committee performed well in general, most also felt that Committee results could be improved. Their suggestions for doing so were principally on matters that can be described as "committee management." The other issues were related to party matters. (Both areas are discussed below.) While members recognized that implementing their suggestions would take Committee time, they felt that the improvement would be worth it. Put another way, they felt that there is value in investing some Committee time and resources in initiatives to improve Committee results.

Part Four: Committee Management

The suggestions regarding committee management that were proposed and discussed can be grouped into four areas:

- *Shared understanding of Committee role:* devoting Committee time to developing a better collective understanding of Committee roles and priorities (the same idea applies to major studies)
- *Capacity building:* devoting Committee time to strengthening members' knowledge base by including more briefing sessions and identifying opportunities for members to hone certain of their skills (for example, in questioning reluctant witnesses)
- *Annual reporting:* periodically reviewing what the Committee has accomplished, synthesizing—perhaps for each business line—conclusions, and reporting to the House on issues and achievements from its work over the year
- *Reviewing Committee resources:* considering the adequacy of Committee resources and their application

Actions to address the first two areas of management improvement—shared understanding and capacity building—can be incorporated into the Committee's agenda with little further discussion. Perhaps the most convenient way to start the process of building a shared understanding is at the start of a new session of Parliament with new Committee membership—such as with an orientation event. Improvements in such initiatives could be made based on experience with early events.

Annual reporting, particularly if the Committee wishes to go beyond describing outputs, likely would require further thought and discussion. Reporting could include synthesizing findings by business lines or measuring indicators of impacts and results. There is little experience among Canadian parliamentary committees in annual reporting. Accordingly, further study, such as by a PAC subcommittee or working group, might be helpful. The Parliamentary Centre has advocated such reporting and is continuing to track practices elsewhere.

There are widely divergent views on resource issues such as adequacy, application, and sourcing. Although all these issues have been raised by PAC members and by members of other committees, the diversity of views suggests that an in-depth study would be a useful step.

Part Five: Political Party Issues

The predominant concern expressed by Committee members and others was that the Committee's interparty squabbling during periods of the Sponsorship Program study were not in the interests of any of the parties and did not help to generate public respect for Parliament. This concern was not about undertaking the study of the Sponsorship Program, nor was it about political parties taking different positions. Rather, it was that the procedural discussions seemed to become a self-interested interparty competition with little apparent concern for the public good.

Two specific suggestions were made to build a more knowledgeable and stable Committee. The first was for the Committee to develop selection standards for PAC members that would be sent to party leaders for their consideration. The second was that this guidance be extended to include criteria for substitution of members at PAC meetings. Such changes were not seen as sufficient to address the concern with excessive partisanship, but rather as contributing to a more professional atmosphere more evidently aimed at serving Canadians. The Committee also was urged to seek improved practices for selecting and questioning witnesses, the issues that seemed to divide along party lines and trigger the most negative exchanges.

It is important to reemphasize that these discussions did not suggest that interparty competition should not take place in Parliament or its committees. Interparty competition is a key feature of Canadian democracy and healthy democracies elsewhere. Rather, the concern was that it had become an impediment to the purposes of the Committee, had undermined informative debate and deliberation, and was embarrassing for participants.

Part Six: Concluding Observations

This case study of the activity and results of one Westminster model public accounts committee illustrates a number of points outlined in the previous chapter—the importance of ex post scrutiny, at least when supported by an independent and professional audit office and committee staff, the importance of requiring officials to answer publicly for their stewardship of public resources, the value of transparency to the public, and the benefits and risks of partisanship. It also points out that even well-performing PACs have considerable scope to improve their performance.

7

Parliament and Supreme Audit Institutions

Rick Stapenhurst and Jack Titsworth

Introduction

Building strong accountability institutions is a key challenge of development and is critical to controlling corruption. Among state institutions, the supreme audit institutions (SAIs) play a central role because they help promote government accountability and transparency through sound public financial management.

SAIs are national agencies responsible for auditing government accounts. Their constitutional mandate, reporting relationships, and effectiveness vary from country to country and, within countries, according to current government policies, but their primary purpose is to act as overseers of governments' management of public funds, as well as the quality and credibility of reported government financial information.

Given this mandate, SAIs are well situated to help curb corruption. In many countries, they are viewed as the independent watchdogs of the public interest, and their audits are often potent deterrents to waste and abuse of public funds. They help reinforce the legal, financial, and institutional framework of public finance that, when weak, allows corruption to flourish, and they act as the anchor of a predictable framework of government behavior that reduces arbitrariness in the application of rules and laws.

This chapter discusses the role of SAIs in promoting accountability and transparency in government and thus, in curbing corruption. The first section reviews the different types of SAI, the different types of audit, and the role of audits in the budget process. The second section considers the nexus between the different types of SAI and national parliaments. The third section reviews the conditions for success of SAIs and SAI limitations, while the fourth section more explicitly examines the role of SAIs in curbing corruption.[1]

Different Types of SAI

There are three principal auditing systems that are practiced around the world: the Westminster, the audit board, and the Napoleonic. In the Westminster system, used

---

[1] This chapter updates and expands Stapenhurst and Titsworth (2001).

principally in Commonwealth countries (Australia, Canada, and New Zealand, as well as many African, Caribbean, Pacific, and South Asian countries), the office of the auditor general is an independent body that reports to parliament. This office, which consists of professional auditors, submits periodic reports to parliament on the financial statements and operations of government entities, but with less emphasis on legal compliance than in the Napoleonic system (see below). These auditors are not civil servants, although their terms and conditions of employment are normally similar to those of their civil service peers. Auditors general usually report to parliament annually, although in Australia, Canada, New Zealand, the United Kingdom, and some other countries, reporting is more frequent. Within parliament, a specialized public accounts committee (see chapter 4) reviews the audit reports, investigates further incidents of waste and abuse of funds, and recommends to parliament corrective government actions.

The board system, prevalent in non-Commonwealth Asian countries, is similar to the Westminster model in that it helps parliament exercise its oversight role. Indonesia, Japan, and the Republic of Korea, for example, have a board system comprising an audit commission, which is the decision-making body, and the general executive bureau, which is the executive organ. The president of the board acts as the auditor general. The board of audit is a constitutional organization independent of the executive; its primary mandate is to analyze the state's expenditures and revenues and report its findings to parliament.

The French have exported the Napoleonic system to the Latin countries of Europe, as well as to many South American and francophone African countries. The SAI—called the *cours des comptes* (court of accounts)—has both judicial and administrative authority and is independent of both the legislative and executive branches of government. The institution is part of the judiciary; it makes legal judgments on compliance with laws and regulations and exercises a budget control function to assure that public funds are well used. The court of accounts audits the accounts of government departments and agencies, commercial and industrial entities under the purview of government ministries, and social security bodies.

Different Types of Audit

Audits can be classified into three basic types: attest or financial auditing, compliance auditing, and performance or value-for-money auditing.

In financial auditing, the auditor attests to the accuracy and fairness of presentation of financial statements. Auditors plan and perform attest audits, using their knowledge of accounting and auditing and of the government organizations that are being audited. As part of these audits, they gather evidence to support the amounts and disclosures in the financial statements. Ultimately, the auditor adds credibility to financial statements by providing an unqualified audit opinion on the financial statements, or at least providing useful information explaining any reservations.

In compliance auditing, the auditor verifies that the government's income and expenditures have been authorized and used for approved purposes. The audit team reviews transactions to determine whether the government department or agency has conformed to all pertinent laws and regulations. This includes checking the spending authority in the annual budget and any relevant legislation.

Performance or value-for-money auditing confirms whether taxpayers have received value for their tax revenues. Often, the audit team works closely with an advisory committee of subject matter experts that offers advice and reviews audit results. Performance auditing seeks to ensure that administrative procedures adhere to sound management policies, principles, and practices. Also, it looks to see that the best use is made of human, financial, and other resources, including procedures, information systems, and performance measures used by audited organizations, and that the organization's performance helps achieve its institutional objectives. The performance-auditing mandate varies among SAIs. Sometimes it is confined to reviewing operational efficiency or the extent to which due economy has been observed in the use of resources, while in other cases, it extends to reviewing the effectiveness of government programs in achieving their objectives. Furthermore, some SAIs audit the accuracy and reliability of performance indicators contained in annual reports and other documents.

Financial, compliance, and performance audits combine to form an audit framework (comprehensive auditing) that, over time, provides a complete view of an organization. Audits that promote honest, accountable, and productive government can be described as constructive audits; they encourage the government to manage revenue and expenditures so as to achieve effective results. These audits ask the right questions about accomplishments, failures, and economic efficiency. The most effective audits contribute to the transparency of government programs.

Audits and the Budget Process

Audits are an integral part of the budget process. The budget sets out the government's fiscal policies: revenues, expenditures, and the economic policies on which these are based. As a public document, it requires public disclosure, evaluation, and auditing. Here SAIs play a key role. On the basis of the report issued by the auditor general or the court, a public accounting is issued describing how the budget has been implemented and managed.

The Role of Parliament

In the Westminster system, the SAI is a core element of parliament's oversight function (see box 7.1). Effective oversight requires public scrutiny of expenditures and revenues. Because few Members of Parliament have the skills to undertake this function, parliaments typically rely on SAIs to audit public accounts on their behalf, requiring the auditor general to report regularly on their findings. A multiparty public accounts committee (PAC) usually reviews reports by the office of the auditor general, considers testimony by witnesses from government departments and agencies, and sends its report to the full parliament for comment and action. There are often recommendations or instructions that require follow-up action by both the auditor general and government accounting officers.

In the board system, the audit board prepares and sends an annual report to the cabinet that is submitted to parliament. Board staff attend all the deliberations on fiscal accounts and are expected to explain the board's opinion.

In *cours des comptes*–style SAIs, parliaments do not automatically receive the auditors' reports, although they may receive a report on the work of the court.

Box 7.1 *The Auditors General–Parliament Nexus in Commonwealth Countries*

A study group facilitated by the Commonwealth Parliamentary Association recommended that auditors general (AGs) should have the status of officers of parliament, thereby helping ensure both the independence of the AG from the executive and the relationship of the AG with parliament as a whole and not just with a single committee, such as the public accounts committee (PAC). The study group argued that the AG could potentially have a working relationship with the departmental or sectoral committees, too. In some countries, such as Canada and Ghana, the AGs have established parliamentary liaison offices to foster closer working relationships with parliamentarians.

That said, it is inevitable that the relationship between parliaments and AGS tends to find its principal form in the AG's relationship with the PAC. Across the Commonwealth, 85 percent of PACs depend primarily on the AG's report to guide their work, and the AG has been described as the "friend, philosopher, and guide" to the committee.

Source: McGee 2002.

However, four forms of collaboration between the court of accounts and parliament are possible:

- The president of the court of accounts may, at his or her discretion, pass the court's findings to parliament's finance committee.
- A parliamentary committee may ask the court to conduct a specific management audit, which typically audits the economy, efficiency, and effectiveness of the processes in the organization(s) being audited.
- The court's annual report, presented to parliament and submitted to the country's president, addresses the legal concordance between the general accounts of the finance department and the treasury.
- In a separate document, the court prepares an annual report for parliament on how the resources made available by the previous year's finance act have been used.

Conditions for Successful SAIs

Several features are crucial to the success of an SAI.

Supportive Environment

SAIs function within a wider institutional setting; therefore, they are effective only to the extent they are permitted to conduct their work and the degree to which their reports are used to promote accountability. In many countries, the public accounts themselves are poorly maintained, parliaments may be weak, and the finance ministry may not ensure that audit queries or observations are addressed. Flagrant abuses identified by the SAIs are often not prosecuted, and in some cases, SAIs' work may be sabotaged.

Clear Mandates

Auditing mandates should be rooted in a set of rules and boundaries agreed to by parliament. Audit acts that define parliament's objectives are one way of communicating and authorizing an audit mandate (see box 7.2). Failure to establish legisla-

---

Box 7.2 *Common Features of Audit Mandates*

The purpose of setting out an audit mandate is to assure parliament that it will receive independent credible audit assurance and other useful information about the management of public funds. Audit legislation often contains these features:

- Criteria for the selection of an auditor general, president of the court of accounts, or chairman of the board of audit
- Terms of service
- Provision for retirement or dismissal
- Scope of audit (that is, when and what to report on)
- Reasonable access to records
- Immunity from liability
- Requirement to report regularly
- Right to hire and fire SAI employees
- Right to contract out for professional services
- Provision of an adequate budget

Source: Dye and Stapenhurst (1998)

---

tive auditing requirements leaves SAIs vulnerable to criticism about their mandates. Before drafting legislation, SAIs and governments must determine the auditors' independence, the reporting responsibilities, the scope of audits, and the entities to be audited—elements shaped by national legislation and domestic conditions. In Westminster parliamentary systems, an audit also ensures that the SAI addresses all the issues parliament wants scrutinized by an independent body.

Independence

Independence is a basic feature of SAIs in industrialized countries, although not without political pressure from time to time. Independence must be clearly enunciated, and the personal independence (based on appointment and secure tenure) of the auditor general (sometimes referred to as a "chair" or "president") or court of audit members must be clearly established in legislation and acknowledged in tradition. Autonomy is essential for an auditor general, given the need to report directly to parliament without interference from other government branches. The leader of an SAI needs legal and traditional status to ensure that senior government bureaucrats will make information available and respond appropriately to recommendations. Independence can be strengthened by setting out the role of the auditor general in the country's constitution (as India, Indonesia, Japan, Uganda, and Zambia have done). In Japan, the Board of Audit is independent of the Cabinet. The Board has three commissioners who are appointed by the Cabinet and attested to by the Emperor. Each commissioner, who hold the same status as state ministers and supreme court judges, holds office for a seven-year term, and his or her status is assured during this term. In Indonesia, the chairman, vice chairman, and members of the Supreme Audit Board are appointed by the president on their nomination by Parliament. In the United Kingdom, removal of the comptroller and auditor general is held by the monarch on the resolution of both houses of Parliament. Similarly, in Canada and India, it takes both houses of Parliament to terminate the employment of the auditor general before his or her normal retirement time.

In the Napoleonic model, the autonomy of the *cour des comptes* is guaranteed by its status as a court, its magistrate members' security of tenure, and its right to design its own program of activities. In Belgium, for example, members of the court can only be removed by the Parliament; in Portugal, only the president can remove the head of the *Tribunal de Contas*; and in Luxembourg and Austria, the removal of the president requires a decision by the Constitutional Court.

Another dimension of independence is the freedom to determine the scope of audits. In developed countries, there is little or no influence by the executive government on the choice of issues to be audited. Those being audited should have no influence on the choice of whom or what gets audited. Likewise, the substance of the audit report should be the sole decision of the SAI. Although discussion and negotiation are integral parts of the process, deciding on the report's final contents is the audit office's responsibility.

Adequate Funding, Means, and Staff

SAIs require adequate funding, equipment, and facilities. In the developing world, where such resources are often inadequate, there is a potential for SAIs to operate more efficiently. Budgetary constraints often inhibit upgrading and maintenance of staff skills (for example, few developing countries set annual targets for performance audit training). However, it is unlikely that increased efficiency alone would generate enough savings to provide competitive salaries and modern technologies. Governments must recognize the costs as well as the high returns of audits and provide commensurate funding.

To ensure high-quality work, SAIs need well-qualified, adequately remunerated staff who are encouraged to continuously improve, especially in their areas of expertise. For example, auditors could enhance their skills in fraud detection and information technology through a combination of training, education, and experience. In some developing countries, SAIs are overstaffed with untrained auditors who add little or no value to the audit process.

The number of authorized personnel should be determined independently from government control (for example, in the board model, the audit commission determines the number of workers in the general executive bureau).

Although responsible for commenting on the economy, efficiency, and effectiveness of government operations, few SAIs engage in self-evaluations. Most do not track the resources that are consumed by audits or overall operating costs. Budgets are rarely produced for performance audit projects and administration or for training and methodology development. This is especially true in developing countries, where few SAIs have a capital budget and where—because of the lack of use of timesheets, for example—there is no database for determining the cost of performance audits, administration, or training. To help maintain their credibility, SAIs should be managed in such a manner that a performance audit of their own operations would result in a favorable report.

Sharing of Knowledge and Experience

International exchanges of ideas, knowledge, and experience are an effective means of raising the quality of audits, harmonizing standards, sharing best practices, and generally helping SAIs fulfill their mandates. To this end, international congresses and training seminars, regional and interregional conferences, and international publications have promoted the evolution and development of the auditing function. Moreover, SAIs should liaise closely with enforcement officials of government agencies to ensure that they share skills and insights and become more adept at uncovering corruption.

Adherence to International Auditing Standards

Audits are more effective when SAIs adhere to appropriate professional auditing standards, such as those promulgated by the International Organization of Supreme Audit Institutions (INTOSAI) or international professional accountancy bodies.

Limitations

SAIs face different limitations because of countries' distinct constitutional, legal, political, social, and economic systems, making it impossible to offer universal remedies. The main limitations are as follows:

- Limits on independence.
- A shortage of qualified personnel (a severe problem for many SAIs whose staff cannot keep pace with the changing scope, techniques, and complexities of their work).
- A lack of adequate monitoring and follow-up of audit findings. Control over public funds is less effective if audit queries or recommendations are not followed up by parliament and acted on by the executive branch.
- Limits on the scope of audits. Restricted audits limit the effectiveness of SAIs' interventions, as well as the motivations for their existence. In some cases, SAIs cannot audit enterprises if the state has only a limited financial interest, and in others, they cannot conduct external control over international organizations or security and defense spending.

Role of SAIs in Curbing Corruption

While no one institution, acting alone, can significantly reduce corruption, audits can be a powerful force to combat corruption. Although preventing corruption may not be an explicit responsibility of some SAIs, audits may detect fraud and abuse (see box 7.2). Fostering strong financial management, based on reliable reporting and internal control systems, is a crucial part of detecting and preventing corruption, because it promotes transparency and accountability in government programs and actions.

Perhaps the main contribution of SAIs to preventing corruption is the psychological factor of deterrence, coupled with required reporting on criminal and corrupt activity in the public sector. Indeed, an increasing number of SAIs—among others, in Bhutan, China, the Czech Republic, Estonia, Germany, India, Indonesia, Lithuania, Malaysia, the Netherlands, the Philippines, Romania, the Slovak Republic, South Africa, Spain, Sweden, and the United States—are required to report criminal and corrupt behavior in the public sector. It is noteworthy that this list suggests that some *developing* country SAIs are ahead of their counterparts in the industrial world when it comes to addressing corruption.

Box 7.3 *South African Arms Deal*

A few years ago, a corruption scandal rocked South Africa. In the course of its review of the Auditor General's Report of September 15, 2000, the Standing Committee on Public Accounts (SCOPA) raised crucial questions relating to irregularities in a multibillion-dollar arms deal with various European arms manufacturers.[2] The auditor general, along with the public prosecutor and the National Directorate of Public Prosecutions, were instructed by Parliament to investigate the matter further.

Among other allegations, European companies are said to have provided discounted motor vehicles to key public officials (including to the former African National Congress [ANC] chief whip and chair of the Parliamentary Committee on Defense) and provided funds to the ANC. In addition, a contract for four new navy ships was mishandled as the government delegated the tendering of a large contract for key equipment to a private consortium (a subcontractor was accused of being allowed to drop its price to secure the contract after the tender had closed).

The subsequent report by the auditor general was criticized by opposition MPs and much of the media as having been "heavily edited" and "doctored"—with significant reported differences between an earlier draft report submitted to the executive and the final report submitted to Parliament. Although the auditor general denies that "any changes were made to the report based on pressure from the President or the executive," this case does highlight the need for SAI independence from the executive (both constitutionally and in practice) and the potential for both the supreme audit institutions and parliaments to investigate and expose incidents of fraud and waste in public finance.

It should be noted, too, that the potential for political interference in the audit process is not just a developing countries phenomenon. Grasso and Sharkansky, for example, describe the political pressures brought to bear on the audit activities of the U.S. General Accounting Office and Israel's state comptroller.

Sources: IDASA 2003; Grasso and Sharkansky 2001.

Within the International Organization of Supreme Audit Institutions, there has been increased interest in corruption and fraud, with the development of new audit methods to prevent corruption, where possible. There must be a focus on whether the checks and controls devised by governments are adequate and actually working. Three areas in which auditors have been quite successful in identifying corrupt practices are in detecting situations in which managers are drawing pay for "ghost" workers; in identifying substandard construction through inspection; and in exposing "grand corruption" in large government contracts (see box 7.3).

Bibliography

Dye, Kenneth, and Rick Stapenhurst. 1998. *Pillars of Integrity: Importance of Supreme Audit Institutions in Curbing Corruption.* Washington, DC: World Bank Institute.

Grasso, Patrick, and Ira Sharkansky. 2001. "The Auditing of Public Policy and the Politics of Auditing: The U.S. GAO and Israel's State Comptroller." *Governance* 14 (1, January): 1–21.

---

[2] The British billion (a million million) is different from the American billion (a thousand million). The author is using the British meaning here.

IDASA. 2003. *Democracy and the Arms Deal Part 3.* Cape Town: Institute for Democracy in South Africa.

International Organization of Supreme Audit Institutions. 1977. "Lima Declaration of Guidelines on Auditing Precepts." Document adopted at the Ninth Congress, Lima, Peru (October).

Manning, Nick, and Rick Stapenhurst. 2002. "Strengthening Oversight by Parliament." PREMnote 74, World Bank, Washington, DC.

Mbanefo, Uche. 1998. *Strengthening African Supreme Audit Institutions: A Strategy Paper and Action Plan.* Washington, DC: World Bank.

McGee, David G. 2002. *The Overseers: Public Accounts Committees and Public Spending.* London: Pluto Press.

Sahgal, Vinod. 1998. *Strengthening Legislative Audit Institutions: A Catalyst to Enhance Governance and Combat Corruption.* Ottawa: Office of the Auditor General of Canada.

Stapenhurst, R., and J. Titsworth. 2001. "Features and Functions of Supreme Audit Institutions." PREMnote 59, World Bank, Washington, DC.

Wehner, Joachim. Forthcoming. "Principles and Patterns of Financial Scrutiny: Public Accounts Committees in the Commonwealth." *Commonwealth and Comparative Politics.*

8

The Role of the Media in Curbing Corruption

Rod Macdonell and Milica Pesic

Introduction

As chapters 2 and 4 noted, a critical element of a country's anti-corruption program is effective media. The media have a dual role to play: they not only raise public awareness about the causes, consequences, and possible remedies of corruption, but they also investigate and report incidents of corruption. In this regard, the media depend on parliament to promote a favorable legal environment for the media. In addition, parliament often finds an ally in the media for overseeing government and ensuring accountability. It is important, too, that parliament itself is open to the scrutiny of the media.

This chapter is divided into three parts. The first examines the tangible effects of journalism on corruption. It highlights eight ways that the media can directly affect the incidence of corruption: exposing corrupt officials, prompting investigations by authorities, exposing commercial wrongdoing, reinforcing the work of anti-corruption offices, providing a check on anti-corruption offices, promoting accountability at the polls, pressuring for change to laws and regulations, and encouraging officials to avoid adverse publicity. The second reviews the intangible effects of journalism on corruption. The final part considers ways in which the media can be strengthened, in particular what parliament can do to ensure a strong and independent media.[1]

Tangible Effects of Journalism on Corruption

Exposing corrupt officials is probably the most effective way in which the media can shine a spotlight on wrongdoing.

Exposing Corrupt Officials

The most obvious examples of journalism's potential for curbing corruption can be seen when politicians or other senior public officials lose their jobs as a consequence of the public outcry or legal proceedings that follow reporting on corruption.

Certainly, the world was reminded in 2005 of the infamous Watergate case and the resignation of President Richard Nixon in 1974, brought about in large part by the brilliant investigative journalism of *Washington Post* reporters Bob Woodward

---

[1] This chapter draws upon and substantially updates Stapenhurst (2000).

and Carl Bernstein. This case came back into the public limelight when the key unnamed source of the two journalists, Mark Felt, whose identity had been protected for 31 years, acknowledged that he had been the source known as "Deep Throat." The exposés of the journalists brought about the resignation of the most powerful man in the United States, the most powerful nation in the world. Their stories demonstrated that this form of journalism is a formidable tool. And although Watergate spawned a generation of investigative reporters and the uncovering of all sorts of wrongdoing and systemic malfunction in many countries, Nixon was the only head of government to be forced out of government by the fruits of investigative reporting.

That remained so until 2000, when investigative reporting caught up with then-President Joseph Estrada of the Philippines. The Philippine Center for Investigative Journalism (PCIJ) carried out a brilliant investigation of the assets of Estrada, which provided the evidence that was used in his impeachment trial, a trial that resulted in the ouster of the movie actor–president after a "people power" uprising in January 2001. He was put under house arrest in April 2001 and has remained so for several years while he faces trials for plunder, perjury, and violating the country's anti-corruption law. (A case study of the PCIJ's Estrada story can be found at http://www.worldbank.org/wbi/governance/pubs/estrada.html.)

The PCIJ struck again in May 2003 when it ran an in-depth report on the extravagant lifestyles of tax collectors of the Philippines Bureau of Internal Revenue. The series demonstrated that the officials were living way beyond the means afforded them by their modest salaries. The article had impact. In the words of Yvonne Chua of the PCIJ:

> After publication of the story, government agencies conducted formal investigation on tax collectors, which led to suspensions of a number of them. Others were transferred. Some opted for retirement. Lifestyle checks on other public officials became a priority among the government anti-corruption initiatives. PCIJ's lifestyle check became a template of sorts for investigators in government and civil society and other journalists (Coronel 2002).

In Thailand, spurred on by the PCIJ's landmark work, the *Prachachart Turakij*, a Bangkok-based business biweekly, looked into the inaccuracies in the assets declaration of Interior Minister Sanan Kachornprasart and brought about his resignation in March 2000. Kachornprasart was of one of Thailand's most powerful politicians. In 2001, the same newspaper reported how Thai Prime Minister Thaksin Shinawatra hid his assets in the names of, among others, his driver and maid. That exposé nearly caused him to lose his post, but he was acquitted by the Constitutional Court in a split vote in August 2001 (Coronel 2002).

Examples of this kind of outcome are not hard to find—particularly from contemporary Latin America, where a surge in media reporting on corruption in the 1990s contributed to the removal of three heads of state from office: Ecuador's Abdala Bucaram, Venezuela's Carlos Andres Perez, and Brazil's Fernando Collor de Mello. In addition, cabinet ministers in Colombia and members of the U.S. House of Representatives, for example, ended up losing their jobs as a result of media reporting.

In December 2004, the U.K. Home Secretary David Blunkett resigned after media reports that his office had fast-tracked a visa application for his ex-lover's nanny. Mr. Blunkett insisted that he had done nothing wrong, and his close friend and ally, Prime Minister Tony Blair, said he had left government with his integrity intact. What did Blunkett do? He sent an e-mail to the office dealing with visas saying the application should "receive no favors," but move "slightly quicker."

When public officials lose their jobs because they have been found guilty of corruption, a variety of related deterrents to corruption—such as public humiliation and loss of prestige, social standing, and income, among others—are simultaneously reinforced. Furthermore, the political turbulence that follows the ousting of high public officers helps increase the standards of public accountability and thereby provides an additional deterrent to corruption.

Contrast these outcomes—resignations, investigations, and prosecutions of prominent office holders—with what had transpired in Indonesia in recent years. There, an independent news media faced persistent censorship and repression for years—conditions that allowed grand corruption and unsustainable economic practices to flourish unchecked, culminating in the 1997 economic crash and the nationwide political upheaval that followed. Lin Neumann of the Committee to Protect Journalists has noted that the crisis finally forced former President Suharto "to acknowledge the degree of involvement in the economy by his own family," despite his stressing for decades that "such a discussion could lead Indonesian journalists to jail. The Suharto children thus acquired major interests in everything from cloves . . . to toll roads, to a subsidized national car company, telecommunications, and media without having to defend themselves in the press."[2] The "only widely trusted Indonesian publication, *Tempo* magazine, was closed by Suharto in 1994," Neumann continued, because "its reporting on the Suharto family, economic corruption, and human rights abuses in East Timor were an embarrassment to the regime."[3] (The magazine was allowed to begin republishing in 1998. It ran into more trouble in September 2004 when its editor, Bambang Haymurti, was found guilty of defaming a businessman whom *Tempo* alleged stood to benefit from a fire in a textile factory. The conviction of Haymurti is under appeal.)

Had a vigorous independent press been allowed to do its job properly and expose the pervasive corruption that so characterized the Suharto regime of Indonesia, some of the most egregious corruption-tainted investment and economic policy decisions that helped propel Indonesia into its economic crisis might not have been made, or at least might have met a more compelling challenge.

Prompting Investigations by Authorities

Even if it does not typically result in the ousting of a public officeholder or bureaucrat, hard-hitting reporting by independent-minded reporters sometimes provides the initial seed that prompts official bodies to launch formal investigations of their own. Such was the case after a series of *Miami Herald* stories in 1996 that "established how a prominent American bank may have abetted the kind of corruption

---

[2] Investigative Reporters and Editors (IRE), Investigative Journalism Online Resource Center, File No. 13876.
[3] IRE, File No. 14544.

that undermines democracy throughout Latin America."[4] The series was instrumental in prompting a criminal investigation by the U.S. Justice Department. Likewise, stories published in 1997 by the *Dallas Morning News* on allegations of contract fraud and mismanagement by top officials in Dallas public schools helped precipitate an investigation by the Federal Bureau of Investigation (FBI) into school corruption. In a similar case, the FBI and Arkansas State Police launched an investigation following publication of a 1986 series in the *Arkansas Democrat-Gazette* that identified corruption throughout a local municipal court system.[5]

The Brazilian Parliamentary Commission of Inquiry, which ultimately led to former President Collor's demise, was also set up partly in response to the findings of investigative press reports.

Exposing Commercial Wrongdoing

In other instances, the media can reveal commercial abuses, such as the report by Bamidele Adebayo of *The News* magazine, in Nigeria, which exposed a financial swindle of a Brazilian bank of US$181 million. Adebayo won the Center for Public Integrity's International Investigating Award for the October 2001 article that revealed the intricacies of a so-called "419" swindle, a scheme that has given Nigeria a black eye because scam letters sent out by fraudsters exploit and defraud unsuspecting foreign victims.

Exposing commercial abuses can have consequences beyond drawing the public's attention to the corrupt acts. For instance, in a lawsuit that was triggered by a media report into the corrupt activities of General Electric, the court ordered GE Capital to pay $100 million for unfair debt collection practices, as part of a 1999 class-action lawsuit settlement. The suit alleged that GE Capital solicited agreements from bankrupt creditors to pay their credit card debts without notifying bankruptcy courts of the agreements.

Reinforcing the Work of Anti-Corruption Offices

Sometimes journalists' stories can play a critical role in reinforcing the effectiveness of public anti-corruption bodies. Simply reporting in a regular, detailed way on the work and findings of these bodies can reinforce public scrutiny of them and, hence, the independence of such bodies from vested interests within the power structure, which might otherwise be tempted to interfere in their work. The publicity that journalists bring to the work of such bodies may also encourage witnesses to wrongdoing to step forward and testify about what they know. To illustrate, in Italy, the press played a key role in disseminating the findings of anti-corruption magistrates, thereby helping to shape the widespread public sentiment that has powered anti-corruption reforms.

Providing a Check on Anti-Corruption Offices

At the same time, there is a danger that journalists may become too close to the official anti-corruption bodies that provide a good source of punchy, dramatic stories.

---

[4] IRE, File No. 4097.
[5] IRE, File No. 3183.

The potentially problematic nature of such relationships is evident when one considers that these very bodies can themselves turn out to be corrupt. It is crucial for journalists to maintain independence from the police, prosecutors, the courts, and other public bodies charged with rooting out, prosecuting, and issuing rulings on corruption cases. Thus journalists can cast their critical gaze on these bodies themselves, expose weaknesses within them, and (ultimately) reinforce their effectiveness in curbing corruption. In the U.S. city of Detroit, for example, a radio station's investigation of corruption and irregularities in the local bankruptcy court was credited with leading to the dismissal and retirement of several judges, lawyers, and bankruptcy trustees, as well as a change in the way judges are assigned to cases.[6]

Promoting Accountability at the Polls

Even when reporting on corrupt activities by public figures does not lead directly to indictments, it can still help shape public hostility that can lead to electoral defeat for individual politicians or, indeed, for entire governments. The "cash for questions" scandal in the United Kingdom is a case in point. In 1994, a *Sunday Times* reporter posing as a businessman persuaded two Conservative Members of Parliament to express willingness to accept a payment of more than US$1,000 in return for lodging parliamentary questions. The ensuing uproar contributed to the public disgust over sleaze in public life that led to current Prime Minister Tony Blair's landslide victory over the Conservative incumbent John Major in the 1997 parliamentary elections (Barbash 1994).

In Ukraine, former President Leonid Kuchma was accused of numerous wrongdoings (including the killing of a journalist who investigated Kuchman's deeds); however, the accusations did not lead to his resignation. Nevertheless, when the electoral commission determined that Kuchman was suspected of electoral fraud during a subsequent election, the public withdrew its support for him and elected instead a pro-European Union (EU) opposition leader, Viktor Yushchenko.

Pressuring for Change to Laws and Regulations

Investigative journalism can also curb corruption by identifying weaknesses in laws and regulations that create a climate favorable to corruption. In so doing, authorities are prompted to change those laws and regulations. This was how WTLC Radio in Indianapolis concluded a series of pieces in 1984 and 1985 that examined past corruption in the state government of Indiana and criticized weaknesses in existing laws, which it said could lead to more corruption. The radio station offered up its own list of recommendations, including the establishment of a new public watchdog body and expanding the authority of the state ethics commission and attorney general.[7]

Moreover, when officials stonewall journalists, media outlets sometimes become a strong force that can pressure for improved disclosure. Such disclosure, or the potential for it, can often act as a deterrent to corruption. In Canada, the *Montreal Gazette's* lengthy court battle to gain access to the expense accounts of elected members of the provincial legislative assembly can be seen in this light (Macdonell 1993).

---

[6] IRE, Investigative Journalism Online Resource Center.
[7] Ibid.

Avoiding Adverse Publicity

Sometimes, mere inquiries by journalists—in the absence of a story's publication or of conclusive proof of wrongdoing—can lead to a tangible response from authorities eager to protect their reputations. Such was the case in 1996 when the *Minneapolis Star-Tribune* began making inquiries about the relationship between a local strip club and several vice-squad police officers. The officers were alleged to have "received special gifts and favors from the . . . club while failing to pursue serious violations that could have closed the business." [8] The police department responded to the inquiry by launching an internal investigation of its own.

Intangible Effects of Journalism on Corruption

Most often, though, the impact of the media's efforts to uncover and report on corruption is probably less tangible and more indirect than the preceding examples might suggest.

Michael Johnston (1997) has observed that weak political competition generally plays a role in sustaining the "most serious cases of entrenched political and bureaucratic corruption." Hard-hitting, independent journalism, however, can act as a counterweight to corruption that would otherwise flourish in the absence of such competition. It does this simply by presenting a variety of points of view and thus informing public debate in a way that enhances political and economic competition. As Johnston (1997) has observed, "[s]tronger political and economic competition can enhance accountability, open up alternatives to dealing with corrupt networks, and create incentives for political leaders to move against corruption."

In making such information public, the media often work closely with organized civil society: nongovernmental organizations, trade unions, pressure groups, lobbies, and citizens' groups, among others. These organizations carry out key monitoring and policy analysis, which reporters can then broadcast to the public.

Two other factors closely correlated with high levels of corruption are "low levels of mass participation in politics and weak protection of civil liberties" (Johnston 1997). Here, too, independent news media have an obvious, if indirect, counterweight role to play. This is particularly so when the news media foster debate of the sort that encourages members of the public to get involved politically and when news media outlets take the lead in pressing for enhanced civil liberties in which they have a strong vested interest—like freedom of expression.

A skills-building exercise in which journalists in Ethiopia, Mauritius, Tanzania, and Uganda took part in recent years illustrates this principle well. The exercise, as part of a workshop sponsored by the World Bank Institute, has sent out local reporters to "test" various repositories of public documents for the transparency with which they handle those documents and make them available to journalists. Finally, journalists can reinforce the record-keeping function of the state through their regular use of public documentation. [9]

---

[8] Ibid.

[9] For a more detailed description of this exercise, see Macdonell and Norris (1997).

How Can The Media Be Strengthened?

Realizing that the media are a critical element in a country's anti-corruption strategy begs the question of what can be done to encourage an independent media. This section examines how the media can be strengthened and, in particular, what parliament can do to support this objective.

Private versus Public Ownership

Some analysts have suggested that privatization of state-owned news media can be a means of strengthening their autonomy and, hence, their capacity to curb corruption. In Mexico, for example, shortly after the government relinquished state control over all television in 1989 and eased controls on the import of newsprint, the news media began reporting more aggressively on public corruption. For one private network, TV Azteca, its expanded coverage of corruption helped boost its audience share from 5 to 25 percent. The government-owned network has responded by covering more such stories itself (Simon 1998).

However, privatization may not always produce the desired results—particularly when it takes place in a poor nation with a small, entrenched business elite that has close ties to the government. As Lawrence Kilimwiko (1997), Chairman of Tanzania's Association of Journalists and Media Workers, has observed, "[d]espite the facade of liberalization—with four TV stations, seven radio stations, and over eight daily papers—there is government voice everywhere. We might be boasting of [a pluralistic] media," he noted in his presentation at an investigative journalism workshop, "but in reality they are all led by one voice, with journalists being turned into megaphones [for] the views of the owners and their allies in the state at the expense of the public good." One method that the Tanzanian government uses to retain a measure of control is the issuing of licenses, with the government being "very selective in issuing of media licenses to a few people who are known to be strongly aligned to maintaining the status quo" (Kilimwiko 1997).

Publicly owned media, on the other hand, do sometimes aggressively assert their independence—even in poor countries. In Benin, for instance, the state-owned newspaper *La Nation* is protected from government interference by a constitutionally empowered oversight body comprising state and nongovernment appointees known as the *observatoire de la déontologie et de l'éthique dans les médias*.[10] Likewise, although journalists at Uganda's state-owned *New Vision* newspaper have been known to complain that political considerations color the paper's news judgment and its reporters' assignments, it has been known to publish hard-hitting reporting on allegations of corruption within government, such as on business ties between a property magnate and the Minister of State for Primary Education (Wasike 1998). Public broadcasting corporations of such countries as Australia, Canada, South Africa, and the United Kingdom also have developed loyal and respectful audiences, thanks to the independence of their journalism.

---

[10] Conversations between Alexander Norris (journalist/facilitator) and Beninese journalists, Introductory Investigative Journalism Workshop, Cotonou, Benin (1997).

The ideal solution is perhaps a mix of private and public news media with a wide diversity of ownership enforced through a strong antitrust law. The *Cape Town Principles for an Informed Democracy* (2002) affirms that the public "should have access to a variety of print, broadcast, and Internet-based media to end reliance on government information or party-run information sources." Parliaments are in a prime position to facilitate diverse media ownership, whether by passing legislation privatizing state-run media or facilitating the entry of private media into the marketplace. Furthermore, parliaments, when exercising their oversight function, can ensure that the government provides state-run media with the resources and independence required to perform their vital function. Irrespective of who owns the media outlets though, the owners "must recognize that ownership entails a commitment to inform which is at least equal to the need to earn a profit" (Bouchet and Kariithi 2003).

Protection of Journalists

Journalists who seek to expose corrupt activity often must face moral and physical threats. In Kenya, for example, the division of society into ethnic groups creates a sense of fear among Kenyan journalists, which factors into their reporting of corrupt practices; meanwhile, denouncing corruption committed by a member of the same ethnicity carries with it a set of different considerations in that the reporting may affect their ethnic community (Githongo 1997). This creates a sense of moral obligation that might impede journalists from presenting free and accurate reports.

Journalists may also publish reports on corrupt practices at the risk of their own lives. The case of Kazakh journalist Askhat Sharipzhanov is just one example. After interviewing Altynbek Sarsenbayev, the Information Minister, and Zamanbek Nurkadilov, a leading member of the opposition to President Nazerbayev, Sharipzhanov was run down by a car driven by Kanat Kalzhanov. Several days later, he died. Kalzhanov received a relatively light sentence of only three and a half years with hard labor. Reporters Without Borders subsequently called for the investigation into Sharipzhanov's death to be reopened because many details found by an independent body had not be taken into consideration by the court.

Examples of journalists being harassed, jailed, or killed after writing about corruption are depressingly easy to find. Figures from the International News Safety Institute (INSI) show that 2004 was the bloodiest year in a decade for the news media. A total of 117 journalists died gathering news around the globe—42 of them in Iraq. Two-thirds of the 75 who died somewhere other than Iraq were targeted because of their work. "Democracy owes an enormous and growing debt to these members of the free press. . . . It's high time that countries with journalists' blood on their hands took effective action to find and prosecute their killers," said INSI Director Rodney Pinder.[11]

According to the International Federation of Journalists (IFJ), in 2004, 129[12] journalists were killed worldwide, the worst 12-month toll on record: "Behind each tragic death is a story of widespread intimidation and violence against journalists being carried out on a scale never seen before," said White. "We honour each of

---

[11] INSI Web page: http://www.newssafety.com/.

[12] It is not clear why there is a difference between INSI fatality figures and the IFJ's. Certainly, different organizations have different criteria to determine whether a journalist was killed while covering the news (for instance, the well-known New York-based Committee to Protect Journalists counts only journalists, not other media workers such as cameramen).

those who have died, from the dedicated and courageous correspondents to the support staff who make up the media team."[13]

In a study of journalists killed between 1993 and 2002, the New York–based Committee to Protect Journalists (CPJ) found that 16 percent of the journalists murdered in that time frame were killed covering warfare, while almost 80 percent were targeted because of their work, killed by people who wanted to silence them and put an end to their work.

Clearly, the protection of journalists' rights and their safety is critical to ensuring that journalists can fully contribute to curbing corruption. Steps in this direction have been taken in South Africa, where the Open Democracy Laws contain provisions for the protection of whistle-blowers from reprisals (Martin and Feldman 1998). This is just one example of the kind of legislation that parliament can encourage the passage of to protect journalists and their sources. Ultimately, parliaments must try to work toward creating an environment in which authorities are willing and capable of prosecuting those actors who intimidate or harm journalists. Parliament can encourage the passage of human rights legislation, including the establishment of accountability institutions such as human rights commissions, as well as ensuring that the criminal law provides adequate protection for journalists. Furthermore, when providing oversight of key institutions, such as the police and security forces, parliament could pay special attention to the responses of these agencies to such incidents to make sure that those who perpetrate violence against journalists are brought to account.

Access to Information

Access to information can be defined as the ability of the citizen to obtain information in the possession of the state (Martin and Feldman 1998, 7).[14] Information allows citizens to make informed judgments about government activities and thereby hold officials accountable. As former U.S. President Wilson noted, "Everyone knows that corruption thrives in secret places and avoids public places, and we believe it is a fair presumption that secrecy means impropriety" (IFJ 1996). Therefore, freely accessible information pertaining to government activities is necessary to ensure accountability of government officials.

Generally, governments have little difficulty in providing information to the public that reflects well on itself. The problem arises when the information reflects the opposite; here, "voluntary disclosure by government" does not work because both politicians and bureaucrats often try to hide embarrassing information.[15] While governments should seek to encourage attitudinal changes, which would relax restrictions on disclosures, the problem with administrative guidelines is that discretion remains; legislation guaranteeing access to information is the only alternative. The principle therefore needs to be set in stone. It is for this reason that a study group composed of representatives from WBI and the Commonwealth Parliamentary Association, in partnership with the Parliament of Ghana, drafted a series of recommendations in July 2004 aimed at enhancing the role of access to information.

---

[13] http://www.ifj.org/default.asp?Index=2903&Language=EN.

[14] The next three sections draw on chapter 14, "Information and Public Awareness," in Pope (1996).

[15] See, for example, "Ministers to Defer Truth on Nuclear Power Stations," Guardian (United Kingdom), August 21, 1995: "Sensitive financial information about the country's oldest and dirtiest nuclear reactors is being kept under wraps by the Government until it has privatized the industry's more modern atomic power stations."

"Recommendations for Transparent Governance" (2004) provides a framework for greater transparency in government, in particular through the implementation of access-to-information regimes. The cornerstone of such regimes is access-to-information legislation. As a central actor, parliament can seek to influence the drafting of the legislation so that it complies with the "Recommendations" and review the legislation on a regular basis to ensure that it is providing maximum disclosure and the transparency it intended to bring. Furthermore, parliament could use its oversight role to ensure the effective implementation of the legislation, namely by requiring public bodies to provide annual reports on their compliance with the legislation, holding the responsible minister to account for any failures in implementation, and overseeing the functioning of the independent administrative body tasked with implementation of the regime.

In accordance with the "Recommendations," any access-to-information legislation should ultimately establish the following:

- A right of access based on the notion of maximum disclosure, and if access is refused, a right of review to an independent administrative body, such as an Office of the Ombudsman
- Practices and procedures to be observed, including a deadline by when authorities must respond to a request for information, a requirement that reasons be given if a request is refused, and the identification of those categories of information to which access is guaranteed

Arguments against such legislation include those regarding cost and efficiency; however, it is necessary to consider the costs of failing to enact such legislation, which includes a lack of accountability and transparency and a fertile environment for corruption. Parliament can seek to reduce the cost of adherence to access-to-information regimes by promoting a culture of openness, encouraging the implementation of effective records management in those government agencies subject to such legislation, and requiring such agencies to undertake routine publication of key information so that it is easily accessible to the community.

On January 1, 2005, the United Kingdom's Freedom of Information Act come into force, giving all citizens in the United Kingdom new rights to see what goes on in their name, with their money. Under the Act, some 100,000 public bodies—from schools, police forces, hospitals, local councils, and waterway authorities to the government departments—must reveal documents that, until now, have been kept secret. More than 50 countries have enacted similar laws requiring the government to reveal information to the public.

It is traditional for official secrets to be exempt from disclosure for the purposes of national security, foreign relations, economic stability, and law enforcement; however, what constitutes an official secret is a matter for debate. There is always potential for corrupt officials to use one of these exemptions as an excuse not to disclose information. In the United Kingdom the culture of official secrecy is strong—until the late 1980s, all government information, including what kinds of biscuit were served to the prime minister, was technically an official secret—and that culture has been transmitted throughout the Commonwealth. In Malaysia, for example, the Internal Security Act defines any reporting of military activities without permission as a breach theoretically punishable by imprisonment, and the principle of national responsibility says that anything the government considers undesirable cannot be covered by journalists in their news reporting. Ultimately, to avert these exceptions being used to cloak corrupt activity, any decision made by public authorities not to disclose information on the grounds of one of these exemptions should be subject to judicial review.

Some preconditions are required to enjoy access to information. The main preconditions are political stability, an independent judiciary, and the presence of adequate infrastructure and data. Political stability is necessary because it makes politicians more secure and less averse to citizen involvement in decision making. An independent judicial system is required to act as an intermediary between the government and the people and hold the government accountable. Good communications infrastructure is important for access to information, including physical (for example, radio and television) and personal (for example, education) infrastructure (IFJ 1996). While the role played by the media in spreading information has already been discussed, the importance of literacy is not to be underestimated, given that access-to-information legislation presumes a generally high literacy rate.

The above preconditions are more likely to be met by developed countries. Developing countries, in general, are more likely to suffer political instability, weak judiciaries, inadequate infrastructure, and unreliable data. Nonetheless, the liberalization of access to information in developing countries would be an important step for ensuring government accountability and transparency, as well as strengthening press freedom.

Media Accountability

While accountability of public officials is important, the media should also be held accountable for their actions. Journalists, who champion human rights, probity, and democratic principles, must themselves adhere to these high standards. Unfortunately, this is not always the case. For instance, in many developing countries, "envelope journalism" is almost a daily practice. Journalists receive money in return for filing stories that please the "envelope donors."

Six media and public relations organizations have joined forces in an effort to stamp out bribery in journalism and the media. The International Federation of Journalists (IFJ), the International Press Institute (IPI), Transparency International (TI), the Global Alliance for Public Relations and Communications Management, the Institute for Public Relations Research and Education, and the International Public Relations Association have released a Charter of Media Transparency that calls for written policies on gift taking, the clear separation of editorial and advertising content, and an end to bribery for media coverage throughout the world.

Editors also experience pressure to publish questionable material. As such, it is imperative that editors are assured editorial freedom. The situation could be greatly improved if editors and journalists were properly paid for their work, thereby reducing the incentive to accept inducements to provide favorable coverage. When the government or media owners are unable to provide decent salaries for editors and journalists, support from outside donors may be a solution. In November 2004, the European Commission (EC) donated 2 million euros to members of the Serbian media who were willing to report about wrongdoings with respect to environmental pollution, organized crime, and trafficking in humans.

Obstacles to media accountability nonetheless exist. First, the media must publish news to remain profitable, which may push some media houses to "sell" their wares.[16] Second, the reluctance of public officials to disclose information results in journalists using less-accountable means of information gathering. Third, an oppressive judicial system reduces media accountability. The fear of being put in jail or of having to pay large amounts because of a libel suit may cause the media to refrain from publishing certain matters, even though they may be in the public interest.

Freedom of the Media

The media has a dual role with regard to curbing corruption: to raise public awareness about corruption and to investigate and report incidents of corruption in a professional and ethical manner. To carry out this dual role, the media must be free.[17] In addition to having access to information, journalists must investigate and report without fear of reprisals. Beyond the risk of physical harm, reprisals can include actions to censure journalists, close publications, or hamstring finances. Such "covert coercion" encourages a culture of self-censorship or safe reporting that offends no one in office, but does not provide meaningful information to the community.

Many countries require the registration of newspapers or journalists, with some governments rescinding licenses at will. Section 17(1) of Tanzania's Newspaper Regulations, for example, does not permit newspapers to change their address, the provisions of their constitutions, or even their aims and values; two tabloids were banned under this regulation in June 1998. Furthermore, licensing can act as a form of censorship because it allows authorities to license only those media agencies or journalists that support the government's position. There should not be any limits as to who may enter the practice of journalism. Parliaments should recognize that licensing journalists is not compatible with freedom of expression and refrain from legislating in this area (Bouchet and Kariithi 2003, 23).

Governments can, and do, put pressure on the economics of the newspaper business. In many developing countries, the main source of advertising is the government; in recent years, Bangladesh, Malawi, Uganda, and Zambia—among others—have either restricted advertising to specific newspapers or withdrawn all advertisements except those appearing in the state-owned press. Elsewhere, governments have restricted and controlled newsprint imports, applied punitive tax audits, or restricted access to the infrastructure (such as frequencies, transmitters, or aerials) needed to broadcast. Parliament must be aware of such methods used by governments to curb the freedom of the media and seek to counter any such attempts when fulfilling its oversight function.

Some governments level charges of contempt of parliament, the head of state, or even the country as a whole. In Cameroon, it is an offense to abuse and insult the members of the National Assembly. In Kenya, until its recent repeal, sedition legislation had a similar effect. In March 1998, the Kenyan Broadcasting Minister told media houses that they were taking "advantage" and warned that they "did not

---

[16] "The problem of 'journalism for sale' or paid-for material posing as legitimate news reporting is one of the greatest challenges facing media today," said IFJ General Secretary Aidan White. See http://www.hdfnet.org/index.cfm?fuseaction=message&messageID= 14520&lang=en&cat_id=70.

[17] This section draws on chapters 1 and 2 of Commonwealth Press Union (1999).

appreciate [their] responsibility for protecting [then-] President Moi's image." Contempt of parliament is an offense so vaguely and broadly defined that it poses a serious challenge to freedom of expression; parliaments should refrain from using their discretionary power to hold journalists in contempt, except in the most serious of cases. In particular, it has been suggested that parliament should not seek to bring contempt charges against any journalist who reports on information leaked from parliament, but rather discipline the Member who leaked the information (Bouchet and Kariithi 2003, 27).

A set of principles to counteract these restrictions, the Charter for a Free Press, was approved by journalists from 34 countries at the Voices of Freedom World Conference on Censorship Problems in 1987. The United Nations Secretary-General at the time, Boutros Boutros-Ghali, declared that the charter's principles "deserve the support of everyone pledged to advance and protect democratic institutions." He added that the provisions, while nonbinding, express goals "to which all free nations aspire."[18] The charter prescribes full protection of journalists under law.

Press Councils

In many young and fragile democracies, the media are less experienced than elsewhere, and there may be a tendency for the media to be less than "responsible" (IFJ 1996). In this regard, there may be merit in the establishment of press councils. Press councils can provide an open forum for the public to chastise the press when it is irresponsible and thereby influence its behavior. Press councils must be independent and directed by people widely respected for their nonpartisan standing and their integrity. These bodies should not have powers of legal sanction, which could enable them to become powerful censors. They should, rather, have the prestige and integrity that give their public reports a strong moral force.

Because a press council has no power to force anyone to do anything, its effectiveness depends on the cooperation of all groups involved. An independent press council is responsible for the self-regulation of the news media in any given area, free from government interference or judicial supervision. It should be independently funded; have voluntary universal industry commitment; be based on a code of conduct written and approved by the industry itself; and uphold freedom of expression, the public's right to know, and the media's right to publish without prior restraint (Beales 2002).

A very fine line exists between responsible and irresponsible journalism. The moral force of a press council is thus a better way to secure a responsible press, rather than providing governments and courts with wide-ranging powers to curb the press. Parliament should seek to support the media's independence, rather than pass legislation that curbs the media's freedom.

Self-Regulation by the Media

The independence of the media is vital to a functioning democracy and is essential if the media is to fulfill its role of keeping decision makers accountable. Media independence, however, does not mean that the media should not be regulated; it does

---

[18] Boutros Boutros-Ghali, speech given at the Voices of Freedom World Conference on Censorship Problems, London (January 16–18, 1987).

mean that particular attention must be paid to how the media is regulated to ensure its continued independence. Self-regulation has worked in some countries and not in others and remains a contentious issue. Nevertheless, "there is a strong consensus among media practitioners and also many NGOs that it offers the best guarantee of protection from interference" (Bouchet and Kariithi 2003, 19). The IFJ "Tirana Declaration" (1999) on media, ethics, and self-regulation supports the position that ethical journalism must be guided by codes of principles for the conduct of journalism developed by media professionals themselves. This is further supported by World Bank research, which suggests that successful media self-regulatory systems are underpinned by consensual codes of conduct (Islam 2002). Of course, there is no single model for self-regulation that can be copied throughout the world; the most appropriate model for each situation must take into account the local social, cultural, and ethical issues.

If self-regulation is adopted, then it is for parliament to create the legal framework that guarantees freedom of expression, which enables journalists to practice freely. However, if government opts for statutory regulation and seeks to establish a regulatory authority, parliament should consider whether statutory regulation is appropriate under the circumstances. If it has been chosen as a last resort, than parliament should ensure that the authority is protected by strong guarantees of independence, both in statute and in practice. Parliament should also provide ongoing oversight of its operations to guarantee its continued independence.

Numerous media organizations focus on freedom of the press. The Southeast Asian Press Alliance, Canadian Journalists for Free Expression, the Committee to Protect Journalists, the International Federation of Journalists, and the World Press Freedom Committee are but a few of the organizations that work to help governments put in place laws and arrangements that foster a free press.

Investigative Journalism Training

The American organization, Investigative Reporters and Editors (IRE), defines investigative reporting as "the reporting, through one's own initiative and work product, of matters of importance to readers, viewers, or listeners. In many cases, the subjects of the reporting wish the matters under scrutiny to remain undisclosed."[19]

Investigative journalism can also be defined as "the collection and processing of facts about current events for dissemination to the public through the medium of newspapers, magazines, radio, and so on" (Katorobo 1995, 51). Its implementation requires journalists to have excellent skills that must be mastered and learned. In particular, research, analytical, and communication skills must be learned by the practitioners in an effort to make their work more effective. Furthermore, journalists must acquire the capacity to make sound and balanced political and social judgments. Failure to do so would jeopardize the reliability of their work.

If journalists are expected to report news fairly and accurately, they must possess the tools and appropriate knowledge for it. This becomes especially important when they are required to provide an easy, although truthful, explanation of the news to the public.

---

[19] http://www.ire.org/contest/.

Media practitioners who have not acquired all the qualities that such a job requires should receive appropriate training. Training becomes especially valuable when it aims at avoiding errors and deficiencies in reporting. The most common errors occur in the collection of facts and data, in analytical processing of the data, in drawing logical conclusions from observed facts, and in the statement of events. These errors can be easily avoided with training that would also improve the quality of journalism and enhance media credibility (Katorobo 1995, 51). Together with providing appropriate tools, training must make journalists understand the nature of corruption and the need to fight corrupted practices.

The World Bank Institute (WBI) facilitated tens of investigative journalism workshops and videoconference trainings for more than 2,000 journalists from nearly two dozen countries.[20] The objective of these workshops is twofold: to raise the awareness of journalists of the critical importance of the issue of corruption and its harmful impact on development and to improve the skills of journalists so that they can investigate and report incidents of corruption in a professional and ethical manner.

Other organizations have recognized the importance of investigative journalism training. In September 2005, the U.S. government announced a two-year Investigative Journalism training program for 225 students in South Africa that is aimed at assisting in that country's anti-corruption efforts.[21]

Conclusions

The role played by the media in curbing corruption has proved to be extremely valuable (please refer, for example, to the case study by John Smith that follows this chapter). Often, reports on corrupt practices by government officials have provided the starting point for investigations, judicial proceedings, or resignations. More broadly, media reporting has improved the level of pluralism and accountability in society.

The media are often referred to as the "fourth estate," after the clergy, the nobility, and the commons. As Kilimwiko (1997, 73) notes, "it is through the mass media that a nation communes with itself and with other nations beyond. It is in that way that the authorities within a nation . . . sense the problems and aspirations of the people they are established to serve. Conversely, it is through the same channel that the people sense the capacity and policies of those authorities."

However, if the media are to reach their full potential as the fourth estate and keep public officials accountable, the media must be strengthened and—most important—its independence must be assured. Parliament has a vital role to play in facilitating an environment that nurtures an effective media, whether by enacting access-to-information and freedom-of-expression laws or by encouraging media self-regulation (rather than government regulation). At the same time, parliaments themselves should open up their own proceedings to scrutiny by the media—thereby facilitating greater public access to parliamentary information.

---

[20] Workshops have been held in Benin, Ethiopia, Malawi, Mali, Mauritius, Tanzania, Uganda, and Ukraine with journalists from these countries, as well as from Albania, Burkino Faso, Cameroon, Comoros, the Republic of Congo, Côte d'Ivoire, Georgia, Latvia, Madagascar, Niger, Senegal, the Seychelles, and Turkey. Support for these workshops has been provided by the governments of Canada, Denmark, France, and the United Kingdom, as well as by the United Nations Development Programme (UNDP).

[21] http://pretoria.usembassy.gov/wwwhpr15j.html.

Bibliography

Barbash, Fred. 1994. "Scandal Over Paid Questions Rocks British Tories." *Washington Post* dispatch published in *Montreal Gazette* (October 21): A8.

Beales, Ian. 2002. *Imperfect Freedom: The Case for Self-Regulation in the Commonwealth Press*. London: Commonwealth Press Union.

Bouchet, Nicolas, and Nixon Kariithi. 2003. *Parliament and the Media: Building an Informed Society*. Working Paper, World Bank Institute, Washington, DC.

Cape Town Principles for an Informed Democracy. 2002. Proposed during the Indian Ocean Rim Conference on "Parliament and the Media: Securing an Effective Relationship," Cape Town, South Africa (April 14–18).

Coronel, Sheila. "Opening a Pandora's Box: The Emergence of a Free Press in Southeast Asia." *Development Dialogue* (2001:1) Dag Hammarskjöld Foundation. Uppsala, Sweden.

Commonwealth Press Union. 1999. *The Independence of the Commonwealth Media and Those Working Within It*. London: CPU.

CPJ (Committee to Protect Journalists). 1998. http://www.cpj.org/.

Githongo, John. 1997. "The Role of Journalists in Combating Corruption in Kenya." Unpublished paper presented at World Bank Institute seminar, Cotonou, Benin (January).

HRW (Human Rights Watch). 1998. http://www.hrw.org/.

IFJ (International Federation of Journalists). 1996. "The Right to Know: Access to Information in African Countries." African Regional Conference (July 25–27).

———. 1999. "Tirana Declaration: Media Ethics and Self-Regulation." http://www.ijnet.org/Director.aspx?P=Ethics&ID=158580&LID=1.

IRE (Investigative Reporters and Editors, Inc.) Investigative Journalism Online Resource Center. http://www.ire.org/resourcecenter/about.html.

Islam, R. 2002. *The Right to Tell: The Role of Mass Media in Economic Development*. Washington, DC: World Bank Institute.

Johnston, Michael. 1997. "What Can Be Done about Entrenched Corruption?" Paper prepared for the Annual World Bank Conference on Development Economics, Washington, DC. (April 30–May 1).

Katorobo, James. 1995. "Investigative Journalism: The Mutual Roles of the Media and the Civil Service in Exposing Misconduct." In *Investigative Journalism in Uganda I: Final Workshop Proceedings*, Uganda (August 14–19).

Kilimwiko, Lawrence. 1997. "Corruption in the Media." Paper presented to the first Investigative Journalism Workshop for Female Journalists, Bagamoyo, Tanzania (February 16–22).

Klitgaard, Robert. 1996. "Bolivia: Healing Sick Institutions in La Paz." In *Governance and the Economy in Africa: Tools for Analysis and Reform of Corruption*, ed. Patrick Meagher. University of Maryland Press: College Park.

Langseth, Petter, Rick Stapenhurst, and Jeremy Pope. 1997. "The Role of a National Integrity System in Fighting Corruption." Working Paper 400/142, Economic Development Institute (EDI), World Bank, Washington, DC.

Larsen, Alex, and Flemming Ytzen. 1997. "Freedonia: Investigative Journalism." Case Study, World Bank Institute, Washington, DC.

Macdonell, Rod. 1993. "New Chief Judge of Montreal Municipal Court Gets Mandate to Improve Work Ethic." *Montreal Gazette* (November 26): Al.

———. 1997. "Bouchard Releases Expense Account." *Montreal Gazette* (March 27): A3.

Macdonell, Rod, and Alexander Norris. 1997. "Public Documentation Exercise." In *Rapport sur le seminaire sur le journalisme d'investigation tenu a Port-Louis, Ile Maurice, du 29 septembre au 8 octobre 1997*, report submitted to the Economic Development Institute (EDI) of the World Bank, Washington, DC.

Marsden, William, and Jennifer Robinson. 1987. "Possible Conflict Exposed, Latulippe Quits as Minister." *Montreal Gazette* (June 30): Al.

Martin, Robert, and Estelle Feldman. 1998. "Access to Information in Developing Countries." A study prepared for Transparency International, Berlin.

Neumann, A. Lin. 1998. "High Price of Secrecy: Restricting the Press Worsened the Economic Crash." *Columbia Journalism Review* 37 (March/April). http://archives.cjr.org/year/98/2/asia.asp.

Pope, Jeremy, ed. 1996. *The TI Source Book*. Berlin, Germany: Transparency International, 1996.

Powell III, Adam Clayton. 1998. "Competition Essential to Press Freedom, Broadcast News Executives Say." *Free!* Freedom Forum online newsletter (May 29): http://www.freedomforum.org/search/default.asp?ps=100&qs= %22Competition+essential+to+press+freedom%22.

"Recommendation for Transparent Governance." 2004. Conclusion of a CPA-WBI Study Group on Access to Information, held in partnership with the Parliament of Ghana, Accra, Ghana (July 5–9).

Shugaar, Anthony. 1994. "Italy's New Hall of Mirrors." *Columbia Journalism Review* 33 (July/August).

Simon, Joel. 1998. "Hot on the Money Trail." *Columbia Journalism Review* 37 (January/February).

Stapenhurst, Rick. 2000. "The Media's Role in Curbing Corruption." World Bank Institute. http://www.worldbank.org/wbi/governance/pdf/media.pdf.

Wasike, Alfred. 1998. "Sudhir Buys Back Muhwezi Shares." *The New Vision*, Kampala, February 6, 1998, Al.

Woodward, Robert. 1994. "Sleaze Sinking British MPs: British Regard for Politicians Low." Reuters news dispatch, published in the *Montreal Gazette* (July 15): A12.

Case Study on the Role of Parliament and the Media in the Fight against Corruption

John Smith

Background

Uganda, a country of 24 million people and a gross national income (GNI) per capita of US$320, is one of the poorest countries in the world. When the National Resistance Movement (NRM) government took power in Uganda in 1986, it inherited a country traumatized by civil war and insecurity. The situation was made worse by high levels of lawlessness, corruption, and mismanagement. The civil service, once hailed as one of the best in Sub-Saharan Africa, had become oversized, inefficient, demoralized, and unresponsive.

The new government castigated past governments for plundering the nation, and it promised fundamental changes, with one of the key challenges being the fight against corruption. Government, with the assistance of various development partners, developed a strategy to combat corruption and ensure good governance. This included public service reform; creation of institutions to fight corruption; efforts to purge the police, judiciary, and other government bodies of corrupt elements; and privatization.

A new constitution was promulgated in 1995, and an expanded and more representative Parliament was elected largely by universal suffrage. The new Parliament, exercising powers it had acquired under the constitution, took on a leading role in the fight against corruption.

In addition, with the favorable political and economic climate and the focus on transparency, a free and vibrant press emerged. For the first time, the media were able to challenge government and expose corruption in ways that enhanced public scrutiny and increased government accountability.

Perhaps the most significant corruption cases the Parliament handled involved two senior cabinet ministers, Brigadier Jim Katugugu Muhwezi, Minister of State for Primary Education, and Sam Kutesa, Minister of State for Finance in charge of Privatization. The pair were accused of defrauding the government of millions of dollars and of having taken kickbacks, peddled their influence, and evaded taxes. Media reports on the scandal sparked an outcry from the public, civil society, and parliamentarians. Within less than two years, the two ministers had been censured and forced to resign.

This case study examines the roles of the Parliament and the media, working together, in curbing corruption, and it lays particular emphasis on the cases of the two ministers. It addresses the challenges and lessons to be learned and highlights the unique role that was played by Parliament and the media to get to the bottom of the two corruption cases.

Institutional Setup in Uganda

The institutional framework for anti-corruption in Uganda involves various institutions, including Parliament, the Ministry of Ethics and Integrity, the Inspector General of Government (IGG), the Auditor General (AG), the judiciary, and law enforcement.

Uganda's 309-member Parliament comprises a collection of interest groups. Among these are representatives of women, the disabled, workers, youth, and the army, ex oficios like the country's prime minister as well as directly elected representatives (who form the majority). Several committees within Parliament are charged with overseeing the operations of government. Standing committees include the Public Accounts Committee (PAC), which is empowered to scrutinize government accounts based on the AG's annual reports. Under the constitution, government departments and agencies may be required to submit their accounts to the PAC for scrutiny and publication. Despite these mechanisms, the AG's powers were initially limited to reporting on bad accounting practices and were constrained from reviewing classified expenditures such as defense and military intelligence operations. Thus, operating without oversight, security agencies were provided with unchecked powers—which experience elsewhere has shown is a prime environment for fraud and embezzlement.

Unlike the AG, the office of the IGG[1] plays a more proactive role as the main government anti-corruption watchdog. With a staff of auditors, accountants, lawyers, and investigators, plus powers to cause arrests and prosecution of suspects, the IGG is perhaps the best-resourced agency to fight corruption. The effectiveness of the department is, however, dogged by various constraints such as underfunding, a growing culture of untouchables (powerful personalities close to the president), and ineffective laws hampering the IGG's powers. Such laws include the Leadership Code, which requires political leaders to declare their wealth to the IGG, but does not require them to show means of income used to acquire the property (see chapter 9). In addition, Parliament has, in the past, not taken timely action on the biannual reports submitted by the IGG's office as required by law. The Office of Minister of Ethics and Integrity mainly plays the role of policy coordinator, standard setting, and development and review of anti-corruption legislation. They are currently in the process of finalizing the "whistle-blower" and qui tam laws among others.

Allegations against the Ministers

In March 1998, following a scandal that involved allegations of rampant corruption, Parliament passed the first-ever motion to censure a cabinet minister. Minister Muhwezi, a lawyer, an ex-policeman, a soldier in the ruling government's National Resistance Army, and the former Director General of the powerful Internal Security

---

[1] Uganda's first Inspector General of Government became a champion in the fight against corruption. He subsequently was elected to Parliament, became the chair of PAC—and became the first chair of the African Parliamentarians Network Against Corruption (see chapter 14).

Organization (ISO), was later forced to resign. Allegations of Muhwezi's impropriety were first brought to light when an outspoken opposition MP revealed that the minister was a shareholder in Meera Investments, a company owned by a local businessman, and for which he had influenced the granting of an annual tenancy contract with the Uganda Revenue Authority worth 600 million Ugandan shillings (U Sh) (US$350,000). The media publicized the allegations, casting doubt on the minister's credibility, by alluding to a case in which, while serving as ISO chief, he had arrested the same businessman over shoddy foreign exchange deals and accused him of trying to bribe him with US$10,000.

Parliamentarians who signed a petition expressing loss of confidence in the minister, accused him of using his influence to benefit business people. It was also alleged that the minister was involved in various incidents of using his influence to acquire properties. Indeed, his total worth was reported to be U Sh 6 billion (US$3.5 million) at the time. The media suggested that Muhwezi could have made most of his fortune while serving as head of ISO, prior to his appointment as Minister of State for Education.[2]

The list of Muhwezi's possessions that the petitioners presented to Parliament included two farms, one at Nyakagyeme (in Runkungiri district) and another in his wife's ancestral home, each of which was estimated at U Sh 300 million (a combined total of more than US$350,000); two other farms, both estimated at U Sh 150 million (approximately US$85,000); another farm in Mpigi district worth U Sh 600 million (US$350,000); a palatial home in his upcountry village estimated at more than U Sh 1 billion (US$600,000); another house in Kampala, valued at U Sh 200 million (about US$115,000); two commercial buildings in Kampala, one worth U Sh 500 million (around US $300,000) and the other worth more than U Sh 700 million (about US$540,000); plot 11 Luthuli Avenue, rented by the Ugandan Revenue Authority (URA) at US$3,500 a month; several plots of land, both in the capital of Kampala and upcountry, worth more than U Sh 600 million (US$350,000); a hotel in Rukungiri district, southwestern Uganda, valued at U Sh 700 million (US$540,000); several other properties in London and Washington, DC; as well as shares in several thriving local companies. Contrary to the Leadership Code, the minister was accused of owning shares in foreign-owned companies, including a subsidiary of William Obrain, a U.S. company. Crucial to the investigations of this wealth—a point the petitioners were repeatedly raising—was the very short time within which the minister had acquired the properties.

Muhwezi's counterpart and Minister of State for Finance in charge of Privatization, Kutesa, was charged with overseeing the divestiture of the cargo-handling operation of the Uganda Airlines Corporation (UAC). UAC had a 50 percent stake in Entebbe Handling Services (ENHAS), the company that handled its cargo operations, while Kutesa—in an apparent conflict of interest—owned the rest of the shares in the same company. In addition to being a shareholder, Kutesa was also chairman of the board of directors of ENHAS. This conflict of interest was contrary to clause 8(1-3) of the Leadership Code. A Parliamentary select committee, charged with investigating the privatization process, produced a lengthy report accusing Kutesa of directly influencing the decision to sell the airline's 50 percent share to ENHAS, falsifying the company's accounts, and evading taxes.

---

[2] It will be remembered from above that security expenditures are "classified" and not subject to scrutiny by the Auditor General.

Role of Parliament

Following allegations against Muhwezi of complicity in the controversial URA rental deal, Parliament became interested in the matter and referred it to the Parliamentary Rules, Privileges, and Discipline Committee. Although the Committee did clear Muhwezi, other MPs continued their investigations, often leaking information to the media, whose coverage of the events kept the spotlight on the minister, prompting even further investigations of his wealth. A group of MPs, keen to see the case to its logical conclusion, were busy drafting a petition of censure and gathering signatures from colleagues. Revelations about Muhwezi's conduct and massive wealth galvanized support for the petition to the extent that more than 90 signatures of MPs in support of the censure were gathered in two days. The petition document, expressing lack of confidence in the minister, was, as required by the constitution, submitted to the Speaker of Parliament for passing on to the president.

The ensuing months were characterized by parliamentary debates, extensive media coverage, and behind-the-scenes strategy meetings of the two distinct camps that had emerged in Parliament: petitioners and nonpetitioners. On March 4, 1998, months after the censure process started, in a vote of 148 for and 91 against, the House passed a motion of censure against the minister.

Empowered by the successful result of Muhwezi's censure, Parliament continued to expose cases of corruption involving ministers. A few months after the Muhwezi censure, another Minister, Kirunda Kivejinja, Minister without Portfolio, preempted Parliament's moves to censure him by resigning his post. Kivejinja was accused of using his influence to divert 2,000 liters of fuel belonging to the state-owned Uganda Railways Corporation.

In December the same year, the Minister of State for Finance in charge of Privatization, Matthew Rukikaire, also resigned after Parliament threatened to censure him for failure to adequately oversee the privatization of the Uganda Commercial Bank, the country's largest commercial institution, in which billions of Ugandan shillings were lost in a sale gone bad.

When the House reopened after a Christmas break in February 1999, the case of Sam Kutesa was at the top of the agenda. A month later, in a vote of 152 for and 94 against, Kutesa became the second minister to be censured.

Box 1 *"Sweet 16"*

Nothing illustrates the alliance between Parliament and the media better than an incident in which a group of 16 MPs, part of the group that had championed and signed the petition document submitted to the Speaker, changed their minds and sought to dissociate themselves from it. One parliamentarian leaked this information to the media, which published the legislators' names, causing them public embarrassment and shame. The "sweet sixteen," as fellow MPs later baptized them, had secretly written to the Speaker of Parliament describing the petition bearing their signatures as a contestable document. On reading the media story about the 16, one angry MP was quoted in the press as saying, "We are appealing to the public to take note of those MPs who cannot take a firm stand against corruption and graft. . . . Our people are tired of corruption, but why are our leaders resisting the tide of transparency?"

Source: Author's research.

Role of the Media

As chapter 8 showed, the media can play a critical role in curbing corruption. The media proved to be invaluable in exposing these corruption scandals. Both the government-owned *New Vision* and the privately owned *Monitor* (now *Daily Monitor*) consistently put the stories on their front pages, thereby demonstrating that the media were capable of playing a key watchdog role.

Newspaper editorials and commentaries focused public attention on issues of accountability. An editorial in the *New Vision* of March 6, 1999, called on Kutesa to "resign now." It is little wonder that two other ministers, Kivejinja and Rukikaire, resigned before they could be censured.

Media reports galvanized public interest and awareness on corruption. Using a freedom-of-information law, the media managed to obtain information and publish balanced reports. This was possible in part because information was gathered by ordinary citizens, MPs, and parliamentary staff and leaked to the media, which amplified it and thereby engendered more information. The numerous letters to the editors in the print media and live radio and television debates involving telephone call-ins by members of the public provided an invaluable channel for receiving civil society's views. Providing the much-needed analytical approach, media reports bolstered the petitioners' case. Accordingly, Parliament, the media, and civil society each played a complementary role (see box 1).

In instances where the media were privy to sensitive information and hesitant to publish it, this information would be passed on to vocal legislators who would take it to the floor of Parliament. The media would then freely report it, cashing in on the privileged nature of parliamentary proceedings. Conversely, less courageous parliamentarians, uncomfortable expressing their views on sensitive matters, resorted to leaking information to the media. This collaborative pattern was important in broadening the media's reach and adding to the list of subjects available to comment on in the anti-corruption war.

Lessons Learned

Both censures of senior ministers in Uganda resulting from corruption sent an important message that a strong parliament and the media, working together, can hold government to account.

The media plays an important role in providing relevant information and maintaining public interest in, and attention to, corruption issues, influencing subsequent punitive or corrective action. Persistent media coverage demonstrated that the public often needs a reason to believe that an issue is important; otherwise, it can become apathetic. One way the ministers were successfully brought to justice was that the media kept raising the issue of a "smoking gun," by referring to their massive wealth.

Parliament began to see the media as a partner, not only providing useful information on debatable issues, but also catalyzing public support for its cause. Clearly, Parliament found itself increasingly benefiting from the media and vice versa.

Media coverage of anti-corruption issues can influence different decision makers, including the judiciary, to effect necessary punitive measures. Although both Ministers Muhwezi and Kutesa opted to challenge their censures in constitutional courts and to sue the media for defamation, the cases were either defeated or abandoned, demonstrating that with a strong partnership between law makers, the media, and ordinary citizens, corruption can be defeated.

Measures to curb corruption without legal safeguards to guard against the reoccurrence of abuses are not sustainable. Unfortunately, weaknesses in the constitution allowed space for a continuation of the abuses. A next step for Parliament should have been to strengthen the constitution. Parliament needed to cash in on the euphoria immediately after the victory over the two ministers to amend the constitution and create enabling legal safeguards barring people either censured by Parliament or forced to resign public office because of corruption from assuming such offices again. Failure to do this besmirched the record of the Sixth Parliament because the two individuals were later reappointed ministers. The current Constitution under article 235 provides for disqualification from reappointment for breach of the Leadership Code. The Leadership Code Act (2002) stops the reappointment of these leaders for a period of 5 years following dismissal.

For legislation on "access to information" to be effective in the exposure or identification of corruption cases, it is important that the law to be clear and conclusive in its provisions to facilitate timely and complete access to relevant information by parliament, the press, and any other concerned parties. The law had a two-way effect in these cases, in that although existing provisions hindered access to primary or "classified" relevant information, it facilitated the effective use of secondary information by both the media and MPs, which automatically became privileged under the National Assembly Powers and Privileges Act when presented in Parliament.

A final lesson from the censures is that availability and enforcement of constitutional provisions to expose and punish corruption can go a long way in enhancing public accountability. The censures were the product of the liberal voices in Parliament who, empowered by the provisions of Article 118 of the new constitution, were able to censure the ministers.

Conclusion

Coverage of these cases provided new sources of information for journalists as the number of people in different government departments willing to volunteer information about corruption increased. As a result, newspaper coverage of corruption rose because of continued provision of information by volunteers. Parliament and the media demonstrated that their roles as watchdogs are complementary and can be mutually reinforcing.

9

Anti-Corruption Commissions

John R. Heilbrunn

Introduction

Numerous governments have adopted anti-corruption commissions despite growing evidence that such commissions fail to reduce corruption. Why do policy makers allocate scarce revenues to establish a commission that consumes resources and possibly undermines the credibility of their commitment to reform?

A cynical response is that policy makers are not seriously committed to enacting effective reforms. At an extreme, the reasons may be as simple as malice and greed: political leaders are engaged in looting the economy, and an appearance of reform allows them to postpone the adoption of meaningful efforts. A more common scenario is that policy makers are risk averse and reluctant to enact reforms that might threaten domestic constituents who profit from systemic corruption. Meanwhile, governments in developing countries need international investments, and international donors often require policies to reduce corruption as a prerequisite for continuing development assistance. Establishing an anti-corruption commission may represent an effort to satisfy international donors and placate domestic calls for reform, even if for only a short while.

Evidence of dysfunctional anti-corruption commissions is manifest in the numerous agencies that lack independence from the executive, receive inadequate budgetary support from the legislature, have no procedures for forwarding cases of corruption for prosecution by the relevant judicial authorities, and fail to submit regular reports to the legislature. Herein lies the dilemma: whereas it may be desirable to enact policies to reduce corruption, a weak commission leads to a reputation for token reforms, which undermines the political leadership's credibility. Indeed, it is easy to explain why anti-corruption commissions fail in so many places. It is far more difficult to explain why any succeed.

This chapter argues that anti-corruption commissions often fail to reduce public sector venality. It will be noted that those governments that have established successful anti-corruption commissions have done so in response to demands for reform from a broad base of domestic constituents, including legislators and actors in civil society organizations. Such demands generally occur after a precipitating crisis has caused deep economic hardship and a national consensus emerges that reforms must be implemented. Without such a crisis, building domestic coalitions is a challenge for even the most popular leaders, as chapter 10 will show. When support is more tenuous, policy makers have an incentive to weaken reforms and avoid any threat to powerful—yet corrupt—constituents.[1]

This chapter examines the four types of anti-corruption commission:

- The *universal model,* with its investigative, preventive, and communicative functions, is typified by Hong Kong's Independent Commission Against Corruption (ICAC).
- The *investigative model* is characterized by a small and centralized investigative commission as operates in Singapore's Corrupt Practices Investigation Bureau (CPIB).
- The *parliamentary model* includes commissions that report to parliamentary committees and are independent from the executive and judicial branches of the state (for example, the New South Wales Independent Commission Against Corruption).
- The *multiagency model* includes a number of offices that are autonomous, but which together weave a web of agencies to fight corruption. The United States Office of Government Ethics, with its preventive approach, complements the Justice Department's investigative and prosecutorial powers, and together these organizations make a concerted effort to reduce corruption.

The chapter then looks at commissions in various countries that have adapted these models to their particular circumstances. In its conclusion, the chapter formulates some possible responses to the question of why governments would adopt a problematic approach to fighting corruption.

The Universal Model: Hong Kong's ICAC

Since its establishment in 1974, the Hong Kong Independent Commission Against Corruption (ICAC) has enjoyed resounding success in fighting corruption (Klitgaard 1998, 98–100). It was established after a botched investigation into corruption of the colonial police led to Police Superintendent Peter Godber's flight from prosecution. Shortly thereafter, Governor Sir Murray MacLehose empaneled a commission under the chairmanship of Justice Alastair Blair-Kerr (de Speville 1997), which concluded that corruption was systemic among high-level officials and police officers. In response to these problems, the Commission recommended the establishment of a special agency to investigate allegations of corruption, prevent bribery in business and government, and educate citizens about corruption through outreach programs.

Political authorities recognized that "an essential part of the strategy was to ensure that the legal framework within which [the ICAC] was contained was as strong, clear, and effective as it could be made" (de Speville 1997, 23). Existing legislation was revised, and new laws were passed to set up an anti-corruption agency with a mandate to investigate any allegations of corruption and forward evidence to prosecutors.

To ensure the agency's credibility, new laws criminalized corruption by defining a lengthy list of offenses that include the obstruction of justice, theft of government resources, blackmail, deception, bribery, making a false accusation, and conspiracy to commit an offense. Most pertinently, the legislation gave authorities discretion to

---

[1] This chapter synthesizes Heilbrunn (2004).

conduct searches, examine bank accounts, subpoena witnesses, audit private assets, and detain individuals, and it also permitted officials to seize passports and property and incarcerate suspects when evidence suggests a risk of flight. Although such powers violate fundamental tenets of due process embedded in Western legal thought, the particular circumstances in Hong Kong at the time were thought to require special provisions to prevent suspects from escaping prosecution.

Putting into operation stringent laws requires solid budgetary support. For example, in 2001, the ICAC was appropriated the equivalent of US$90 million, an amount that was viewed as fully justified when compared with the costs of unchecked corruption (Chan 2002). This allocation paid the salaries of approximately 1,200 contracted officers; such officers' contracts are independent of civil service rules, and there are prohibitions on officers entering the civil service after they leave the Commission. The agency benefits from low turnover: more than half of its officers have been with the ICAC for more than 10 years. A stable employee base has contributed to the development of internal expertise in fighting corruption.

The ICAC controls corruption through three functional departments: investigation, prevention, and community relations. Largest among the departments is the Operations Department, which investigates alleged violations of laws and regulations. The Corruption Prevention Department funds studies of corruption, conducts seminars for business leaders, and helps public and private organizations identify strategies to reduce corruption. It has also funded several thousand studies for public sector agencies and businesses in Hong Kong (de Speville 1997), which inform the public about how officials adjust to changes in laws and regulations. The role of the Community Relations Department is to build awareness of the societal costs of corruption by poster campaigning, television commercials, and films that dramatize the work of ICAC officers.

The ICAC's reporting hierarchy includes the Special Administrator, the ICAC Director, and three oversight committees: the Operations Review Committee, the Corruption Prevention Advisory Committee, and the Citizen Advisory Committee on Community Relations. The ICAC is required to submit regular reports that follow clear procedural guidelines for investigations, seizures of property, and the duration of inquiries, and the oversight committees seek to ensure that ICAC's investigations are undertaken with the highest levels of integrity.

When first established, the ICAC had marginal success: domestic constituents mocked its efforts, and its public pronouncements lacked credibility. However, the repatriation and successful prosecution of Peter Godber increased the ICAC's credibility, and citizens began to report incidents of bureaucratic corruption. Since that time, the ICAC has built an impressive record of investigations that have resulted in numerous convictions. Nowadays, Hong Kong is considered one of the least corrupt jurisdictions in East Asia, despite its free-wheeling market economy.

The Investigative Model: Singapore's CPIB

Corruption was commonplace in Singapore throughout its colonial history. When police inspectors stole 1,800 tons of narcotics during the 1950s, British administrators passed the Prevention of Corruption Ordinance and established the Corrupt Practices Investigation Bureau (CPIB) (Tan Ah Leak 1996, 151). This ordinance was intended to signal investors that the administration in Singapore would not tolerate corruption. However, enforcement was spotty, the CPIB was weak, and Singapore kept its reputation for freewheeling and corrupt capitalism. In response, in the 1970s, the Singaporean government reorganized the CPIB and gave it considerable powers to curb endemic corruption, focusing especially on investigation and enforcement. Evidence of the CPIB's success in reducing corruption is testified by Singapore's highly favorable investment climate, which "typically ranks among the top twenty recipients of foreign investment in the world in absolute terms" (Findlay, Fong, and Kim 1993, 127).

A capacity to reverse reputational costs is all the more remarkable, given Singapore's history. In 1959, the British granted Singapore autonomy from Malaysia, and independence followed shortly thereafter. At independence, recognizing that a credible commitment to fighting corruption was essential to attract investment and build an environment conducive to economic growth, the government implemented a set of reforms to regulate citizens' behavior and impose strict punishments for corrupt practices (Mauzy and Milne 1990, 8). Despite the proclaimed reforms, corruption continued to be a serious problem in Singapore through the mid-1970s, when another series of scandals disclosed once again that police officials were implicated in the narcotics trade.

These scandals prompted the government to strengthen laws. The CPIB was devoted entirely to the investigation of corrupt acts and the preparation of evidence for prosecution, and since then, the staff complement has grown from 9 to more than 75 law enforcement professionals (Quah 1997, 139). The outcome is that corruption in Singapore has been reduced to levels rivaling those of the lowest countries in Europe.

The CPIB derives its power from legislation that grants it remarkable discretion. First, the 1960 Prevention of Corruption Ordinance gave it a mandate to investigate allegations of corruption and prepare cases for prosecution. This ordinance has been amended seven times and renamed the Prevention of Corruption Act (chapter 241 of the Statutes of Singapore). The 1989 Confiscation of Benefits Act expanded government powers to seize assets of civil servants accused and convicted of taking bribes, and it prohibited illegal payments, as well as the solicitation and acceptance of bribes. The 1989 Confiscation of Benefits Act prohibited illicit payments to civil servants and expanded government powers to seize the assets of public officials convicted of taking bribes.[2] Together, these acts give the CPIB discretion to seize assets and establish the preconditions wherein an individual convicted of corruption is punished by lengthy prison terms and substantial fines.

Among the CPIB's unique characteristics are its small size, its narrow emphasis on investigation, and its service to a semiauthoritarian regime. With approximately 75 staff members, the CPIB lacks the resources of Hong Kong's ICAC, and it has accordingly relied on strategies of deterrence backed by heavy penalties: a conviction for corruption may carry a US$100,000 fine and up to five years in prison (Ali 2000). Finally, the CPIB was an effective tool of President Lee Kwan Yew's semiauthoritarian regime, which made economic growth its primary policy objective.

The organization of the CPIB is highly hierarchical. At the top is the president, who receives all reports and may act as the final arbiter of whether the CPIB takes action against alleged corruption. Below the president is the Anti-Corruption Advisory Committee, to which report the director, deputy director, assistant directors, and special investigators of the CPIB.

---

[2] See http://www.cpib.gov.sg/.

Fighting corruption was contentious, and Singapore's political leadership encountered resistance when seeking an appropriate ministerial location for the CPIB. Between 1955 and 1970, the CPIB reported to four different ministries, demonstrating the difficulty of implementing a meaningful set of reforms to combat corruption (Quah 1997, 845). Although the agency moved from ministry to ministry after its establishment, its present location in the executive branch has endowed it with a great deal of influence.

Whereas some observers argue that putting the CPIB directly into the executive branch indicates a high level of commitment on the part of Singapore's political leadership, it might also be seen as part of the structure of semiauthoritarian rule (Mauzy and Milne 1990, 83). Its reporting hierarchy reinforces the executive's influence while reducing the CPIB's independence. Indeed, countervailing measures that might control the CPIB or (at a minimum) place some constraints through oversight mechanisms are absent.

A litmus test to assess an anti-corruption commission's accountability might be the activities of oversight bodies. In Singapore, oversight mechanisms are less clearly defined than in Hong Kong, for example; nonetheless, public sector corruption has declined significantly. Indeed, one commentator has noted that while legislation may not have eliminated corruption, it "is a fact of life rather than a way of life. Put differently, corruption exists in Singapore, but not a corrupt society" (Quah 1997, 841).

Singapore is a special case because its anti-corruption commission created a climate conducive to international investments while its citizens live under a semiauthoritarian regime that in other circumstances might be inimical to high levels of economic growth. Despite the centralization of power, the CPIB demonstrates the government's commitment to combating corruption: first, this commitment signaled domestic constituents that corruption would not be tolerated; second, international investors received assurances that their investments were secure. However, what is crucial about this type of agency is that it operates without the accountability constraints active in a democratic polity.

The Parliamentary Model: The New South Wales ICAC

Prior to 1980, corruption had been uncommon in New South Wales, Australia; however, the narcotics trade in Southeast Asia presented huge profits for smugglers who bribed police and judges in countries throughout the region. New South Wales (NSW) was vulnerable to these pressures, and in the 1980s, it was revealed that a chief magistrate, a cabinet member, and numerous public officials had accepted bribes from drug traffickers.[3] A recognition of the influence of narcotics smugglers prompted law enforcement officials in NSW to contact their counterparts in Hong Kong, after which it was decided to establish an anti-corruption agency.

Political leaders in NSW wished to establish an agency with many of the same core functions performed by Hong Kong's ICAC, but with a greater emphasis on prevention (Grabosky and Larmour 2001, 182). Parliament held extensive debates on the proposed commission and whether it was the best means to respond to a

---

[3] See www.icac.nsw.gov.au for reports on the background, organization, and record of the NSW ICAC.

rash of scandals involving the police and narcotics money. The first bill lapsed when the Parliament went into recess without having reached closure on its debates over the measure. In 1988, Parliament again took up debate on the legislation and passed the initial ICAC bill in July. Following further amendments, the bill was sent to the Premier in August who, in September, announced the nomination of Commissioner Ian Temby as the head of ICAC. In March 1989, the ICAC commenced operations.

Legislation governing the ICAC has been amended several times since March 1989. In 1990, the ICAC's methods and scope of investigation were clarified. In 1994, an extension of the definition of corruption to include Members of Parliament was added to the law, which inserted new language into the code of conduct for Members of both Houses of Parliament. In 1996, further amendments were passed to improve witness protection powers.[4] Even with these changes, a series of scandals among the police involving bribery and protection schemes again led in 1997 to the establishment of an independent investigative agency called the Police Integrity Commission (Grabosky and Larmour 2001, 177). Although the Police Integrity Commission is independent from the ICAC, the anti-corruption agency lends its expertise on prevention and public outreach. The dual commissions attest to the difficulties that anti-corruption agencies face in circumstances involving the large profits available from drug trafficking.

Since the ICAC was established, it has effectively built public trust through its emphasis on leadership in government and the private sector. Moreover, the ICAC has adopted three principles as the basis of corruption prevention. First, prevention is better than the cure. Second, prevention is better than punishment. Third, prevention is better than management.[5] To complement these principles, the ICAC has published a series of Corruption Resistance Reviews that it disseminates on the Internet and through government offices. These reviews help prevent corruption by giving advice to private and public sector actors about the costs of venality.

The organizational hierarchy of the ICAC includes a commissioner, an assistant commissioner, and directors of four operational units: the Investigation Unit, which conducts investigation analyses and assessments of alleged incidents of corruption; the Legal Unit, which serves as a liaison to the Parliamentary oversight committees; the Corruption Prevention, Education, and Research Unit, which operates in areas of corruption prevention, education, research, and the relations with the media; and the Corporate and Commercial Services Unit, which provides private sector actors with information through its information technology, information services, records and property, and other branches.

Accountability in the ICAC is imposed through the submission of annual reports to Parliament and through internal and external audits on ICAC operations. The ICAC operates under the supervision of two parliamentary committees: a Joint Committee and an Operations Review Committee. Responsibilities of the 11-member Parliamentary Joint Committee include supervision and review of ICAC activities;[6] its members represent the parties in Parliament and are selected from both cham-

---

[4] See www.icac.nsw.gov.au for copies of legislation and background on parliamentary debates.

[5] Gifford, presentation at the Boyanna Residence.

[6] Information on the Parliamentary Joint Committee is available at www.icac.nsw.gov.au.

bers. The Committee submits regular reports on specific issues to Parliament, as well as special reports in response to questions from either chamber. It is also responsible for the answering of citizens' complaints that are made to the Office of the Ombudsman or Parliament.

By contrast, the Operations Review Committee holds the ICAC accountable for its actions, investigations, and general comportment as a government agency. Its eight members have the task of advising the commissioner whether to continue, suspend, or terminate an investigation. Any investigation must first be vetted by the Committee after a review of written documentation of evidence. If the Committee finds merit with the evidence, it gives approval for an investigation to be launched. Follow-up on investigations comes in the form of oversight by this committee—which is a critical source of accountability. Every three months, it determines the appropriateness of ongoing investigations, reviews ongoing investigations, and communicates its findings regularly to the commissioner.

Other methods to enforce accountability include term limits for the commissioner, budgetary accountability to the Treasury, and the existence of privacy and freedom-of-information laws. In addition, the ombudsman inspects telephone intercepts and records of investigations to prevent any abuses of power. The effect is an agency operating in "the context of a vibrant Westminster-style democratic system" that ensures a high degree of integrity for the Australian state (Grabosky and Larmour 2001, 187). Although the ICAC has had a mixed record of successful prosecutions, its major contribution has been as a prevention agency that changed the norms of how business is conducted in New South Wales.

The Multiagency Model : The United States Office of Government Ethics (OGE)

Corruption in U.S. history has prompted reforms and laws against bribery and corruption. These reforms have followed such incidents as the decades-long scandals of Tammany Hall in New York City during the 19th century, which prompted passage of the 1888 Pendleton Act, which ended patronage practices and defined codes of conduct for the civil service; Teapot Dome, which gave impetus to the Progressive Movement's reforms and congressional oversight of the executive; and the Lockheed and Abscam scandals, which preceded the 1977 Foreign Corrupt Practices Act (FCPA), which prohibits the payment of bribes by American corporations operating overseas. [7] Indeed, hearings and convictions from the Lockheed and Abscam scandals led to the establishment of the Office of Government Ethics (OGE) as part of a multiagency approach to curb bureaucratic corruption.[8]

The OGE represents one component of a multiagency approach to fighting corruption. Its legal foundation is the 1978 Ethics in Government Act, with its codes defining conflicts of interest that prohibit senior officials from accepting employment with federal government contractors, serving on boards of companies that contract with the federal government, and profiting from their official positions for

---

[7] On the Credit Mobilier scandal, see Noonan (1984, 460-500). On Tammany Hall, see Mandelbaum (1965) and Mushkat (1971). Published sources abound on the Teapot Dome Scandal, including Noggle (1962) and Stratton (1998).

[8] Noonan (1984, 652-80) provides an outstanding account of these hearings.

a period after leaving office. The OGE cooperates with a variety of offices in the executive branch, including the Office of Management and Budget, Government Accountability Office, and police agencies in the Justice Department. Its mandate is to deter conflicts of interest by disseminating information on laws and regulations that govern public sector employment.

Originally, the OGE was to be housed in the Office of Personnel Management. However, in 1988, the Office of Government Ethics Reauthorization Act was passed to establish the OGE as an autonomous office, reporting to both the president and Congress. The OGE is responsible for informing public servants about conflicts of interest and resolving any issues that may occur. In partnership with federal police agencies and the Justice Department, the OGE fosters high ethical standards for public servants and strengthens the public's confidence that official business is conducted with impartiality and integrity. The OGE's organizational goal is to create an ethical environment by coordinating multiagency cooperation while acknowledging the autonomy enjoyed by individual agencies (Davis 2002).

The OGE enforces a set of laws that define conflicts of interest and specify penalties for violations. It defines the length of time between when an official leaves office and accepts employment with firms that conduct business with the government, delineates the terms under which a government official may advise a private company, and regulates other activities that involve elected or appointed officials and private sector companies. Unlike anti-corruption commissions in many countries, the OGE has no investigative function, but serves to inform public officials about actions that might represent potential conflicts of interest. As a consequence, its role is entirely preventive, and its operations are to improve bureaucratic understanding of laws and regulations. When it determines evidence of malfeasance, it submits such evidence to the Department of Justice for investigation and prosecution.

Other Experiences

The more functions an anti-corruption agency seeks to fulfill, the greater its demand for revenues. Despite the expensive nature of *universal anti-corruption commissions*, the successful establishment of Hong Kong's ICAC has encouraged other governments to create similar organizations. Indeed, governments in Bosnia-Herzegovina, Guinea, Mauritius, and the Republic of Korea have established similar commissions. These governments have tried to replicate the three-tiered functions of investigation, prevention, and education. However, low levels of political commitment, disarticulation among branches of state, and severe budgetary constraints often prevent the establishment of large anti-corruption commissions with comprehensive mandates, and as a consequence, such commissions typically fail to reduce corruption.

Among the states that have adopted the universal model, Botswana stands out as a successful example. Botswana's commission evolved out of a series of scandals that revealed that senior officials in the ruling Botswana Democratic Party had accepted bribes. In September 1994, the Botswana National Assembly enacted the Corruption and Economic Crime Act to establish the Directorate on Corruption and Economic Crime (DCEC) (Republic of Botswana 1994).

Botswana has a highly developed bureaucratic state that governs without the controls imposed by a dynamic associational milieu or media (Molutsi and Holm

1990, 332). The legislature lacks crucial elements of independence from the executive and is generally perceived to be subservient to the president's prerogatives. Not surprisingly, the DCEC reports to the president, who approves the release and dissemination of an annual report. This reporting structure is indicative of centralized executive authority, which may account for the government's extraordinary success in managing its diamond resources. This, in turn, has brought the government substantial revenues, enabling it to overcome the budgetary impediment typically presented by universal anti-corruption commissions (Maipose and Matsheka 2002).

The DCEC has a mandate to investigate, prevent, and educate the public on all issues related to economic crimes and corruption. Its statutes specify that the DCEC is an independent agency that provides community outreach programs to public and private sector actors on the costs of corruption. Although the DCEC has an investigative function (recently enhanced), its annual reports reflect an emphasis on prevention and community outreach. It has no role in the prosecution of corruption cases; however, evidence is forwarded to judicial authorities for action.

Other governments have adopted the *investigative model* with its enhanced police function, which presents a potential for an abuse of state power. Not surprisingly, the model tends to be established in countries with centralized executives free from the institutional uncertainties of regular and competitive electoral cycles.[9] Investigative commissions are common in authoritarian or semiauthoritarian regimes wherein the executive has dominance over the other branches of government. Many African states have established such commissions that report directly to the president.

Among transition economies, Lithuania's Special Investigative Service (SIS) stands out. The Lithuanian government established the SIS in 1997 to investigate alleged incidents of corruption and to report to the president and to Parliament (Junakas 2001). The agency was intentionally modeled on the Singapore CPIB: its director reports to the president, its officers have unusual police powers to investigate political venality, and—in cooperation with the Government Ethics Agency and the Office of the Ombudsman—it has a free hand to investigate incidents of corruption in the public sector.

The *parliamentary model* presupposes the operation of a functioning parliament with budgetary capacity to fund parliamentary committees that provide critical checks on executive power. In countries with the parliamentary model, anti-corruption agencies are accountable to the legislature; however, lack of independence may create serious difficulties for such agencies. In Thailand, for example, Parliament established the National Counter Corruption Commission (NCCC) in the late 1970s to report incidents of corruption (Piriyarangsan and Phongpaichit 1996). However, the proliferation of "crony operated establishments" distributed funds to business interests, which in turn had access to the executive (Krueger 2002, 2). Indeed, the reliance on cronyism undermined the NCCC and created an economic vulnerability unsurpassed in other Southeast Asian governments (Hicken 2001, 163–182).

After the financial crisis, Thailand adopted a new constitution that established a bicameral legislature with a House of Representatives and a Senate. However, the legislature has been relatively weak because of the continued influence of cronies

---

[9] The concept of elections as institutionalized uncertainty comes from Przeworski (1991, 14).

linked to the government (Rock 2000, 182–83). Indeed, it has been suggested that the single greatest impediment to resolving crony capitalism in Thailand is that the NCCC is subservient to the executive, which has a decisive influence in determining the commission's composition.[10] While parliamentary oversight is a potential control on the NCCC, extensive strengthening of the Thai Parliament is necessary for it to exert substantial influence.

Another variant on the parliamentary model focuses on committees that disseminate reports of venality as a means to educate the public and thereby promote prevention. An emphasis on public disclosures is exemplified by the Warioba Commission Report in Tanzania. Public outrage with police corruption exploded in the early 1990s when street vendors in Dar es Salaam had to pay bribes to the militia, an action that violated "societal norms of economic justice in which the poor ought to pay the least for whatever good or service being sought" (Tripp 1997, 182). In response, the 1995 Law on Ethics for Public Leaders empaneled a Presidential Commission of Inquiry Against Corruption, also known as the Warioba Commission. With funding and support from the World Bank, the Tanzanian government released the Warioba Commission Report, which implicated numerous officials, including the former-President Ali Hassa Mwinyi, ministers, and high-level civil servants (Economist Intelligence Unit 1997, 10). Despite this, however, and since that time, Tanzania has scored little success in its efforts to reduce corruption, as evidenced by its ranking in the Corruption Perceptions Index (CPI) of Transparency International (TI).[11]

A third variant of the parliamentary model is that of legislatures that establish commissions to oversee executive investigative commissions. In Bulgaria, for instance, the Parliament established an anti-corruption commission to oversee a second commission that reports to the Council of Ministers. These efforts responded to self-imposed pressures to provide "proof" that the government was taking serious measures to fight corruption as part of its ambitions of joining the European Union.

A duplication of agencies poses a significant problem for countries where budgetary constraints limit parliamentary operations and the executive has unchecked power. Therefore, it is not unlikely that countries may end up establishing parliamentary anti-corruption commissions that are poorly funded when compared with the executive-funded commissions. This phenomenon has been quite common in Eastern Europe, where some parliaments have undertaken oversight functions usually performed by national accounting courts, supreme audit agencies, and financial inspectorates (which organizationally fall under the executive).

Several countries, particularly those with a federal political system, have implemented the *multiagency approach*. Some have constitutions that establish a federal political system. Examples of these countries include Argentina, India, and Nigeria. In these states, an anti-corruption commission is linked to federal authorities, and prosecution is conducted by the judiciary. The commissions have had uneven success. Nigeria's efforts, for example, have been problematic because of

---

[10] The Government of Thailand, The Constitution of Thailand, Part 2: The National Counter Corruption Commission, Section 297.

[11] Out of the 100 countries that TI ranked, Tanzania was 75 in 2002, 82 in 2001, 77 in 2000, and 82 in 1998. See the CPI at www.transparency.org.

powerful interests in federal, state, and local governments that oppose any anti-corruption reforms.

Uganda is a notable example of the adoption of a multiagency approach. In response to pressures from international donors, the government established a triad of organizations to fight corruption through its Inspector General of Government (IGG), Auditor General, and Human Rights Commission (World Bank 1998). Although the IGG is supposed to eliminate bribery in the public sector, Uganda's falling ranks in the TI's CPI suggest that systemic corruption is persistent and actually getting worse.[12] The continuity of systemic corruption in Uganda attests to an embedded malfeasance among powerful members of society who profited from privatization policies and access state marketing boards (Tangri 1999, 26–27).

Benin, too, has adopted a multiagency model led by an anti-corruption commission. Its strategy has been for the *Cellule pour la Moralisation de la vie Publique* (Office for the Improvement of Morality in Public Life—CMVP) to work in conjunction with control agencies in public finance, audit agencies in the judiciary, and parliamentary offices (Tchané 2000, 77–89). Beninese officials tried to build on international experiences that have demonstrated the need to reduce incentives and opportunities for corruption in the public sector. However, sanctions and oversight committees are effective only when officials are adequately paid and their careers hold real promise—which has not been the case in Benin—and chronic budgetary shortfalls continue to pose an impediment to reform.

Unraveling the Puzzle

The cases explored in this chapter suggest some reasons why policy makers create anti-corruption commissions. Often, a precipitating crisis forces political leaders to undertake significant reforms. In Hong Kong, New South Wales, and Singapore, narcotics scandals caused the precipitating crises that pushed policy makers to establish commissions with broad powers that were independent of the police. A more piecemeal approach occurred in the United States, as anti-corruption reforms responded to particular scandals involving patronage, executive discretion, and conflicts of interest. In each of these circumstances, successful reforms required a committed leadership willing to enact policies that citizens recognized as desirable. Since the late 1990s, these four types of commission have been replicated in numerous countries with questionable success.

The cases presented in this chapter highlight the difficulty of transferring organizational arrangements that operate efficiently in one country to another. This failure, in most instances, is the result of the fact that political leaders and reformers are responding simultaneously to multiple constituencies and (in particular) the international donor community, which is tired of "leakage" of its development assistance. However, the performance of countries like Argentina, Bangladesh, Brazil, India, Tanzania, Thailand, and Uganda, all of which have enacted anti-corruption reforms, bespeaks the difficulty of enacting meaningful reforms. It is evident that policy makers' incentives in these countries do not include offending entrenched constituents who may oppose sustainable anti-corruption reforms.

---

[12] In 1998, the CPI ranked Uganda 73. In 2000, the CPI ranked Uganda 80, 89 in 2001, and 94 in 2002.

Perceived vulnerability to electoral defeat has a major influence on whether politicians will enact controversial reforms, especially anti-corruption legislation. If political leaders believe that taking meaningful measures against corruption may result in their loss of office, they have an incentive to block reforms. One method to slow meaningful reforms is to establish an anti-corruption commission that communicates a willingness to fight venality while at the same time underresourcing it so that it is bound to fail. Another tactic adopted by some governments is to view corruption as an educational problem: their activities take a normative approach that stresses the immorality of corruption while at the same time failing to prosecute corrupt politicians and officials. And finally, a fundamental difficulty is the high operating costs of anti-corruption commissions.

Conclusion

Anti-corruption agencies are part of a number of tools and strategies that can be adopted to reduce venality. Some of the prerequisites for their success include the independence of a commission; a clear reporting hierarchy that comprises executive officials, parliamentary authorities, and public oversight committees; and governments' commitment to enact reforms that may be politically difficult.

The first key variable that might explain a failure to reduce corruption through the establishment of an anti-corruption agency is the absence of laws that are necessary for its success. Without legal tools, a commission cannot succeed. Many governments fail to enforce existing laws, or the commissions have no mandate to enforce such laws. Second, a commission must be independent from interference by the political leadership (Johnston 1999, 218). In some circumstances, a commission linked to the executive branch is used to settle old scores with political rivals. Alternatively, if the agency is linked only to the Parliament, a competitive relationship may develop between parliamentarians and national crime investigators. The result is that the anti-corruption commission loses credibility.

Third, it is necessary to have a clear reporting hierarchy. An optimal hierarchy might be one in which reports are delivered by the director of the organization to oversight committees and then simultaneously shared with the legislature and the government. However, some governments prefer to receive reports without the bother of any hierarchy. This arrangement means that the executive branch monopolizes the information and eliminates any accountability of independent agencies. In Ghana, for instance, the constitution stipulates that the auditor general reports directly to the president in a confidential report that the executive may release at his or her discretion. As a consequence, the audits lack transparency, and the president withholds information that may potentially be damaging to the administration.

Finally, the presence of oversight committees may be crucial to the effective organization of an anti-corruption commission. In Hong Kong, oversight committees provide a control over the ICAC and prevent it from persecuting political opponents of the government. The two committees found in New South Wales attest to the potential of parliaments in controlling potential excesses of anti-corruption agencies.

Bibliography

Ali, Muhammed. 2000. "Eradicating Corruption: The Singapore Experience." Paper prepared for presentation at the Seminar on International Experiences in Good Governance and Fighting Corruption, Bangkok, Thailand (February 17).

Botswana, Republic of. 1994. "Corruption and Economic Crime Act." *Botswana Government Gazette.* Gaberone: Government Printer (August 19).

Chan, Thomas (Director of the Department of Corruption Prevention, Hong Kong ICAC). 2002. Presentation at Boyanna Residence, Sofia, Bulgaria (October 29).

Constitution of Thailand, The. 1997. Part 2: The National Counter Corruption Commission, section 297. Translation in *Thailand Government Gazette*, 114, part 55 A (October 11), Bangkok, Thailand.

Davis, F. Gary (Former Chief Counsel, the Office of Government Ethics). 2002. Presentation prepared for the Workshop on Anti-Corruption Agencies at the Boyanna Residence, Sofia, Bulgaria (October 29).

de Speville, Bertrand. 1997. *Hong Kong: Policy Initiatives against Corruption.* Paris: OECD Development Centre Studies.

Economist Intelligence Unit. 1997. *Tanzania* (First Quarter): 10.

Findlay, Ronald, Pang Eng Fong, and Linda Kim. 1993. "Singapore." In *Five Small Economies*, ed. Ronald Findlay and Stanislaw Wellisz. Washington, DC: World Bank; New York: Oxford University Press.

Grabosky, Peter, and Peter Larmour. 2001. "Corruption in Australia: Its Prevention and Control." In *Where Corruption Lives*, ed. Gerald E. Caiden, O. P. Dwivedi, and Joseph Jabbra. Bloomfield, CT: Kumarian Press.

Heilbrunn, John R. 2004. "Anti-Corruption Commissions: Panacea or Real Medicine to Fight Corruption?" Working Paper 37234, World Bank Institute, Washington, DC.

Hicken, Allen. 2001. "Governance and Growth in Thailand." In *Corruption: The Boom and Bust of East Asia*, ed. J. Edgardo Campos. Manila: Ateneo de Manila University Press.

Johnston, Michael. 1999. "A Brief History of Anticorruption Agencies." In *The Self-Restraining State: Power and Accountability in New Democracies*, ed. Andreas Schedler, Larry Diamond, and Marc Plattner. Boulder: Lynne Rienner Publishers.

Junakas, Valentinas (Director of the Lithuanian SIS). 2001. Presentation at the 10th International Anti-Corruption Conference, Prague (October 7–11).

Klitgaard, Robert. 1988. *Controlling Corruption.* Berkeley and Los Angeles: University of California Press.

Krueger, Anne O. 2002. "Why Crony Capitalism Is Bad for Economic Growth." In *Crony Capitalism and Economic Growth in Latin America: Theory and Evidence*, ed. Stephen Haber. Stanford, CA: Hoover Institution Press.

Leak, Tan Ah. 1996. "The Experience of Singapore in Combating Corruption." In *Uganda International Conference on Good Governance in Africa: Empowering Civil Society in the Fight against Corruption*, ed. Petter Langseth and Fiona Simpkins. Washington, DC: World Bank.

Maipose, G. S., and T. C. Matsheka. 2002. "Explaining African Growth Performance: The Botswana Case Study." Photocopy, University of Botswana, Gaberone.

Mandelbaum, Seymour J. 1965. *Boss Tweed's New York*. New York: John Wiley and Sons.

Mauzy, Diane K., and R. S. Milne. 1990. *Singapore: The Legacy of Lee Kuan Yew*. Boulder: Westview Press.

Molutsi, Patrick P., and John D. Holm. 1990. "Developing Democracy When Civil Society Is Weak: The Case of Botswana." *African Affairs* 89 (356): 323–40.

Mushkat, Jerome. 1971. *Tammany: The Evolution of a Political Machine 1789–1865*. Syracuse, NY: Syracuse University Press.

Noggle, Burl. 1962. *Teapot Dome: Oil and Politics in the 1920s*. New York: W. W. Norton.

Noonan, Jr., John T. 1984. *Bribes*. New York: Macmillan Publishing Company.

Piriyarangsan, Sungsidh, and Pasuk Phongpaichit. 1996. *Corruption and Democracy in Thailand*. Bangkok: Silkworm Books.

Przeworski, Adam. 1991. *Democracy and the Market: Political and Economic Reforms in Eastern Europe and Latin America*. New York: Cambridge University Press.

Quah, Jon S. T. 1997. "Singapore's Experience in Curbing Corruption." In *Political Corruption: A Handbook*, 4th edition, ed. Arnold J. Heidenheimer, Michael Johnston, and Victor T. Le Vine. New Brunswick, NJ: Transaction Publishers.

Rock, Michael T. 2000. "Thailand's Old Bureaucratic Polity and Its New Semi-Democracy." In *Rents, Rent-Seeking Economic Development: Theory and Practice*, eds. Mushtaq H. Khan and K. S. Jomo. New York: Cambridge University Press.

Stratton, David H. 1998. *Tempest over Teapot Dome: The Story of Albert Fall*. Norman: University of Oklahoma Press.

Tchané, Abdoulaye Bio. 2000. *Lutter contre la corruption: Une impérative pour le développement au Bénin dans l'économie internationale*. Paris: Éditions l'Harmattan.

Tangri, Roger. 1999. *The Politics of Patronage in Africa: Parastatals, Privatization, and Private Enterprise*. Trenton, NJ: Africa World Press.

Tripp, Aili Mari. 1997. *Changing the Rules: The Politics of Liberalization and the Urban Informal Economy in Tanzania*. Berkeley and Los Angeles: University of California Press.

World Bank. 1998. "Uganda: Recommendations for Strengthening the Government of Uganda's Anti-Corruption Program." Poverty Reduction and Social Development Division, the Africa Region, the World Bank, Washington, DC.

Case Study: The European Parliament's Role in the Resignation of the Santer Commission

Katia Stasinopoulou

Introduction

The twin issues of accountability and democratic deficit are a topical and recurrent element of debates on the European Union (EU). Analysis of EU affairs is often underscored by a perception of the EU and its institutions as an inefficient bureaucracy that lacks sufficient democratic checks and balances and that has resulted in a "disconnection" between EU institutions and its citizens.[1]

As the only democratically elected EU institution, the European Parliament (EP) is perhaps best suited to addressing issues related to the EU's accountability, mismanagement, and alleged democratic deficit. This case study will therefore focus on a 1999 landmark of EU history: the European Parliament's role in the resignation of the European Union executive, the European Commission. The study illustrates the EP's effectiveness in taking advantage of its democratic mandate and enforcing, among other things, its powers of oversight. The resulting crisis became a catalyst for institutional reform, an overhaul of financial and personnel management, and increased accountability in the European Commission.[2]

This case study will set the scene by describing the institutional responsibilities of the Commission and the European Parliament. It will then analyze the role played by Parliament in the Commission's dismissal and its implications. Finally, it will discuss what conclusions can be drawn from the event.

Part One: The Roles of the European Commission and the European Parliament

The institutional actors of the EU—the Parliament, the Commission, the Council of the EU, the Court of Auditors, and the Court of Justice—have an interdependent relationship that comes to the fore in the context of legislative procedures. However, for the purposes of this case study, we will narrow our focus to the two main institutions involved in the dismissal of the Commission.[3]

---

[1] House of Commons European Scrutiny Committee, *Democracy and Accountability in the EU and the Role of National Parliaments,* Thirty-third Report of Session 2001-2, HC 152-xxxiii-I, pp. 13–15.

[2] Hereafter, also referred to as the "Commission."

[3] The Council shares legislative powers with the EP; it comprises ministers representing their respective Member States and has a rotating presidency. The European Court of Justice ensures the uniform application and interpretation of EU law. The European Court of Auditors examines the accounts of the EU's revenue and expenditure and checks that the EU budget has been managed soundly.

The Commission and Parliament share a common institutional perspective, which is demonstrated by close working arrangements and agreements between the two institutions.

The European Commission is the executive arm of the European Union. It is politically independent and defends the interests of the EU as a whole. The Commission is referred to as the guardian of the treaties.[4] It initiates legislation, represents the EU in certain international forums, implements the budget and decisions of the Parliament and Council, and enforces European law. It has a five-year term and is led by a president and a commissioner from each of the 25 Member States. The President assigns a commissioner to oversee each policy area and can reshuffle the college of commissioners if he or she deems it necessary. Parliament must be consulted on the nomination of each commissioner and, as we shall in the next section, occasionally makes its opposition felt strongly.

Since 1979, the Members of the European Parliament (MEPs) have been elected every five years by direct universal suffrage.[5] The EP is one of the key institutional actors of the EU and has seen a gradual increase in its supervisory, budgetary, and legislative powers:

- *Supervisory role.* It is the Parliament's supervisory role that is cardinal to this case study. In 1999, the EP drew on its oversight powers to force the Commission to resign by threatening to adopt a "motion of censure," which to be carried would have required a two-thirds majority of votes cast, representing more than half the total number of MEPs.[6] Another supervisory power is the creation of ad hoc committees of inquiry to investigate alleged "contravention or maladministration of EU law," as was the case with mad cow disease. The Parliament was also instrumental in the creation of the European Anti-Fraud Office (OLAF) (see box 1).
- *Budgetary role.* A fundamental component of parliament's democratic responsibilities is its input in the budget cycle. The EP's powers in this area have increased, and it is the joint budgetary authority alongside the Council. It is committed to a "zero-tolerance" approach to fraud and mismanagement. Parliament supervises the Commission's financial and administrative activities, and its Budgetary Control Committee monitors EU spending. However, the EP's most important power relates to the "discharge" of the budget. According to this procedure, the Commission must submit the previous year's accounts to the Parliament for approval.
- *Legislative role.* The most common procedure for adopting legislation is "codecision," in which the EP has equal footing with the Council in certain areas. This is arguably the most powerful element of the EP's legislative arsenal and was the product of successive treaty amendments. Other procedures include "cooperation," whereby the EP can give an opinion on legislation and if there is a second reading, it can adopt, reject, or amend the pro-

---

[4] The successive EU treaties are the backbone of the EU. The European Convention of the Future of Europe attempted to regroup all the treaties into a single Treaty for a European Constitution (2004); however, as a result of political difficulties, the text has not been ratified by all Member States, which means that it is effectively on hold.

[5] Before 1979, MEPs were nominated by their respective national parliaments.

[6] Article 201, Rule 34 of the Parliament's Rules of Procedure.

Box 1 *European Anti-Fraud Office (OLAF)*

The European Anti-Fraud Office (OLAF) replaced the Anti-Fraud Coordination Unit (UCLAF) on June 1, 1999. Its main responsibility is to fight fraud, and to this end, it enjoys independent investigative status. OLAF's mission statement is to protect the EU's interests and to "fight fraud, corruption, and any other irregular activity, including misconduct within the European Institutions." It conducts external investigations relating to economic operators and internal investigations relating to EU institutions. OLAF works closely with the relevant national authorities in Member States, can provide technical support with regard to their anti-fraud activities, and is involved in the design of the EU's anti-fraud strategy and strengthening relevant legislation.[7]

posal by absolute majority. According to the "assent" procedure, the Parliament approves or rejects the legislation in question without suggesting any amendments. Finally, during "consultation," the EP gives an opinion and puts forward amendments.

Part Two: The Collective Resignation of the Santer Commission and Its Repercussions

The 1999 crisis that provoked the resignation of the Santer Commission had its origins in alleged financial mismanagement. President Santer[8] took office in 1995 against a backdrop of questionable practices and increasing tensions. He pledged to address the issue through institutional reforms, but was ultimately unsuccessful in dealing with the roots of maladministration.

Parliament was keen to draw on its budgetary and supervisory powers to address the continuing allegations of financial mismanagement in the Commission. Its concern regarding the allegations was reflected by the Budgetary Control Committee's decision in December 1998—further to a special report by the European Court of Auditors—to withhold discharge of the budget, which is tantamount to a vote of no confidence. The crisis was compounded when in December 1998, a Commission official in the financial control unit informed the EP of alleged mismanagement of EU finances.[9] In response, Parliament considered a motion of censure against the Commission at the plenary session of January 14, 1999. Although the motion was not carried, it was a tactical move that underlined the gravity of the crisis and sent a strong warning to the Commission.

By flexing its muscles throughout this crisis, the EP demonstrated its considerable powers of oversight and enhanced its institutional credibility. Later that month, the EP also appointed a five-member Committee of Independent Experts to investigate these allegations (see box 2). The Committee's report, published on March 15, 1999, criticized the institution for its lack of accountability and transparency and for

---

[7] For further information, see OLAF's Web site: http://europa.eu.int/comm/anti_fraud/index_en.html.

[8] During 1995–99, the Commission was headed by a Luxembourger, Jacques Santer.

[9] The Dutch official in question, Paul van Buitenen, was suspended for several months on half pay. He subsequently became a Member of the European Parliament for the Group of Greens/European Free Alliance.

Box 2 *Committee of Independent Experts*

On January 27, 1999, the leaders of the EP's political groups appointed five members of a Committee of Independent Experts, whose main task was to establish responsibility for the alleged mismanagement in the European Commission. The Committee was allowed to work in full independence and had no contact with the media or MEPs while it was investigating the allegations. In addition, the Commission pledged to provide it with any documents it might need. The Committee's report was submitted to the president of the Parliament, then to the president of the Commission, and eventually made public. It was followed by a second report that focused on the functioning and administration of the Commission.

---

tolerating a culture of impunity. It did not include concrete allegations of bribery, but singled out a number of senior commissioners for cases involving favoritism, nepotism, and incorrect appointment procedures.[10] The report highlighted an accountability vacuum at the senior management level of the European Union's executive branch. It concluded that no one seemed willing to take responsibility for the well-documented cases of fraud and mismanagement.[11] In addition, the report mirrored a shift in the focus of the conflict, from initial concerns related to budgetary issues to the broader issue of democratic accountability and collective responsibility of the Commission.[12]

The EP reacted to the report by issuing the Commission an ultimatum. It either must resign en masse or accept a four-point plan:[13]

- An independent review of fraud investigations within the Commission
- A new code of conduct to determine the relationship between commissioners, their cabinet, and the EU civil service
- An enhanced role for the European Parliament that would allow it to work with the Commission to reform management procedures
- A new mechanism allowing the Commission to bring forward votes of confidence

Rather than face the ignominy of a protracted battle, the Commission chose to resign preemptively on March 16, 1999.

The credibility of the EU depends largely on the integrity and independence of the Commission, not only because of its exclusive right to initiate legislation but also because of its representative function in certain international forums. Unsurprisingly therefore, the Commission's image in the EU and abroad was tarnished

---

[10] For further details on the allegations, see chapter 8, Committee of Independent Experts, *First Report on Allegations regarding Fraud, Mismanagement, and Nepotism in the European Commission* (1999).

[11] The Committee's reports are available at http://www.europarl.eu.int/experts/default_en.htm.

[12] Nils F. Ringe, *The Santer Commission Resignation Crisis: Government-Opposition Dynamics in Executive-Legislative Relations of the EU,* prepared for the 2003 Annual Meeting of the European Union Studies Association, March 27–29, 2003, p. 5.

[13] http://news.bbc.co.uk/2/hi/uk_news/politics/253139.stm.

by the institutional crisis. However, the resignation became a catalyst for the implementation of much-needed institutional reforms and contributed to the reinvigoration of the institution. Through these reforms, the EU was also able to address broader policy considerations at a critical moment of EU history. The resignation coincided with preparations for the introduction of the single European currency and the enlargement of the EU, both major developments that called for greater accountability and enhanced management practices.[14]

Analysts argue that the rapid nomination of Romano Prodi—a former Italian Prime Minister—to head the new Commission demonstrated that Member States clearly wanted a new president with stronger leadership skills and more political clout than Jacques Santer.[15] The Prodi Commission was formally appointed on May 5, 1999, and in an attempt to restore the institution's credibility, Prodi promised sweeping institutional reforms, increased accountability, and greater transparency. The strategy for reforms was formally presented in the Commission's white paper, "Reforming the Commission," which emphasized the importance of accountability and of "maintaining high standards of ethical behaviour, thereby contributing to confidence of the public in the functioning of the European Institutions."[16] More specifically, Prodi set up an interinstitutional committee to monitor standards of behavior in the Commission, Parliament, and Council and an audit unit in the Commission to oversee how funds are spent. He also introduced reforms in training, promotion, recruitment, and disciplinary procedures and created a new provision to ensure that the commissioner's cabinets are international. To reinforce accountability, President Prodi assigned Commissioner Neil Kinnock to oversee a portfolio that specifically dealt with personnel and budgetary issues and institutional reforms. Kinnock was also given the title of "vice president," which consolidated the high status of his job.

A further important consequence of the 1999 crisis is demonstrated by the EP's increased role in the 2004 hearings of the Barroso Commission.[17] During the proceedings, MEPs objected strongly to several nominees on the grounds of, among other things, conflicts of interest, insufficient qualifications, and allegations of financial irregularities. To avoid an EP veto of the entire college of commissioners, President Barroso was forced to reshuffle the portfolios and accept new nominations, while some national governments were faced with the humiliating rejection of their nominees. Barroso's reaction to the Parliament's opposition highlighted the Commission's commitment to good governance and democratic legitimacy. Moreover, the hearings allowed MEPs to take full advantage of their political mandates to supervise the executive and thus leave their imprint on the democratic process.

---

[14] Two of the most important events of recent EU history are the introduction of the single currency, known as the euro, which became legal tender in 13 Member States on January 1, 2002, and the accession of 10 new countries on May 1, 2004.

[15] Hussein Kassim and Anand Menon, "European Integration since the 1990s: Member States and the European Commission," paper prepared for the ARENA seminar, University of Oslo, February 11, 2004, pp. 26–27.

[16] Commission white papers set out official proposals for action in specific policy areas. European Commission, "Reforming the Commission: A White Paper," COM (2000) 200, March 1, 2000. http://europa.eu.int/comm/off/white/reform/index_en.htm.

[17] A Portuguese national, José Manuel Barroso, was confirmed as Commission President in November 2004.

Conclusion

The institutional crisis brought about by the resignation of the Santer Commission highlighted that the EU is capable of effective collective action and provided an opportunity to focus on the Commission's democratic and management shortcomings. In the aftermath of the dismissal—and as a direct result of EP actions—the Prodi Commission implemented significant reforms to address the mismanagement, which might otherwise have continued unabated. These reforms have contributed to ensuring that six years after the crisis, the Commission still strives to uphold principles of transparency and accountability. A recent example of the lasting legacy of the crisis was the dynamic role played by the EP in the 2004 Commission hearings.

The European Parliament's important role in the resignation of the Santer Commission has most definitely raised its interinstitutional profile. Secondly, the episode clearly demonstrated the Commission's respect for the EP's increased supervisory and budgetary role. In addition to showcasing the considerable powers of the Parliament, the crisis also sent a clear message to EU citizens that MEPs are committed to tackling corruption in the EU executive. It could also be argued that as the only democratically elected institution, it is incumbent on the European Parliament to use its powers of oversight to lead the way in matters relating to transparency and anti-corruption. Finally, the resignation of the Santer Commission illustrated that by fighting instances of fraud and insisting on accountability, MEPs are fulfilling their democratic mandate and addressing the EU's democratic deficit.

Part IV
Representation

10

Building Coalitions: Parliaments, Civil Society, and Corruption Control

Michael Johnston

Introduction: Sustaining Reform

Societies rarely bring corruption under control through penalties, morality campaigns, or administrative improvements alone.[1] Anti-corruption coups and "one-man show" crusades are even less successful, weakening civil society, the press, political competition, and accountability. Too often they substitute intimidation for transparency. Long-lasting corruption control must draw on the energies and self-interest of citizens themselves, enabling them to resist exploitation. Equally, it requires that that those who speak for the people effectively demand accountability, exercise oversight, and check official abuses. Vigorous civil societies and strong, socially rooted, credible parliaments can be effective partners for good governance.

In 17th-century England, Parliament began to curb royal abuses of power in the course of a long struggle with the Crown over issues as diverse as taxation, religion, and crown patronage (Roberts 1980; Peck 1990; Johnston 1993). The elected chamber—the House of Commons—was chosen by a very few people; many places did not have Members to call their own. Further, Parliament was not designing better government, but rather defending its own autonomy and prerogatives—in effect, insisting on its place in an emerging web of processes that were transforming governance. The result was a fundamental expansion of the political process and new notions of accountability, driven by sustained political contention.

Such a process cannot simply be proclaimed; rather, it must draw on lasting interests. It involves real contention—in the English case, a series of impeachments, a regicide, civil war, and (near century's end) a reconstitution of the monarchy itself. Also, it involves real costs and risks. But political partnerships of this sort bring major segments of society into politics, build stronger linkages between citizens and those who speak for them, and create new institutions and standards capable of enforcing acceptable limits for the uses of wealth and power.

---

[1] This chapter is an adaptation, in part, of Johnston and Kpundeh (2002).

This chapter considers ways to maximize the anti-corruption power of parliaments by emphasizing their role as centers of the "ecology of governance."[2] That role requires partners—specifically, social action coalitions that mobilize citizens and major social interests. In this context, "parliaments" is taken to mean national legislatures generally, although at times contrasts between Westminster and presidential/separation-of-powers models will be made. Social action coalitions are self-conscious, freely organized, active, and lasting alliances of elites, organizations, and citizens sharing partially overlapping political goals and a basic commitment to peaceful change. Synergy among the strength of civil society, the vitality and credibility of parliaments, and what is often (in an oversimplification) called "political will" are all essential to improving the quality and openness of governance. Parliaments that channel deep-rooted social interests into free debate and meaningful legislation and that exercise real autonomy and oversight with respect to executive agencies not only speak effectively for civil society but also strengthen its role in the public arena. In turn, parliaments deepen their social roots, enjoy enhanced legitimacy, and develop a political base for moving against corruption. Such partnerships between parliaments and social action coalitions make it possible to draw on the strength and diverse interests of whole societies as forces checking the abuse of wealth and power.

Ends and Means

Parliaments will be most effective at checking corruption—and at building political will in its broadest sense—to the extent that they encourage, protect, and articulate the concerns raised by free and open contention among real interests in society. They must also provide sufficient resources and oversight for executive policy and decisions while asserting autonomy with respect to influence from both above and below. There are at least five basic ways in which parliaments can do those functions: through *representation* of citizens, *legislation*, *oversight* of the executive (and, in some systems, of the courts), *self-regulation* of parliamentary processes, and the *political finance* systems through which members are elected. These are a part of virtually everything that a sound and strong parliament does, but they can also be used in corrupt ways or to conceal abuses already taking place.

This chapter focuses primarily on the representation function in the form of interactions between parliamentarians and social action coalitions. The other functions are no less important, but are addressed in other chapters of this book. Representation gives us more than enough to think about: how parliaments and their Members can strengthen links to social groups opposed to corruption, how those groups can be sustained and strengthened, and how such interactions can check existing corrupt activities and enhance our capacity to prevent future ones are all major issues.

These connections will be explored in several ways in the sections to come. The first part is a reassessment of the notion of "political will," with emphasis on its sources and meaning in a parliamentary setting. The next section examines the civil society sources of political will and the social side of representative processes

---

[2] Global Organization of Parliamentarians Against Corruption (GOPAC): http://www.parlcent.ca/index_e.php (viewed June 2005).

through a discussion of social action coalitions. The third section identifies the incentives that help maintain such coalitions and link them to vigorous, credible, autonomous parliaments. The conclusion proposes some priorities for both action and further study.

Parliaments, "Political Will," and Civil Society

If "political will" is to be more than just a slogan, it must be understood in a broad context. Particularly where democratic politics is in place or emerging in sustainable ways, political will requires leaders willing to attack corruption and supporting constituencies ready to back them up, reward success, and exact a political price for failure or deceit. Building those constituencies and focusing their efforts on corruption issues is a complex matter of deploying multiple incentives in pursuit of many goals—not all of them directly aimed at reform.[3]

Active, well-managed parliaments, chosen through open and competitive elections and provided with significant institutional capacity, can build accountability, become an arena for significant but well-regulated political contention, and add force and focus to citizen sentiments and resentments (while restraining their more extreme expressions). Parliaments can scrutinize executive policy and decisions— where necessary, checking excesses of political will—and hold leaders to their promises at a level of detail—and on a day-to-day basis—beyond the reach of reform-oriented interest groups. By allowing specific interests to have their say and then brokering politically sound compromises, parliaments can broaden the political constituency for effective execution of policy and mandates. Leaders are given strong political incentives to follow through on both political and legal commitments and, crucially, can benefit for doing so.

Parliaments at the Center of the Web

Those sorts of connections require broad-gauged thinking by Members and leadership of the world's parliaments. Hectic legislative and electoral schedules, the demands of constituency service and party duties, advocacy efforts by a wide range of social interests, the agendas of executives and their agencies, and the substantive complexities of legislation all make it difficult to focus on *systemic* aspects of politics and recognize reform opportunities.

The exigencies of self-preservation can also deter Members of parliament from taking a stand against corruption. Where funds obtained through corruption provide payoffs to supporters, challenging such systems could undermine the Member's electoral base. If the Member is from the ruling party, moreover, challenging the system can undermine the Member's standing within the party. This could have serious consequences for the Member's political career, especially if the party leadership has the power to determine candidates on the ballot and leadership positions in the cabinet and parliament. Taking a stand against corruption could also have consequences for a Member's safety, especially where organized crime buttresses corrupt networks. Finally, fighting corruption could undermine Members' objective to enrich themselves while in office to secure their own financial position.

---

[3] For a more complete consideration of political will, see chapter 3.

Against this backdrop of demanding responsibilities and the exigencies of self-preservation, the Global Organization of Parliamentarians Against Corruption (GOPAC)[4] is encouraging parliamentarians to take a broader view. Its origins and activities are discussed more extensively in chapter 14 of this volume, but GOPAC's strategy of networking among Members and parliaments and of sharing enlightened views of the legislative and oversight processes through education efforts are essential to the coalition-building activities discussed in this chapter. GOPAC sees parliaments and their members as parts of a web of institutions, communications, and political processes—an "ecology of governance"—drawing together citizens, interest groups and advocates, and all segments of government. Organized, active citizens are critical to that ecology, providing Members and leaders with important resources and reinforcement.

Parliamentarians who take this broad approach will not find life easy in the short run; particularly where corruption is concerned, "going along" is the path of least resistance. But over time, they can focus the energies of society on corruption problems, channeling potentially disruptive social resentments into constructive forces for better policy and improved oversight. In the process, parties and parliaments themselves become more effective. Best of all, Members and parties can do well by doing good, building a more secure popular base for themselves. However, opposing corruption, by itself, is not a sufficient basis for building and sustaining such partnerships. They require a diverse mix of incentives and an understanding of what brings people into the public arena—and produces cooperation—over the long haul. That incentive system, a critical aspect of "the ecology of governance," is the primary focus of this chapter.

The Civil Society Connection: Building Social Action Coalitions

Coalitions are not a new idea. Indeed, they are the default option for anyone seeking to jump-start broad-based reform.[5] Many groups pursue variations on this strategy: with respect to corruption, the best-known effort is Transparency International (TI), but others such as the Asia Foundation have been involved, and agencies such as the World Bank Institute and USAID have actively aided such efforts. Coalition-building drives begin with much fanfare, but often prove difficult to sustain—particularly where they are needed most.

How can we build an anti-corruption force rooted in society, possessing real influence, and sustained by self-interest and credible incentives? Johnston and Kpundeh (2002) suggest that social action coalitions can unite elites and civil society into a strong force for good governance and reform, deepening and rewarding political will while strengthening civil society (for case studies see, among others, Tendler [1979]; Hede, Prasser, and Neylan [1992]; Nickson [1996]; Clay [1997]; Klitgaard and Baser [1997]; and Stapenhurst and Kpundeh [1998]). They are distinct from formal party coalitions (Geddes 1994; Rose-Ackerman 1999), but are more concrete than mere coordination or consultation groups (Wilson 1973, 267–68), because they must be able to resolve internal conflicts, redirect members' actions in limited ways, and offer benefits not available to outsiders. Social action coalitions

---

[4] http://www.parlcent.ca/index_e.php (viewed May 2005).
[5] Thanks to Dr. Emmanuel Gyimah-Boadi for his comments on this point.

as we envision them will have more of a mass base than, say, TI, though many participants will be organizations and some may even be drawn from political parties and government—with the latter connections posing important questions regarding autonomy. In most instances, they will function best when organized within individual countries or, at most, well-defined regions.

The range of possibilities for social action coalitions is reflected in examples as diverse as broad nationalist, feminist, environmental, cultural-revival, and civil-rights movements, and even religious movements such as the "Christian Right" in the United States. More formalized, reform-oriented examples include Ghana's Anti-Corruption Coalition (see below), groups such as Allianza Civica[6] in Mexico, Honduras, and elsewhere and Poder Ciudadano[7] in countries such as Argentina. In some cases—as with the Russian Anticorruption Partnerships (RAP),[8] a new alignment of four previously established reform groups—coalition building is well out ahead of parliament's ability to be an effective anti-corruption partner. The local good-government movement in the United States, while by now a coalition of formal organizations, has historical roots in the mass movement to end slavery (Anechiarico and Jacobs 1996) and was linked at times to groups such as the Anti-Saloon League. America's venerable League of Women Voters (LWV)[9] was launched in 1920 on the foundations of the successful woman suffrage movement, and since then has advanced a good-politics agenda, both in the United States and in other areas, through its Citizen Exchanges. As these examples suggest, there is no one ideal model: some coalitions are loose, some tight-knit, and others have taken shape under the aegis of a single organization (as in the case of the LWV). But what they have in common is that they mold individuals and groups into a sustainable reform-oriented constituency, not only through the pursuit of a public agenda but also with a range of incentives and appeals.

Minimal Conditions

Social action coalitions will not thrive everywhere. They require, at a minimum, a functioning state, rather than misrule by dictators, private armies, or *mafiyas*. Leaders must have a genuine intent to govern well—not as easy a test to apply as it may seem—and to serve rather than exploit their societies. A reasonable level of order is also essential: pervasive violence, famine or disease, or social disintegration can render coalition building impossible and corruption a secondary problem. Meaningful boundaries and legitimate linkages between state and society are essential both to setting limits on official power and private influence and to maintaining the "space" required for a viable civil society and private economy. Where basic civil liberties—freedom to organize, assemble, and voice criticism of the regime (Isham, Kaufmann, and Pritchett 1996)—and freedom from routine coercion are a reality, people and groups will feel more secure about opposing corruption. A reasonably free press can be an essential "watchdog" and is essential to some of the coalition's incentives, as we shall see.

---

[6] http://www.alianzacivica.org.mx/ (viewed June 2005); http://www.caritas.hn/ (viewed June, 2005).
[7] http://www.poderciudadano.org.ar/ (viewed June 2005).
[8] http://www.stopcor.ru/?english (viewed June 2005).
[9] http://www.lwv.org/ (viewed June 2005).

Also useful for coalition building, if not essential, is a crisis or opportunity (Wilson 1973, 275) making action imperative. Hong Kong's famous ICAC—whose anti-corruption strategy included extensive public involvement from the beginning—originated after a corrupt police official's escape touched off mass outrage. Its first step toward winning public confidence was to bring him back to Hong Kong for trial and imprisonment (see chapter 9). But any such crisis will fade—if not, the coalition will have accomplished nothing—making the active support of parliament critical for the long run. Outside support from NGOs, aid partners, and international organizations, including law-enforcement, prodemocracy, and anti-corruption groups, can provide essential resources, expertise, and encouragement. Ultimately, however, opposition to corruption must become the norm—not a response to crisis—and an extension of self-interest rather than a "good cause." Coalitions must become not only self-sustaining but also polycentric. Early opportunities will give way to different, but no less difficult, challenges as the coalition matures.

Strategic Questions

Good ideas and the prospective benefits of controlling corruption are not enough to sustain a coalition or to build strong links between it and parliament. For one thing, reform is in many respects a public good—if corruption is reduced for anyone, it is reduced for all, or at least for many others—and thus raises classic "free-rider" problems (Olson 1965). That is particularly true where fighting corruption means taking issue with entrenched leaders and interests; after all, corruption persists in no small part because powerful people have a stake in it. Ways must therefore be found to motivate and reward a diverse range of potential stakeholders who suffer immediate and tangible costs of corruption and have resources they can mobilize against it. Businesses, both small and larger, are obvious candidates, but may be compromised by corrupt linkages of their own. Other constituencies are potentially important: farmers and stallholders in markets who are subject to police shakedowns are examples. However, those constituencies may be dispersed over large amounts of territory or divided along ideological or communal lines. The best compromise at this level may be to work through leadership and (where they exist) civil society networks, educating people about the costs of corruption while searching for those who find them most oppressive.

Autonomy is a basic issue, too. What sort of relationship should a coalition have with the regime—fighting from the opposition corner or cooperating? To some extent, the answer depends on the political options generally available. Where political and administrative leaders are hostile to reform, cooperation may be impossible, and an anti-corruption coalition can be forced into an opposition role. That, clearly, bears real disadvantages: reform in that setting amounts to mobilizing the weak and divided against the strong. Coalition architects may have to play a waiting game, learning and working the social networks and educating possible stakeholders, but holding off on major initiatives until the political climate improves. In a competitive democracy, strategy can still be complex: an unrelieved adversarial stance will be counterproductive or dangerous, but too little independence will undermine credibility—particularly if allies are found to be compromised themselves.

Relationships with parliamentary parties pose equally complex questions. The most tempting recommendation is for a social action coalition to remain nonpartisan, but that may not be as simple as it sounds. Some parliaments will be one-party bodies (or close to it); others may be dominated by powerful individuals, ethnic groups, or economic interests. In any such case, a completely nonpartisan or neutral stance will either lack credibility or be a sign of irrelevance. Further, the organizations and citizens making up the coalition will have party affiliations or sympathies of their own, and the balance among such outlooks is unlikely to parallel alignments in parliament—particularly where corruption is a haves-versus-have-nots issue, as is often the case. Cases of corruption will involve specific parties, leaders, and client interests, and a coalition that takes issue with such misconduct will almost inevitably be branded a tool of opposing parties or even of extraparliamentary forces. At another level, coalition leaders will have solid reasons to engage with party leaders, both to get reform proposals and investigations onto the parliamentary calendar and to convert promises of anti-corruption support into political leverage. Such links with party leaders will also be valuable signs to coalition members and backers that their efforts are producing results.

As a result, the optimal stance should be a focus on anti-corruption measures, rather than on specific cases or scandals, and should emphasize active engagement with, and support for, all parties and leaders who take credible and specific anti-corruption stances. The coalition can play a major role in supporting follow-through on such commitments and can provide technical anti-corruption advice to leaders or Members. Investigations of wrongdoing should be left for others, however. Such efforts may well get coalitions and leaders in over their heads in legal and technical terms, invite allegations of partisan bias, and divide the coalition's own base of support. After all, one long-term goal is for parliament to enhance its own investigative powers and expertise in anti-corruption areas. The coalition's role is to support such a development, rather than to lead or preempt it. Similarly, the coalition should resist any temptation to issue "seals of approval" to businesses, government agencies, parties, or politicians. The risks of apparent bias and of severe embarrassment from future scandals, along with the resources and expertise required to launch a certification process, make that idea a bad one from the start.

Strategic calculations are also affected by broader constitutional and systemic issues. In a separation-of-powers system, different parties may control parts of government at the same time, heightening the risk of perceived partisan bias; that same difficulty can be multiplied many times over in a federal system. It will also be essential to maintain broad-based membership, leadership, and sources of financing. The level of consensus or structure of divisions in society itself can also be a challenge: as with the partisan-bias issue, a coalition must avoid being viewed as hostile by any one segment. In such settings, an emphasis on anti-corruption expertise and political backing, as opposed to revealing wrongdoing, may be all the more critical. However, these factors create opportunities, also: separation-of-powers systems may have a more independent judiciary (and if they do not, opportunities exist for the coalition to acquire important allies by backing judicial independence in a careful, long-term fashion). Moreover, in a system in which different parties share power, an anti-corruption group may be less likely to antagonize a country's entire political leadership and find itself frozen out of parliamentary and bureaucratic dealings. The key, again, is to position the group as a political and technical resource for anyone willing to tackle anti-corruption issues, while avoiding the temptation to take the lead in unearthing official wrongdoing.

What's In It for Me? Thinking about Incentives

Can we foster broad-based anti-corruption activity sustained by self-interest and a sense of efficacy, rather than moral crusades doomed to become noble failures? Wilson (1973) addressed that sort of challenge by analyzing the incentives that motivate and reward organizational participation. He thus challenged Olson (1965) and others who argued that organizations seeking a broadly shared goal would almost inevitably fall prey to free-rider problems. Wilson, noting that such groups *do* form and persist and that people act out of diverse motives, reasoned that successful organizations must offer members more than just collective goals. He identified four types of incentives (Wilson 1973, 33–51):

- *Material Incentives.* Rewards of tangible value, such as money, goods, or jobs.
- *Purposive Incentives.* The accomplishment of a significant goal—often, the formal purpose of the organization. Members of a group that succeeds in cleaning up a city's parks do create a benefit available to all residents, but still derive a special satisfaction flowing from their membership and contribution toward that goal.
- *Specific Solidary Incentives.* ". . . [I]ntangible rewards arising out of the act of associating that can be given to, or withheld from, specific individuals. Indeed, their value usually depends on the fact that some persons are excluded from their enjoyment" (Wilson 1973, 33–34). Such incentives include offices, honors, and other recognition; the prestige accruing to a donor who provides a "naming gift" to a university ethics center, for example, would be a large specific solidary incentive.
- *Collective Solidary Incentives.* ". . . [I]ntangible rewards created by the act of associating that must be enjoyed by a group if they are to be enjoyed by anyone" (Wilson 1973, 34), but which (unlike purposive accomplishments) are still restricted to the group itself. These include, for example, the prestige of affiliation, sociability and fellowship, and perhaps a degree of exclusivity.

Material incentives may be exclusive or individual (Wilson 1973, 36–37). Exclusive material incentives are available to all members, but only to members (the mutual-assistance schemes created by immigrant organizations in 19th-century American cities or by village associations in African cities today are examples; so are the discounted travel and insurance offered by fraternal and professional groups). Individual material incentives are given to some members, withheld from others, and never offered to outsiders; patronage jobs distributed by a political machine are a classic example. Among purposive organizations, Wilson identifies goal-oriented, ideological, and redemptive organizations (Wilson 1973, 46–47). The first seek specific changes in their surroundings (for example, less corruption), while the second seek sweeping social change (for example, a new system of property ownership). Redemptive purposive groups aim to change both society and their members' lives (Wilson 1973, 47). It is tempting to think of anti-corruption groups as redemptive, but many such groups wall themselves off from the society and fall prey to internal disputes.

A Rich Mix of Incentives

The most obvious incentives for an anti-corruption coalition are purposive: the goal, after all, is better politics and administration. Moreover, reformers will have few material resources, at least initially, while the enticements of corruption will be strong and familiar. However, purposive appeals will not suffice, for two major reasons. First—particularly where corruption is worst—fighting corruption can be risky business. Corrupt interests can monopolize opportunities within an economy that is unlikely to be robust to begin with, and they will defend those advantages vigorously—at times, through intimidation and violence. Many businesses and citizens will put up with illicit deals or tolerate and avoid them because they perceive few alternatives. Second, reform is a public good, as noted, and is often a long-term prospect at best. Purposive appeals will thus fall victim to free-rider problems and must be supplemented by more-targeted incentives.

Even though they may seem unconnected to corruption, these other sorts of appeals are every bit as important to building and sustaining a coalition as purposive goals of reform. Specific solidary incentives (such as offices, honors and citations, and exclusive access to information) can be targeted to particular members and supporters and can be used judiciously to reward parliamentary anti-corruption efforts, also. Collective solidary incentives (such as sociability, prestige, and a sense of mutual support) are also valuable, particularly where civil society is weak. Such appeals—notably, prestige—require an "audience" (and thus a relatively free press) to be effective (Wilson 1973, 40): leaders may hand out all manner of "Corruption-Fighter" awards, for example, but if no one hears of them they are of little value.

Social action coalitions are unlikely to possess extensive individual material incentives, and, absent other sorts of appeals, the material ones they do have may spark internal contention. However, a coalition can create unique exclusive material incentives—things of real value restricted to active members only. The immigrant mutual-aid groups noted earlier were built in difficult circumstances by poor people, but pooled contributions nonetheless provided valuable aid. Coalition leaders could emulate this model by setting up a kind of "corruption insurance" scheme in which business members pool information, resources, and perhaps modest contributions, while agreeing not to pay bribes. The shared information would help businesses avoid corrupt demands, the no-payment pacts would ease the sense that others are gaining short-term corrupt advantages, and pooled funds could compensate for some of the benefits lost by refusing to pay up. More generally, such a scheme could also reduce some of the risks of coalition membership. Those who violate the no-payment pledge could be suspended or expelled from the scheme, a penalty whose magnitude would grow as the coalition became increasingly institutionalized, visible, and prestigious.

What might the overall incentive system of an anti-corruption coalition look like, and which incentives would appeal to which members and constituents? Table 10.1 offers some general ideas:

Table 10.1 *Coalition-Building Incentives, By Type and Target Constituency (categories drawn from Wilson [1973])*

Exclusive	Material — Individual	Specific Solidary	Collective Solidary	Purposive — Goal-oriented[a]
"Corruption Insurance"	Econ. benefits of improved economy	Data/information banks: • on corrupt agencies, officials • on best practices	Prestige, improved image domestically, internationally	Reform as public good
				Better governance
Information: • vulnerability assessments	Security from better governance	Research products	Enhanced autonomy for organizations, press, opposition leaders, civil society groups	Fair political, economic processes; social equity
• prevention within organizations • legal and technical advice		Rewards, recognition	Sociability, fellowship, mutual encouragement	Stronger economic, social institutions
				Enhanced Rule of Law
Prime constituencies: Small firms Domestic entrepreneurs Investors	Citizens generally Civil society NGOs	Professional coalition staff, researchers Benefactors, financial supporters Anti-corruption "champions"	Mass membership Journalists NGO leaders Government elites	Mass membership NGOs Aid/lending partners Democracy groups and supporters

a. Ideological and Redemptive subtypes of purposes not recommended
Source: Wilson 1973.

Putting Incentive Systems to Work

Table 10.1 gives only a general illustration of the range of incentives available to a social action coalition seeking to supplement purposive appeals. Despite the limitations of purposive appeals and scarcity of individual material incentives, such a coalition can offer many other things to a variety of constituencies—and, indeed, it must do so to survive.

Of these, exclusive material and specific solidary incentives may be the least familiar. They will, however, be the most effective at attracting sustained support from small to medium business firms, domestic entrepreneurs, and investors—precisely those to whom a coalition must turn for material resources, and groups that are of obvious interest to parties and Members of parliaments, too. Information can be of real value. It may take the form of technical assistance: vulnerability assessments focusing on corruption risks within or from outside a firm could be performed for active coalition backers. Training programs, advice on auditing requirements and internal control systems, and a data bank on best practices or risk assessments elsewhere can be of real value. Whether these services be provided on a fee-per-use basis or made available to members paying a regular subscription, they are reasons to join and support a coalition and a way to demonstrate the value of the coalition and its permanent staff. Recognition is a similar incentive: coalition leaders should spare no efforts in giving awards, citations, and favorable publicity to key backers, as well as to anti-corruption "champions" in parliament—but, of course, must target them carefully so as to minimize risks of future embarrassments should those recognized turn out to have something to hide.

Other benefits consist of offsetting the costs of corruption itself. The "corruption insurance" proposed above might take several forms: technical assistance, pooling funds for legal assistance and partial compensation of those hurt most by corrupt demands, and active support for whistle-blowers are just a few examples. At another level, the coalition could broker integrity pacts among firms in a sector of industry or among bidders for large contracts, as exemplified by TI's "Islands of Integrity" initiatives. These can create confidence that refusing to pay bribes does not mean that one is not just handing advantages to competitors; pledges could be given added weight by requiring bidders to post deposits subject to forfeit should they engage in corruption. Some of these services could be offered to government officials, though care must be taken, particularly in the early phases, not to antagonize the superiors to whom they report. In both the private and public sectors, such activities can provide a focal point—and a measure of strength in numbers—for those who wish to abstain from corrupt dealings, but have felt isolated in the past.

Collective solidary incentives—sociability, prestige—may seem an afterthought or even a luxury, but in fact they will be essential to maintaining mass support, and with it, the coalition's visibility and legitimacy. It is no accident that the Hong Kong ICAC's highly regarded public education campaigns have long included a component of fun and social activity, particularly for young people. For journalists, honest contractors and officials, and the leaders of participating organizations, a kind of security can flow from membership: those who conceal corruption or practice intimidation may think twice if they know that their critics are backed by a larger group. Conversely, coalition members tempted by offers of money for silence, for example, have something important to lose if they are found out—membership in a prestigious and enjoyable group. Such incentives may be difficult to quantify, but they show how a solid coalition can, through aggressive use of multiple sorts of incentive, build a following that will enhance its standing in dealing with parliament.

Stages of Coalition Building

Both the targets and tactics of anti-corruption efforts, as well as the development of the coalition itself, will be influenced by the character of the society within which they are launched. Moreover, virtually all of the factors in that list have important historical dimensions that will vary from case to case. We can, however, outline general stages in the coalition-building process:

- Formation, in which the core of a coalition is organized, early leaders and "champions" are identified, and an agenda takes shape
- Credibility, in which the coalition demonstrates that it can act effectively and that it is thus worthy of support from a variety of stakeholders and constituencies
- Expansion, a particularly critical stage in which a small organization builds a broader social and resource base while retaining coherence and effectiveness
- Transformation, during which the coalition does not so much grow as become polycentric, taking initiatives on many fronts and drawing strength from many sources

Coalition development, from one phase to the next, is a matter of increasing the diversity of the constituency base and repertoire of incentives, in turn enhancing possible connection points with parliament while reducing the coalition's vulnerability. Indeed, growth for its own sake will create continuing problems of resources and coherence, often at the expense of credibility. A critical challenge, early on, will be identifying "leaders and champions" in both parliament and the private sector, building cooperative relationships among them, and then moving on to visible early successes. The targets, as Klitgaard, McLean-Abaroa, and Parris (2000) point out, should not necessarily be the most serious corruption problems in a society. Attacking those may guarantee defeat: while reformers are often told to "fry a big fish"—that is, go after a prominent corruption ringleader—"big fish" have big friends. Instead, Klitgaard, McLean-Abaroa, and Parris argue for "picking the low-hanging fruit"—that is, making sure that early struggles are won. The fish fry can take place later on, when the coalition has amassed credibility and prestige that can be parlayed into solidary incentives and after its alliances in parliament have had time to gather strength.

The final stage is that of a fully developed coalition sustaining itself while acting on many fronts. Initiative passes from core leadership to many centers of activity. Incentives become complex, and activities polycentric. In this stage, the coalition ceases to follow any one tactical or structural plan; perhaps its boundaries and overall coherence become very difficult to pin down. But at that point, it will have succeeded in mobilizing the broad-based political backing—sometimes contentious and always sustained by self-interest—essential to anti-corruption initiatives in parliament and society at large. It is unlikely that the coalition will put itself out of business, for corruption will never be completely eradicated. But when fully developed, it combines broad-based elite political will with the protean qualities of a strong civil society, integrating its anti-corruption agenda into the basic activities and interests that drive political life and policy making. Such a coalition will be a powerful partner for anti-corruption forces in parliament and will itself be strengthened by its parliamentary connections.

Parliaments and Coalitions Together

Social action coalitions have particular relevance for enhancing parliaments as anti-corruption forces, for they can build a sound social and political foundation for reform—minimizing the risks of, and increasing the incentives for, Members, parties, and leadership to confront corruption. Where such coalitions are in place, anti-corruption legislators are not alone; they can depend on a base of support for their activities and wield a powerful political weapon as they confront corrupt or indifferent officials (or party leaders). Circumventing the free-rider problems of reform at the parliamentary level, in that fashion, can have major demonstration effects for other Members and in society generally. Anti-corruption legislators linked to social action coalitions are in a position, as well, to target the often-diffuse anger of their constituents far more precisely and effectively than citizens alone could hope to do. The result can become a "virtuous circle" in which citizens who act against corruption enjoy enhanced chances of success and reduced risks, while their parliamentary representatives are rewarded for helping accomplish those results.

Such coalitions—particularly where economic resources are scarce and where formal organizations are the target constituents—are not easy to build or sustain. Their many projects and appeals can conflict with each other, and potential backers' agendas will overlap only partially. Still, social action coalitions allow reform constituencies to "borrow" size and resources from each other when they do work together. Critically, they reduce costs and risks for those, both in and outside of parliament, who make the first move against corruption. Then, over the long run, they sustain popular backing for reform after initial sensationalism has faded.

Any attempt to spell out the ways that social action coalitions and parliaments can aid each other in fighting corruption will of necessity be both too general and too simple: local realities cannot be ignored, and a basic elaboration of connections will underestimate the synergy and cumulative value that can accrue over time. Nonetheless, a basic way to portray such interconnections and opportunities is to think of the sorts of strengths and resources each side can provide the other, and to emphasize as well those that they can share. That sort of account is symbolized in figure 10.1.

At one level, the coalition-parliament relationship is one of formal representation, but not far beneath the surface, a variety of mutually beneficial exchanges take place. Shared values and commitments are reinforced. Popular support flows to anti-corruption leaders and Members in the form of votes, funds, and organized activity; those indifferent or hostile to reform are denied those benefits. Sophisticated coalition leaders, working with parliamentary allies, will play an essential role in distinguishing between real commitment to fighting corruption and the merely symbolic—or even dishonest—stances of other Members and leaders. Here we see, perhaps most clearly, what the coalition concept adds to the representation process: in theory, those sorts of political rewards and sanctions are what citizens provide all the time, but without the organizing and educating functions of a coalition and its leadership, they are unlikely to do so effectively. The value of such leadership is never more apparent than between elections: continued popular concern and support are essential if promises about corruption are to be translated into action and if investigation and oversight functions are to become more effective. Over the long term, these kinds of backing deepen the legitimacy of a parliament—a critical asset if Members are to challenge existing connections between wealth and power and, as needed, take a stand against executive pressures.

Figure 10.1 *Interconnections between Coalitions and Parliaments*

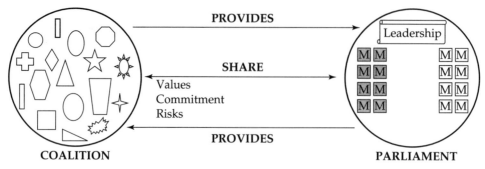

Electoral support and punishments
Political funding, organization
Popular backing, force of numbers
Legitimacy
Grievances, evidence of corruption
Feedback on effects of reform
Policy priorities and mandates

Routes of access, appeal
Investigation, follow-through on grievances
Protection
Support: funding, expertise, information
Coherence, discipline, detailed knowledge
Sustained oversight activities

Source: Author's research.

Other equally important kinds of input have to do with corruption itself. Information on the harm done by corruption, along with an active sense of grievance, requires broad-based social backing of anti-corruption parliamentarians. So does feedback on the effects of reform, particularly because corruption itself is usually impossible to measure directly. That feedback may take the form of perceptions and anecdotal information—constituency staffs, to the extent that Members enjoy such support, will play a critical role here—but over time, it provides a broader picture of the changing quality of services, administration, and political life. (Corruption index scores will not track such changes; indeed, they may deteriorate for a time as a country gets serious about its corruption problem.) If it becomes clear that families are no longer paying bribes for utility connections, business people are experiencing less bureaucratic harassment, and farmers are able to bring their goods to market without having to buy their way past police roadblocks, reform not only will have succeeded but also will have been seen to do so. Better yet, political and coalition leadership will be able to take credit for such successes and will gain credibility in the eyes of ordinary citizens and corrupt figures alike. Finally, citizens working through social action coalitions will be better able to help shape policy priorities—focusing at least some aspects of the legislative process on the broader good—and to back those priorities with solid political mandates (see box 10.1).

Parliaments, in turn, provide essential backing—and in some settings, protection—to the coalitions and their members. Funding for anti-corruption efforts themselves, along with improved legislation and better-targeted policy generally,

---

Box 10.1 *Ghana's Anti-Corruption Coalition (GACC)*

Ghana's Anti-Corruption Coalition (GACC), cooperating under the aegis of the National Governance Programme, links official agencies such as the Serious Fraud Office and the Commission on Human Rights and Administrative Justice (CHRAJ) to a range of civil society groups, including the Centre for Democratic Development and the Ghana Journalists Association. It serves as a public forum and anti-corruption advocacy group, but has also drawn up comprehensive anti-corruption action plans for consideration by governance agencies and parliament, conducts diagnostic surveys, and has participated in the World Bank Institute's anti-corruption training courses. GACC grew out of the 9th International Anti-Corruption Conference in Durban, South Africa, in 1999, where a group of government officials, official anti-corruption agencies, and representatives of civil society agreed on the need for more-extensive connections with civil society. On several occasions, GACC has actively urged parliamentary action and investigations in connection with alleged cases of corruption—as, for example, in May 2005, when questions arose regarding property dealings by President John Kufuor's son. GACC enjoys considerable international backing, but its anti-corruption activities suffer as a consequence of unclear divisions of responsibility among official agencies and the general difficulties that Parliament has in checking the nation's executive. A related challenge in attaining an optimal level of cooperation with government while maintaining autonomy and credibility. Government, for its part, has sought to channel its dealing with the group through the national attorney general's office. GACC's long-term effectiveness is thus unclear, but its persistence in less-than-ideal circumstances since 1999 and its success at keeping a variety of civil society groups as allies make it a particularly important case to watch. It is worth noting that Kufuor's New Patriotic Party claims links with GACC among its successes (GhanaWeb.com 2005; Danish Ministry of Foreign Affairs 2003).

---

are aspects of a close relationship with a broad-based coalition. The same can be said of the sorts of information a parliament can provide to the public and the accumulated expertise it can make available to supportive groups (a professional, well-supported parliamentary staff is a critical resource in this regard). Their potential benefits are clear, as are those flowing from enhanced oversight activities. However, parliament can also provide important avenues of political access, and appeal or recourse from corrupt treatment—essential if citizens are to confront corruption directly, rather than in evasive or illicit ways (Alam 1995). Access and appeal are in turn linked to two broader functions: the first is investigation and follow-through on specific complaints; the second is protection. Even citizens who have heard all manner of anti-corruption slogans in the past and who may be reluctant to file reports because of fear or reprisals can be enlisted as anti-corruption allies if their representatives show a sustained willingness to take complaints seriously and to act on them in visible ways. Those who are pressured because of anti-corruption activities can rely on parliamentarians to publicize and investigate such abuses. If citizens in coalition believe they share the risks of fighting corruption with their representatives and if those parliamentarians know that they can take those risks in the name of, and with the support of, a well-institutionalized citizen coalition, essential steps will have been taken toward sustainable, effective reform.

A final, but very important, kind of support that parliamentarians provide to citizens and coalitions would be the coherence and discipline of effort and the detailed knowledge of policy and process that skilled Members and leaders bring to the legislative and oversight processes. Citizen outrage over corruption is essential, but it is also diffuse; focusing that political and normative energy on specific agencies, officials, budget lines, and programs can make it a compelling force for reform.

Reform Synergy

GOPAC's notion of an "ecology of governance" suggests that as the representation process matures and deepens, it amounts to more than the sum of its parts. Parliament and social action coalitions gather strength and confidence from each other's efforts, and together they constitute an effective counterweight to overbearing executives and corrupt interests. Anti-corruption efforts, representation, and democratic processes themselves can acquire a credibility and normative value that transcends the performance of specific legal, political, or constitutional functions. At that point, reform becomes embedded in, and an extension of, the energies of society and the political process.

Some of the most important connections are based on sharing, rather than an exchange of benefits and incentives. Advocates of democracy generally, and opponents of corruption specifically, must share basic values about the sources and uses of, and interconnections between, wealth and power. The roles of citizens and of civil society, those of state and parliamentary leaders, and the linkages of accountability that link them in GOPAC's "web" must all be matters of basic consensus. That sort of consensus must be built and reaffirmed year by year through the interactions and reinforcing incentives we have discussed here.

In societies where corruption has been brought under control, people refrain from abusive behavior not just (or even primarily) because of a fear of punishment or as the result of a cost-benefit calculation, but rather because they believe in the basic fairness of the institutions and people governing society. They know that if they break the rules or abuse those policies and institutions, they will suffer public disapproval. Worse yet, they will have violated standards and values that their leaders and fellow citizens take seriously and in which they have a lasting personal stake. Those values are the antithesis of corruption, and we strengthen them through social and political interaction. Those interactions will not happen unless people participate—and leaders lead—in ways that address their shared interests and well-being. No leaders and institutions embody those possibilities more clearly than strong, accountable parliaments and their members.

Bibliography

Alam, M. S. 1995. "A Theory of Limits on Corruption and Some Applications." *Kyklos* 48 (3): 419–35.

Anechiarico, Frank, and James B. Jacobs. 1996. *The Pursuit of Absolute Integrity.* Chicago: University of Chicago Press.

Clay, Karen. 1997. "Trade without Law: Private-Order Institutions in Mexican California." *Journal of Law, Economics, and Organization* 13 (1): 202–31.

Danish Ministry of Foreign Affairs. 2003. "Thematic Programme Support Document: Programme for Good Governance and Human Rights (GG&HRP), 2003–2008, Ghana." (November). http://www.ambaccra.um.dk/NR/rdonlyres/1BBF2E36-927F-48A0-9A7F-E12BBBC36103/0/GGHRprogrammedocument.pdf (viewed June 2005).

Geddes, Barbara. 1994. *Politician's Dilemma: Building State Capacity in Latin America.* Berkeley: University of California Press.

Ghana Web. 2005. "Hotel Kufuor: Anti-Corruption Coalition Wants Enquiries." (May 26). http://www.ghanaweb.com/GhanaHomePage/NewsArchive/artikel.php?ID=82396 (viewed June 2005).

Hede, Andrew, Scott Prasser, and Mark Neylan. 1992. *Keeping Them Honest: Democratic Reform in Queensland.* St. Lucia, Queensland, Australia: University of Queensland Press.

Isham, Jonathan, Daniel Kaufmann, and Lant Pritchett. 1997. "Civil Liberties, Democracy, and the Performance of Government Projects." *World Bank Economic Review* 11 (2): 219–42.

Johnston, Michael. 1993. "Political Corruption: Historical Conflict and the Rise of Standards." In *The Global Resurgence of Democracy*, ed. Larry Diamond and Marc F. Plattner. Baltimore: Johns Hopkins University Press.

Johnston, Michael, and Sahr J. Kpundeh. 2002. "Building a Clean Machine: Anti-Corruption Coalitions and Sustainable Reforms." Working Paper 37208, World Bank Institute, Washington, DC.

Klitgaard, Robert. 1988. *Controlling Corruption.* Berkeley: University of California Press.

Klitgaard, Robert, and Heather Baser. 1997. "Working Together to Fight Corruption: State, Society, and the Private Sector in Partnership." In *Governance Innovations: Lessons from Experience: Building Government-Citizen-Business Partnerships*, ed. S. Taschereau and J. E. L. Campos, 59–81. Washington, DC: Institute on Governance.

Klitgaard, Robert, Ronald McLean-Abaroa, and H. Lindsay Parris. 2000. *Corrupt Cities.* Oakland, CA: Institute for Contemporary Studies Press.

Nickson, R. Andrew. 1996. "Democratization and Institutional Corruption in Paraguay." In *Political Corruption in Europe and Latin America,* ed. Walter Little and Eduardo Posada-Carbó, 237–66. New York: St. Martin's Press.

Olson, Mancur. 1965. *The Logic of Collective Action.* Cambridge, MA: Harvard University Press.

Peck, Linda L. 1990. *Court Patronage and Corruption in Early Stuart England.* Boston: Unwin Hyman.

Roberts, Clayton, ed. 1980. *The Growth of Responsible Government in Stuart England.* Cambridge, U.K.: Cambridge University Press.

Rose-Ackerman, Susan. 1999. *Corruption and Government: Causes, Consequences, and Reform.* Cambridge, U.K., and New York: Cambridge University Press.

Stapenhurst, Frederick, and Sahr J. Kpundeh. 1998. "Public Participation in the Fight against Corruption." *Canadian Journal of Development Studies* 19 (3): 491–508.

Tendler, Judith. 1979. "Rural Works Programs in Bangladesh: Community, Technology, and Graft." Transportation Department, World Bank, Washington, DC.

Wilson, James Q. 1973. *Political Organizations.* New York: Basic Books.

11

Political Parties

Riccardo Pelizzo

Introduction

According to a recent conference report, corruption "exists and has always existed," "it is pervasive, and it has far reaching consequences," it "represents one of the most significant obstacles to development," and "it also distorts the proper functioning of democratic institutions." Yet because corruption "is a symptom of deeper institutional weakness," the report also insisted on the importance of strengthening the key democratic bodies fighting corruption ("Report on Wilton Park Conference 748" in 2004, presented in appendix 2 of this book). Political parties are part of this set of institutions, aggregating diverse sets of interests, providing the structure for political participation and representation, and formulating policy options on a national level (Africa Political Party Finance Initiative 2004). However, political parties are also globally perceived to be the most corrupt institutions (Wolkers 2005). Therefore, Members of Parliament, in most cases also members of political parties, have a responsibility to ensure that their parties promote an anti-corruption agenda in their platform and that internally the party abstains from corrupt practices.

This chapter will outline how strengthening and institutionalizing political parties is therefore important in the fight against corruption. The first section provides a fairly detailed discussion of the notion of institutionalization. Particular attention is paid to the fact that the institutionalization of organizations depends on a combination of factors such as the organization's age, generational age, adaptability, complexity, autonomy, and coherence. The second section shows how the notion of institutionalization can be applied to parties and what it means for political parties to become institutionalized. The third section argues that the potential for corruption is inversely related to parties' levels of institutionalization—so that the more a party is institutionalized, the less likely it is to become involved in corrupt practices—and will illustrate the argument with examples taken from developing nations. The final section will advance some suggestions as to what can be done to more fully institutionalize political parties.

Institutionalization of Political Organizations

The notion of institutionalization has been elaborated by Samuel Huntington (1968, 12), who defined institutionalization as the process by which organizations and procedures acquire value and stability. The level of institutionalization of a political system can be defined by the adaptability, complexity, autonomy, and coherence of its organizations and procedures. So the level of institutionalization of any particular organization or procedure can be measured by its adaptability, complexity, autonomy and coherence.

But what exactly is this "adaptability, complexity, autonomy and coherence"?

Adaptability refers to an organization's ability to adapt to changes in the environment in which the organization operates. This adaptability can be measured based on three interrelated indicators. One is the organization's age. In fact, old organizations have had to learn how to adapt to environmental changes to survive, and they can use this adaptive knowledge to cope with present and future changes. This is why older organizations tend to be more adaptable. A second indicator of an organization's adaptability is what Huntington calls the "generational age." This concept first refers to the generation of leaders in power and second reflects an organization's ability to transfer power from one generation to the next. The more often power is peacefully transferred from one generation to another, the more the organization is adaptable. The third indicator gauges organizational adaptability. This term is used to indicate an organization's ability to find and perform new functions, once the objectives that the organization was originally created to achieve have been achieved. In other words, the organization either finds some (new) functions to perform or disappears. In this respect, Huntington noted that "an organization that has adapted itself to changes in the environment and has survived one or more changes in its principal functions is more highly institutionalized than one that has not" (Huntington 1968, 15). To sum up, the level of institutionalization of an organization increases with the organization's age, with generational changes in the organization's leadership, and with the organization's ability to always find new functions to perform.

Institutionalization also reflects an organization's *complexity*. In Huntington's words (1968, 15), "the more complicated an organization is, the more highly institutionalized it is." Complexity refers to two distinct (sets of) characteristics (that is, the number of organizational subunits and their differentiation). A greater number of subunits enhances an organization's ability to "secure and maintain the loyalties of its members." Moreover, differentiation is important because a diverse organization covers a broad range of interests and products and makes it less vulnerable than organizations "[that] produce(s) one product for one market" (Huntington 1968, 18). This means that as the number and the differentiation of the organization's subunits increase, the complexity of the organization increases and so does its level of institutionalization.

The level of institutionalization of an organization does not simply depend on the organization's flexibility and complexity, but also on its *autonomy*. The autonomy of political organizations "is measured by the extent to which they have their own interests and values distinguishable from those of other institutions and social forces." This last point is actually quite important. It means that the organization is institutionalized if it has been able to develop interests, objectives, and procedures "that are not simply expressions of the interests of particular social groups" (Huntington 1968, 20).

Last (but not least), the degree of institutionalization of an organization depends on its *coherence* and *unity*. In Huntington's words, "an effective organization requires, at a minimum, substantial consensus on the functional boundaries of the group and on the procedures for resolving disputes which come up within those boundaries" (Huntington 1968, 22).

The Institutionalization of Political Parties

What Huntington said about the institutionalization of political organizations can also be applied to the political party. Political parties, as organizations, are created by certain individuals (or groups thereof) as means to achieve certain ends (Palombara and Weiner 1966, 3–42). The institutionalization of political parties occurs when parties develop the characteristics mentioned above: adaptability, complexity, autonomy, and coherence. Yet what does this imply?

As noted above, the *adaptability* of an organization reflects the organization's age, generational age, and flexibility to adapt to changes in the environment in which it operates. The same logic applies to political parties. The level of institutionalization of a political party reflects its age (how long the party has been in existence), its generational age (whether and how many times the party has been able to transfer power from one generation to the next one), and whether it has been able to adapt to environmental changes.

The first two points are fairly clear, and the third can be illustrated by the following example. Imagine that a given party is created by a group of individuals to achieve a certain objective (for example, to forbid the trade of the seeds of the baobab trees and protect the survival of these majestic trees). The party is created, it campaigns, it wins some electoral support, and it sends some representatives to the national parliament, where these talented parliamentarians introduce a few bills concerning the preservation of baobabs. Fellow parliamentarians understand the importance of this issue and decide to pass the Protection of Baobabs' Seeds Act. At the end of this stylized process, this party has achieved the objective for which it had been created, and it has no reason anymore to exist, unless, of course, the party is able to identify new objectives to pursue and new functions to perform.[1] When a party finds new activities and functions to perform or when it identifies new objectives to achieve, the party is said to have organizational adaptability.

The *complexity* of political parties reflects the combination of two sets of characteristics. The first set is represented by the number of organizational levels. It is, in fact, believed that the complexity of a party organization increases as the number of organizational levels increases. For example, a party characterized by four organizational levels (national, regional, provincial, local) is more complex than a party characterized by only three levels (national, provincial, local). Complexity, however, reflects not only the number of organizational levels but also the number of units at each level of organization. It is believed that the larger the number of units, the bigger and more complex the party organization is.

But what does it mean for a party to become *autonomous* from the environment in which it operates? According to Panebianco, "There is autonomy when the (party) organization develops its capacity to directly control the processes of exchange with the environment."[2] Therefore, a party controls the processes of exchange with the environment when

---

[1] The most obvious case of a party being able to do so is when the survival of the party organization becomes a value in itself or rather an objective that a party may wish to achieve. On this, see Panebianco (1982, chapter 4). The English translation is available as *Political Parties: Organization and Power,* Cambridge University Press, 1988, chapter 4.
[2] My translation of Panebianco's *Modelli di Partito* (1982, 114).

(a) the party is able to finance most of its activities with the revenue generated by the membership fees and dues—making it less dependent on the external environment to finance itself,

(b) the party has a fairly developed bureaucratic apparatus and selects its leaders from within the party organization, and

(c) the party's elected officials are controlled by (and therefore accountable to) the party leadership and bureaucracy.

Finally, the level of institutionalization increases with the structural *coherence* of the party organization. A political party's structural coherence is low when a party's organizational subunits are quite independent from one another, as well as from the party's central organization. The structural coherence of a political party is high when the party's subunits are interdependent and their interdependence is preserved by the fact that resources are managed and allocated among the various subunits by the party central organization.

Parties' Weak Institutionalization and Potential for Corruption

In many developing nations with little (if any) experience of democratic governance, political parties have not been able to become fully institutionalized. This section will try to illustrate why this may be the case and how parties' weak institutionalization relates to corruption.

As noted above, age is a crucial factor in determining the adaptability and level of institutionalization of an organization. Also, the older one organization is, the more it is institutionalized. The first and most obvious problem that parties in developing and democratizing countries have encountered in their path toward strong institutionalization is that these countries have often had a relatively brief democratic experience. In countries, like the Republic of Korea or Taiwan (China), for example, "political parties also have not had the time to become well-defined."[3] As a result, political parties frequently build their support around patron-client relationships, rather then through well-developed issue-oriented platforms. In countries like Cambodia or Malaysia, the presence of an authoritarian regime has certainly not allowed or favored the institutionalization of political parties and of a competitive party system.[4]

There is a second problem. The fact that developing countries have had such a brief democratic experience means that in most cases the parties that have emerged in the course of the democratic transition are still led by the first generation of leaders. This means that they have had little to no experience in transferring power

---

[3] A more comprehensive discussion of South Korean parties can be found in Laura L. Thornton and David Kovick, "South Korea," in Manikas and Thornton (2003, 263–316). For a discussion of Taiwanese parties, see David Kovick, "Taiwan," in Manikas and Thornton (2003, 317–70).

[4] See Laura L. Thornton, "Malaysia," in Manikas and Thornton (2003, 139–82); and David Kovick and Laura L. Thornton, "Cambodia," in Manikas and Thornton (2003, 41–74). The same point could actually be made about Nepal, where the multiparty democracy established by the 1959 Constitution was suspended in 1962 when the government was dissolved and parties were banned. See Mark Wallem and Ram Guragain, "Nepal," in Manikas and Thornton (2003, 184–85).

from one generation of party leaders to the next. This means that while the party is young, the generation of leaders is not, and this may spark some tensions within the party itself.

Also, political parties in many developing and democratizing nations have not been able to develop complex and articulated party organizations. This means that they have not been able to achieve what Panebianco calls "territorial diffusion": they have not been able to become rooted in the society that they are supposed to represent. Without large numbers of basic units, parties are inherently unable to become what they should be: that is, "a collection of communities, a union of small groups dispersed throughout the country . . . linked by coordinating institutions" (Duverger 1954, chapter 4). Running the danger of becoming "self-centered, inward looking, and exclusive" (Melia 2005), unresponsive and unrepresentative of the people whom they are supposed to speak for, political parties have trouble becoming full-fledged legitimate institutions.

The final reason explaining the weak institutionalization of political parties in some countries is that they have not been able to develop much autonomy (see box 11.1). This problem manifests itself in several ways. Compounding the lack of issue orientation in party platforms mentioned above, in societies historically characterized by patron-client relationships (as for example in Asia and Africa), parties and politicians are often expected to deliver some goods to their constituents. In some cases, parties and politicians are "expected to pay for community and family events, such as weddings and funerals" (Manikas and Thornton 2003, 10). In more extreme cases, citizens expect "patronage and payments in exchange for political support."[5] In such an environment, it is very hard for parties to insulate themselves from the pressures and demands of their constituents. The more a party is insulated from the pressures of the constituents, the more likely it is to resist the pressure to get involved in illicit activities.

The limited autonomy that parties enjoy in developing and democratizing countries is the result of an additional factor. Parties in these countries have encountered major problems in structuring and institutionalizing their internal practices and procedures. In the experience of the Asian countries, for example, this problem emerges because of the "unofficial and often familial, clan-like nature of many parties."[6] Parties in these countries have not developed, established, and systematically applied objective, merit-based mechanisms for selecting and promoting party bureaucrats, cadres, and leaders. In the golden age of mass parties and mass party politics in Western Europe, party leaders were often recruited from among the best party cadres and leaders based on how loyal they had been to the party and how well they had worked for it.[7] This mechanism has demonstrated some shortcomings in consolidated democratic regimes. In fact, party leaders selected from among the party cadres and bureaucrats based on their commitment to their party's ideological stance may sometimes lack the skills to understand, cope with, and possibly solve the problems of contemporary complex democracies. Also, this is why scholars and

---

[5] This is, for example, the case in the Philippines. See Celito Arlengue and John Joseph S. Coronel, "Philippines," in Manikas and Thornton (2003, 217–62). The quote is taken from p. 217.

[6] Laura L. Thornton, "Introduction," in Manikas and Thornton (2003, 10).

[7] See Panebianco (1982, 115). The classic studies on mass parties remain Duverger (1954) and Neumann (1956, 395–421).

> **Box 11.1** *Examples of Interrelated Causes/Consequences of Weak Party Institutionalization*
>
> *Youth of Democracy and Political Parties.* Domination/abuse of power by one political party; confusion of party and nation; marginalization of opposition parties; voter intimidation; little internal democracy; lack of membership, legitimacy, and ideology
>
> *Lack of Ideological, Issue-Oriented Platform.* Donors and members expect financial benefits and kickbacks from contributions to party; patronage networks develop; in many countries, politicians and parties are expected to sponsor or pay for social services for their constituents (schooling fees, roads, weddings, funerals . . .); vote buying (cash or gifts); party switching
>
> *Lack of Internal Procedures and Regulations.* Little internal transparency-accountability-democracy; mismanagement; hijacking of the party line by a few well-placed officials
>
> *Lack of Membership.* Little financial contributions from party members leads to "creative fundraising; lack of legitimacy, representation, and responsiveness; reliance on financial support by vested interests, squeezing out reformers; and misuse of state resources.
>
> *Sources:* Hodess 2001; Bryan and Baer 2005; and Manikas and Thornton 2003.

practitioners have extensively debated the crisis of highly ideological parties and have suggested that parties should abandon their ideological baggage and become sufficiently flexible to cope with a world that demands complex, nonideological answers for complex problems.[8] This said, one should keep in mind that selecting party leaders on the basis of their loyalty to the party and to the party's well-being had also some obvious virtues in the mass parties' golden age. The most important virtue was that a party leader or cadre would not do (and would not allow any of their subordinates to do) anything that could possibly harm the reputation of the party. Imperfect as it could be, this system often prevented parties from (or minimized the extent to which parties were) engaging in extensive illicit practices.

Parties' weak institutionalization (in terms of age, generational age, autonomy, and so forth) is not the only cause of political corruption, but it is certainly one of the causes of party corruption.[9] The internal life of weakly institutionalized parties is neither transparent nor accountable to voters and citizens. Yet parties must serve as models and demonstrate the principles of governance. The behavior of parties toward each other will reflect on the attitude that citizens have toward democracy. Moreover, the internal organization (that is, if they are self-serving, divisive, and intolerant, rather than inclusive, tolerant, transparent, and respectful of rules) will serve as an indication of its behavior in government (Melia 2005). It will also strongly influence the willingness of prospective members to join political parties. Not surprisingly, weakly institutionalized parties tend to have a fairly small mem-

---

[8] A review article on the party crisis debate can be found in Daalder (1992, 269–88). A more recent assessment of the literature can be found in Pelizzo (2003).

[9] One could very well argue that parties' weak institutionalization is both a cause and a consequence of corruption. The argument goes as follows: weakly institutionalized parties are particularly prone to engage in corrupt practices, corruption undermines parties' autonomy from the environment in which they operate, and autonomy is a key component of institutionalization. Therefore, if there is little to no autonomy, there is little to no institutionalization. (I thank Marco Verweij for the useful remark.)

bership base. This means that they must find financial resources other than those generated by membership fees, and when legally collected funds are insufficient to cover the increasingly high costs of politics, parties may have to accept illicit contributions, bribes, and kickbacks. The claim that "corruption is a symptom of deeper institutional weakness" is quite accurate when applied to the corruption of political parties. Parties' corruption reflects the fact that they are weakly institutionalized. Hence, to minimize and possibly eliminate corruption from party politics, it is necessary to eliminate the conditions that make corruption possible (that is, parties' weak institutionalization). But how can parties become properly institutionalized?

Conclusions and Suggestions

The previous section suggested that parties' weak institutionalization in democratizing countries or in newly established democracies is the result of a combination of factors. One is that these countries have a fairly brief experience with democracy and that party democracy and parties have literally not had the time to become fully institutionalized. Yet, institutionalization is not just a matter of time. There are some clear steps that parties should take (and that political reformers and civic activists should advocate). If parties do not develop proper rules and procedures to regulate their internal life, they will not attract party members. If they do not attract members, they will not be able to finance themselves with membership fees. If they cannot satisfy their financial needs legally, they will satisfy them illegally. Numerous measures can be taken to strengthen the integrity and institutionalization of political parties (see boxes 11.2 and 11.3); however, three overarching steps seem

---

Box 11.2 *Nonexhaustive List of Measures for Greater Party Institutionalization*

Political Parties

Codes of conduct and ethical standards for members and officials

- Inner-party democracy: Full membership involvement in election of party leaders, officials, and candidates for public office
- Mandatory disclosure requirements on assets and interests
- Regular, independent, and publicly accessible financial audits
- Independent monitoring, evaluation, and disciplinary committees and processes
- Training and ethical education programs for leaders and party officials
- Term limits for party leaders
- Strengthen issue-driven platforms—develop party platform
- Greater interaction of political parties with civil society
- Educate voters on political parties and anti-corruption measures

Legislators

Effective legislation on, and enforcement of, laws regarding party registration and operation, political finance, electoral provisions, and declarations of assets and interests

- Consider the introduction of public subsidies and funding of political parties, tied to party reforms
- Laws and regulations addressing the ability of public officials to direct government business (that is, ensure competitive bidding practices).

Sources: Manikas and Thornton 2003; Bryan and Baer 2005.

Box 11.3 *Examples of Institutionalizing Political Parties and Curbing Corruption*
           in Malaysia

- *Background.* Political parties are governed by the Malaysia Society Act (1966),
  which requires them to register and submit financial accounts with the Ministry
  of Home Affairs. These accounts are not disclosed to the public and do not
  require parties to reveal their sources of funding. Neither does the law set limits
  to contributions and spending nor bar the ownership of profitable enterprises
  by parties, and it provides for little transparency in internal affairs. However,
  civil-society groups and some political parties have advocated for change and
  have been successful on some matters:
- *Strengthening National Anti-Corruption Efforts.* The Democratic Action Party
  (DAP) has identified the curbing of corruption as one of its key objectives in its
  platform, organized numerous workshops and debates on relevant legislation,
  and provided extensive input on the Malaysian Anti-Corruption Bill of 1997.
- *Selecting Leaders and Candidates.* The Gerakan Party allows party offices to select
  "election observers" for internal party elections.
- *Fundraising.* The United Malays National Organization (UMNO) prohibits
  fundraising by local branches and divisions to avoid undue influence by donors
  and misuse of funds by party members.
- *Strengthening Ethical Standards and Discipline.* The party Islam se Malaysia developed ethics standards requiring leaders to declare their assets and wealth and
  appointed an ombudsman to monitor compliance. The UMNO established a
  disciplinary committee to investigate and punish cases of corruption within the
  party. The DAP requires candidates to resign from their seats should they violate party principles and switch party.

Source: Manikas and Thornton 2003, 21–28.

particularly important: the regulation of the parties' internal life, increased membership, and a stronger party bureaucracy.

Regulating Parties' Internal Life. Parties must adopt formal rules to regulate the selection of cadres, leaders, and candidates. These rules should be ratified in the party's formal documents and implemented. Violations of the internal rules should be sanctioned
by properly designed committees within the party itself. Parties should also devise some
mechanisms to regulate the decision-making process within the party itself. When the
decision-making process is transparent and party members know how the party
achieves a certain decision, they are quite likely to support the party's decision—even if
it is one that they initially opposed—because they see that decision as a legitimate one.

The adoption and the implementation of these rules would address the fact that
parties are somewhat detached from society. According to an NDI study, "some
parties have alienated civic activists and leaders," "the polarization between civil
society and parties is striking," "activists eager to become involved in issue-based
political activity frequently turn to NGOs instead of joining political parties," and
"civic groups are in practice effectively replacing parties by representing citizens on
issues of concern and presenting proposals to the government" (Manikas and
Thornton 2003, 11). Civic activists stay away from political parties not only because
parties are known to be corrupt but also because there seems to be no way in which
parties can be reformed and moralized. The fact that parties lack proper institutional mechanisms for selecting cadres and leaders or for making decisions means
that if civic activists joined parties, they would have little to no power to reform the

parties themselves (Manikas and Thornton 2003, 10–11). Therefore, to attract desirable members, it is very important for parties to develop and adopt some objective, merit-based, and transparent rules and procedures to regulate their internal life.

Membership. This type of reform could have an additional benefit. By increasing parties' accountability to their members, it could give prospective members an incentive to join parties and could expand parties' membership base. This would be quite an important result because even if parties charge minimal membership fees, the expansion of parties' membership base would also increase the party income generated through membership fees and would reduce parties' need to rely on external sources of financial support—which is generally considered to be one of the most important reasons why parties may accept illicit contributions and become corrupt.[10] In other words, by expanding their membership base, parties can take one of the most important steps in the course of their institutionalization: they can directly control how they are financed, or in Panebianco's words, they "directly control the processes of exchange with the environment."[11]

There is an additional reason why the expansion of the membership base is important for political parties: as the membership base expands to include additional social groups (religious, ethnic, socioeconomic, and so on), the party must take into account the sometimes conflicting demands of these various social groups. Its policy stances, decisions, and proposals are "likely to be the result of competition among social forces. A political party, for instance, that expresses the interests of only one social group—whether labor, business, or farmers—is less autonomous than one that articulates and aggregates the interests of several social groups. The latter type of party has a clearly defined existence apart from particular social forces" (Huntington 1968, 20). The fact that the party has an existence independent of that of the social groups that the party represents means that the party is autonomous from them, and as the party's autonomy increases, so does its institutionalization.

Party Bureaucracy. As has been seen, the institutionalization of a political party is strong when the party has high levels of autonomy and structural coherence. In the previous paragraph, it was suggested how a party can be made more autonomous from various social groups. But how is a party supposed to increase its structural coherence? The structural coherence of a party increases as the party develops the ability to control its subunits, keep them accountable, administer the allocation of resources between the various subunits, decide the party line, and ensure that the subunits adopt the centrally decided party line. A party's ability to do all these things depends, in its turn, on its ability to create a centralized party bureaucracy. It is the party's centralized bureaucracy that explains the party position to ordinary members, tells elected officials how to conduct themselves, monitors the behavior of lower-level officials and members, and sanctions what it considers improper conduct.

Transparent internal rules and regulations, the expansion of membership, and the development of a proper party bureaucracy are the conditions without which parties cannot become strongly institutionalized—and without strong institutionalization, parties are particularly vulnerable to engaging in various forms of unethical

---

[10] There is some consensus among scholars and practitioners alike that when legally collected funds are insufficient to cover the increasingly high costs of politics, corruption does not simply happen, it must happen. On this, see the "Report on Wilton Park Conference 748" in 2004, which is included in this book in appendix 2.

[11] My translation of Panebianco (1982, *Modelli di Partito,* 114).

behavior—including corruption. Indeed, as the former President of the Philippines, Corazon Aquino (2003, 1–2), noted herself: "The search for a winning formula against corruption . . . depends a lot on political parties, which are the training grounds of political leaders. It is in the political party where the ideologies and values of young leaders are shaped. . . ."

Institutionalizing political parties, strengthening and reforming them from within, goes hand in hand with the fight against corruption by other political institutions. Such reforms increase the legitimacy and representational value of parties, build the popular trust toward democracy, and lend the national anti-corruption efforts additional credibility.

Bibliography

Africa Political Party Finance Initiative. 2004. *Money in Politics: Supporting the Search for Solutions in Africa.* (November).

Aquino, Corazon. 2003. "Foreword." In *Political Parties in Asia: Promoting Reform and Combating Corruption in Eight Countries,* ed. Peter M. Manikas and Laura L. Thornton, 1–2. Washington, DC: National Democratic Institute for International Affairs (NDI). http://admin.corisweb.org/files/Manikas2003Political_Parties1093601961.pdf.

Bryan, Shary, and Denise Baer, eds. 2005. *Money in Politics.* Washington, DC: NDI.

Daalder, Hans. 1992. "A Crisis of Party?" *Scandinavian Political Studies* 15 (4): 269–88.

Duverger, Maurice. 1954. *Political Parties: Their Organization and Activity in the Modern State.* Translated by Barbara and Robert North. London: Methuen and Co.

Hodess, Robin, ed. 2001. *Global Corruption Report 2001.* Berlin, Germany: Transparency International.

Huntington, Samuel P. 1968. *Political Order in Changing Societies.* New Haven: Yale University Press.

La Palombara, Joseph, and Myron Weiner. 1966. "The Origin and Development of Political Parties." In *Political Parties and Development,* ed. Joseph La Palombara and Myron Weiner. Princeton: Princeton University Press.

Manikas, Peter, and Laura L. Thornton, eds. 2003. *Political Parties in Asia: Promoting Reform and Combating Corruption in Eight Countries.* Washington, DC: National Democratic Institute for International Affairs (NDI).

Melia, Thomas, O. 2005. "Political Parties: Catalysts or Obstacles to Democratic Reform?" Conference panel discussion. June 25–27. World Economic Forum on Democracy. Warsaw, Poland.

Neumann, Sigmund. 1956. "Toward a Comparative Study of Political Parties." In *Modern Political Parties,* ed. Sigmund Neumann, 395–421. Chicago: University of Chicago.

Panebianco, Angelo. 1982. *Modelli di Partito.* Bologna: il Mulino.

Pelizzo, Riccardo. 2003. "Cartel Parties and Cartel Party Systems." Unpublished Ph.D. dissertation, Johns Hopkins University, Baltimore, MD.

Wolkers, Marie. 2005. "Global Corruption Barometer 2004." In *Global Corruption Report 2005.* Berlin: Transparency International (TI).

Part V
Corruption in Political Parties and Parliament

12

Party Political Funding

Michael Pinto-Duschinsky

Introduction

Money is necessary for the proper functioning of democratic politics. Without the necessary funding, politicians cannot articulate their ideas and visions to the public and, therefore, citizens cannot make informed choices during elections. Unfortunately, political financing is rife with corruption, and scandals related to party financing are ubiquitous. Though numerous efforts have been made to reform laws relating to campaign and party finances, success has been rare. A more focused approach to ensure accountability and transparency in political spending might provide policy makers with better results.

The first part of this chapter seeks to familiarize the reader with the complexity of political financing: it examines the extent and variety of forms that political corruption can take. The second part will illustrate some of the attempts made to regulate party funding and combat political corruption. Ongoing debates, based on sometimes erroneous assumptions of underlying trends, have weighed the merits of different models of party financing. It is important to remember, as is explained in the third part of this chapter, that because of country-specific idiosyncrasies, countries should develop their own rules and regulations regarding political financing. Because there is still no "cure" for corruption in party funding, expectations should be realistic. The chapter concludes by outlining a number of measures that legislators can adopt to minimize corruption related to party financing.

Political Finance and Political Corruption

With barely less regularity than the cycle of seasons, each year produces a fresh series of corruption cases arising from political funding.

A few of the scandals of 2003–4 are summarized in box 12.1. The examples are not a scientific sample, and they will soon themselves become dated. However, they strongly suggest that the financing of political life—especially money raised to pay for election campaigns and political party organizations—is a major form of corruption and of alleged corruption.

Each reported example must be regarded with caution. Rumors and false reports abound. Politics is a brutal game, and it is in the interests of candidates and party managers to make accusations against their rivals. Nor do journalists always have the public interest at heart when they report allegations of abuses relating to the funding of political activities. Despite these necessary reservations, it is clear that many charges made in the past have proved to be well founded and that corruption related to money in politics is a crucial issue.

Even the limited selection of examples that are summarized shows that problems of political fundraising occur in many parts of the world, in countries with different levels of economic development and political traditions. It shows also that senior politicians—who often prefer to delegate the job of collecting money to those lower in the political hierarchy—are unable to escape charges of wrongdoing.

Despite a stream of reports from around the world like those in box 12.1 and despite an increasing flow of academic studies, political financing and the abuses thereof remain shrouded in mystery. Many commonly heard notions surrounding them are unproven or wrong. This is partly because "political finance" takes so many forms and is difficult to define and partly because there remain large gaps in research (especially about political money in emerging democracies).

Box 12.1 *Political Finance Scandals: 2003–4*

BRAZIL, February 2004: The Web site of a weekly news magazine (www.epoca.com) publishes a video "that shows a senior government official soliciting campaign contributions for two of the [ruling Workers' Party] candidates and offering lucrative political favors in return." The official was head of the state lottery in Rio at the time of the video (*The New York Times*, February 16, 2004).

COSTA RICA, October 2004: Former President Miguel Angel Rodriguez resigns as secretary-general of the Organization of American States and is placed under house arrest on his return to Costa Rica for alleged corruption. The charges are related in part to the funding of his campaign for election as OAS general secretary and also arise from wider investigations about alleged kickbacks connected with a major telecommunications contract (*BBC News*, British Broadcasting Corporation, October 21, 2004: http://news.bbc.co.uk/2/hi/americas/3764902.stm.).

ECUADOR, November 2004: President Lucio Gutierrez narrowly escapes impeachment by the Congress. Opposition politicians "accused the president of embezzling state funds to campaign for local elections in October" (*BBC News*, British Broadcasting Corporation, November 10, 2004: http://news.bbc.co.uk/2/hi/americas/4001367.stm).

FRANCE, December 2003 and January 2004: Former Prime Minister Alain Juppe receives 18-month (reduced on appeal to 14-month) suspended jail sentence for "his role in a scam in which Paris City Hall funds were used to pay political party allies holding fake jobs in the late 1980s and early 1990s." He was found guilty of allowing employees from the Gaullist party (known at the time as the "RPR") to be put on the payroll at City Hall when President Jacques Chirac was mayor and Juppe was finance director. July 2004: Juppe resigns as president of the ruling UMP Party (Reuters 2004; Sithole 2004; Wyatt 2004).

GERMANY, November 2004: "A key figure in the donations scandal that rocked Germany's Conservative-led opposition four years ago has agreed to return to Germany after being on the run for five years, his lawyer said on Friday. Holger Pfahls, a former German deputy defense minister, was discovered earlier this year to be living in Paris. Earlier this week, the Paris Appeals Court ruled that he could be extradited to Germany after he was arrested four months ago in France on bribery charges. . . . German prosecutors want to talk to him about their investigations into whether he accepted almost 2 million euros in bribes from Karlheinz Schreiber, an arms lobbyist, over the sale of 36 tanks to Saudi Arabia. Schreiber, who is at present living in Canada and fighting extradition to Germany, was a central figure in the party-funding scandal in Germany, which revolved around illegal donations to the

Christian Democrats under former Chancellor Helmut Kohl" (November 19, 2004: www.expatica.com).

LITHUANIA, April 6, 2004: Parliament votes in favor of all three counts of impeachment against President Rolandas Paksas for granting Lithuanian citizenship to a Russian citizen, Yuri Borisov, as an alleged payback for financial and other support during the 2002 presidential election. Paksas is subsequently acquitted on charges of leaking state secrets, but Borisov is convicted in November 2004 "of blackmailing [Paksas] in 2003." The scandal arises partly from the wiretapping by state authorities of telephone conversations in which Borisov is allegedly heard demanding a major reward for a donation by Avia Baltica to Paksas's presidential election campaign of 2002. There are also allegations about the "Russian mafia connections" of Borisov (*Baltic Times*, November 25, 2004: www.baltictimes.com/art.php?art_id=11425; and December 1, 2004: www.baltictimes.com/art.php?art_id=11539).

NICARAGUA, December 2003: Former President Arnoldo Aleman is sentenced to 20 years in prison for corruption. Among other charges, he "was accused of helping to divert nearly [US]$100 million of state funds into his party's election campaign" (*BBC News*, British Broadcasting Corporation, December 8, 2003: http://news.bbc.co.uk/1/hi/world/americas/3299289.stm).

PERU, November 2003: Congress approves charges against ex-President Alberto Fujimori, alleging that he diverted state funds to finance his 2000 presidential campaign.

RUSSIA, December 2003: Studies published in 2004 by the New York–based Open Society Justice Initiative and by the Russian chapter of Transparency International (TI) concluded that President Putin and United Russia had misused "administrative resources" for electoral purposes. In particular, unequal access to the state-controlled media was seen as a dominant feature of the December 2003 elections for the State Duma (Open Society Justice Initiative 2004).

SOUTH AFRICA, September 2004: Vice President Jacob Zuma is implicated in a major corruption case against a businessman, Schabir Shaik, whose trial begins in September in Durban. Shaik is accused of soliciting a bribe from a French arms company for Zuma in relation to the investigation into a major arms deal. Contributions to the ruling African National Congress in connection with the arms deal are also reported (Lang 2005).

REPUBLIC OF KOREA, March 2004: President Roh Moo-hyun is impeached on March 12 on charges related to technicalities of political finance rules. The impeachment is overturned by the Constitutional Court on May 14, 2004. However, in June 2004, a Seoul Court sentenced the "former Millennium Democratic Party (MDP) chairman . . . Chyung Dai-chul to six years in jail and 400 million won in fines on charges of taking illegal political funds from several firms" in the 2002 presidential campaign. An investigation initiated in October 2003 into Korea's latest campaign fund scandal had led by September 2004 to the prosecution of about 74 politicians, including 27 lawmakers, on charges of raising illegal political funds (*Korea Times*, May 14, June 19, and September 8, 2004: cited in www.transparency.org).

Notes:
The inclusion of examples and names does not imply any judgment about the guilt or innocence of those reportedly involved or charged. For additional examples, see Pinto-Duschinsky (2002, 69–75): www.moneyandpolitics.net/researchpubs/pdf/Financing_Politics.pdf and www.boellnigeria.org/politicalfinancebook.html; Hodess (2004), especially the contribution of Walecki (2004): http://www.transparency.org/publications/gcr/download_gcr/download_gcr_2004#download; and Transparency International (2006): www.corisweb.org/article/archive/263.

As a first step, "political finance" must be defined. The narrowest meaning of the term is "money for electioneering." Because political parties play a crucial part in election campaigns in many parts of the world and because it is hard to draw a distinct line between the campaign costs of party organizations and their routine expenses, party funds may reasonably be considered as "political finance," too. Party funding includes not only campaign expenses but also the costs of maintaining permanent offices; carrying out policy research; and engaging in political education, voter registration, and the other regular functions of parties.

Beyond campaigns and parties, money is spent on direct political purposes in many other ways. For instance, account must be taken of (a) political "foundations" and other organizations that, though legally distinct from parties, are allied to them and advance their interests; (b) the costs of political lobbying; (c) expenses associated with newspapers and media that are created and paid to promote a partisan line; and (d) the costs of litigation in politically relevant cases. Clearly, the number of channels through which money may be poured into politics not only leads to problems of definition and research but also makes political financing difficult to control as a practical matter as well. As soon as one channel of political money is blocked, other channels will be used to take its place. Moreover, it is not enough to make a reckoning of the amounts of money raised and spent for political purposes. In addition, it is necessary to include gifts in-kind, such as the provision of free or subsidized television time.

Second, the meaning of "corrupt" political financing is often unclear and thus must be examined. Conventional definitions of political corruption (such as "the use of public office for unauthorized private gain") often do not apply to corrupt political financing. First, the definition of political corruption as "the use of public office" does not apply to all forms of political fundraising. Challengers, for instance, are by definition outside of public office, but may still accept money in exchange for promises to misuse public office should they win at the polls. A second difference between ordinary political corruption and corruption in the field of political financing is that, in the latter case, money is not necessarily used for private gain, but rather for the gain of a political party or of a candidate.

References in common parlance to "corrupt" political financing usually refer to one of the following:

- *Political contributions that contravene existing laws on political financing.* Illegal donations are often regarded as scandalous, even if there is no suggestion that the donors obtained any improper benefit in return for their contributions.
- *The use for campaign or party objectives of money that a political officeholder has received from a corrupt transaction.* In such a case, all that differentiates corrupt political funding from other forms of political corruption is the use to which the bribe is put by the bribe taker. Instead of taking corrupt money for personal uses, the bribe taker gives part or all of the proceeds to his or her party or campaign chest.
- *Unauthorized use of state resources for partisan political purposes.* This is a commonly noted feature of ruling parties' campaigns in established and developing democracies alike. In parts of Africa and the former Soviet Union, the resources available to officeholders, national and local, are blatantly used for electioneering.
- *Acceptance of money in return for an unauthorized favor or the promise of a favor in the event of election to an office.*
- *Contributions from disreputable sources.* Even though there may be no evidence of an exchange of favors or of promises of future favors, the presumption is that tainted sources are likely to have tainted motives. Some of the most dramatic and most fully established examples of criminal sources concern the financing of politics in Central and South America and in the Caribbean by drug dealers.

- *Spending of money on banned purposes such as vote buying.* Research has uncovered significant vote buying in places ranging from Cambodia, Malaysia, and Taiwan (China) in Asia; to Cameroon, Kenya, Uganda, and Zimbabwe in Africa; to Antigua and Barbuda, Costa Rica, Mexico, and Suriname in the Americas; and even to Samoa in the Pacific.[1] Vote buying may take the form of financial payments or of gifts of food and goods.

All the forms of corrupt political funding described above, from illegal contributions to vote buying, have to do with parties and election campaigns. There are, of course, other kinds of suspect ways in which money can play a role in politics (for example, bribes may be given to legislators after their election to influence their votes in the legislature).

Regulations and Subsidies

There is no shortage of regulations and subsidies concerning political money—many of them introduced as a response to scandals. The frequency with which new laws regarding money in politics are introduced is itself an indication of the problems of making workable laws, as well as the widespread lack of will to enforce them.

The main provisions of political finance laws are outlined in box 12.2.

Such provisions sometimes are contained in laws dealing specifically with party finance or election finance. Often they are included in broader laws about elections, political parties, or the prevention of corruption. Media laws and laws about voluntary associations and organizations may also contain provisions about aspects of political financing.

Because of the range of provisions concerning aspects of political finance, there are usually a number of different laws in any one country that deal with the topic. The existence of a variety of separate laws often complicates the task of the regulatory body or bodies responsible for enforcing the laws.

Box 12.2 *Main Provisions of Political Finance Laws*

1. Prohibitions against corrupt and illegal practices (such as vote buying)
2. Financial deposits for candidates for public office
3. Disclosure rules
4. Spending limits
5. Contribution limits
6. Bans on certain types of contributions (such as foreign contributions, anonymous contributions, or contributions from business corporations)
7. Public subsidies
8. Tax relief and subsidies in-kind
9. Political broadcasting rules
10. Rules concerning the funding of internal party contests
11. Rules concerning the funding of referendums
12. Rules concerning the declaration of assets by candidates for public office
13. Measures to control the use of public resources for campaign purposes

---

[1] www.moneyandpolitics.net/researchpubs/pdf/Financing_Politics.pdf, p. 72.

Table 12.1 *Political Finance Regulations and Subsidies in 104 Countries*
(percentage of countries possessing regulations or subsidies)

Regulations	
Disclosure rules (any)	62
Ban on foreign donations (partial or complete)	49
Campaign spending limits (any)	41
Disclosure of individual donors (partial or complete)	32
Contribution limits (any)	28
Ban on paid election advertising on television	22
Ban on corporate political donations (partial or complete)	16
Ban on corporate political donations (complete)	8
Subsidies	
Free political broadcasts	79
Direct public subsidies	59
Subsidies in kind (apart from free political broadcasts)	49
Tax relief for political donations	18

Source: Pinto-Duschinsky 2002, 75.

There has been a general trend over recent decades toward more political finance regulations and more subsidies. The rapidity with which legal changes relating to political finance occur in some country or other makes it difficult to keep abreast of the changes. Therefore, the review of political funding laws on which table 12.1 is based already is slightly dated. However, it provides a good impression of the situation in 104 countries in 2000–2001.

Because public funding is one of the most frequently discussed measures, it merits special attention. The period since the late 1950s has seen the introduction of public subsidies to the extraparliamentary organs of political parties and to individual candidates in a large number of countries. While there have been a few efforts (for example, in Italy and Venezuela in the 1990s) to limit or abolish existing subsidies, the overall trend clearly has been toward state subsidy. Research into all the countries rated as "Free" or "Partly Free" by the Freedom House rankings (a wider sample of countries than those included in box 12.2) established that 59 percent of them had laws in 2002 providing for some direct public funding of parties or candidates.[2] Other findings that emerge are that state aid (as well as other categories of regulations and subsidies) hardly exists in sovereign states with very small populations and that (in most countries) state aid has been popular with the political class and highly unpopular with the electors. State aid is especially common in Western Europe and in the countries that emerged from the Soviet bloc. It is less common in Asia, the Caribbean, and the Pacific.

The amount of state aid and the proportion of political financing derived from this source vary greatly. In certain African countries, cash-strapped governments have eliminated public funding, despite provision for it in the law. By contrast, the public purse provides for the bulk of money for parties and candidates in countries such as Austria.

Public subsidies for electoral politics appear to have produced neither the benefits promised by supporters nor the drawbacks feared by critics.

---

[2] Ibid.

On the one hand, public subsidies have clearly failed to cure the problem of corrupt political funding. Some of the most serious scandals have occurred in countries with generous public subsidies, such as France, Germany, and Spain. A party or candidate that obtains public monies, knowing full well that such monies are equally available to competitors, will not therefore stop looking for more money with which to outspend and outmaneuver political opponents.

On the other hand, the fear of some critics that public funding would cause parties to decline by reducing their incentives to recruit new members and raise money from existing ones has not invariably been justified.

In any case, it is easy to misinterpret the modern phenomenon of public funding laws. Such laws are neither a necessary nor a sufficient condition of the flow of public resources into election campaigns and into party coffers. These laws are not sufficient because, as mentioned earlier, the amounts provided may be insignificant or nonexistent. These laws are not necessary because there are many other ways in which public funds traditionally have been—and still are—directed into politics.

First, in a number of countries, the president or the prime minister traditionally had the use of secret slush funds that could be used for any purpose whatever. In the 19th century, British prime ministers had at their disposal a Secret Service fund that was used, by convention, to subsidize the political campaigns of their supporters. In Imperial Germany, Chancellor Otto von Bismarck's "Reptile Fund" had similar uses, the main difference between Britain and Germany being that Britain abolished its special Secret Service fund in the 1880s while German chancellors continued to deploy such funds until after the Second World War.

Second, in countries such as India, public funds are allocated to members of the national legislature for the formal purpose of carrying out development projects in their constituencies. In practice, the money may all too easily be used as a campaign resource.

Third, holders of paid public offices are required by many political parties and in a considerable number of countries to donate set shares of their salaries to the party. Contributions of such "party taxes" may be recorded in party accounts as membership fees or as donations; in essence, these contributions are a form of indirect public financing.

Fourth, the use of state resources for electioneering functions constitutes a form of indirect public subsidy. A typical practice in a number of African countries is the use of state-owned vehicles to ferry electors to governing-party rallies and to the polls on election day. A time-honored method of seizing the spoils of political office is to employ party supporters on public payrolls. Another and equally widespread opportunity for diverting public funds into party service comes from the resources that are being provided with increasing generosity to members of the legislature in most democracies. Parliamentarians commonly receive public money to employ research assistants and secretaries; often they have free offices and travel privileges. It is hardly surprising that incumbent legislators use at least a portion of these allowances for campaign purposes.

The overall conclusions that emerge about public funding of politics are, first, that the principle of providing direct financial payments from the public treasury to parties and to candidates has become normal. Second, the public funding thus provided varies greatly in extent between different countries and is sometimes insignificant. Third, because there are several other sources of public funding than that which is supplied in direct public subsidies, it is unclear whether the extent and proportion of de facto public funding have been increasing, holding steady, or decreasing.

Laws are one thing; whether they are followed is quite a different matter. In country after country, those investigating political financing receive the warning that laws are a dead letter or are honored in the breach. Evidence for this is the series of unending "reforms of reforms" that have taken place in a number of countries, including France, Germany, Italy, and the United States. The desirable scope of political finance regulations and subsidies is bound to remain a subject of debate. There is little doubt, however, that all too often, laws express objectives (such as transparency of political donations) without considering in sufficient detail how to implement those objectives. There is, in short, too much law and too little enforcement.

Trends: Real and Perceived

The search for legal remedies has not only been a response to scandals but has also followed from a set of widely held (but unproven) assumptions about general trends in the funding of political life. Many commentators, for instance, regard it as self-evident that the costs of politics have been rising in most parts of the world and that the cause of this upward trend has been the development of television and of other mass media as the main forms of modern electioneering. The presumed "arms race" in political spending has been seen as a main cause of corruption in political financing. Yet there appears to have been little systematic research to establish whether costs have actually been rising. Some preliminary cautionary reflections are in order.

First of all, there is the question of the cost of advertising in the mass media. Television and other media play crucial roles in modern political life in many parts of the world. Yet even in those countries, such as the United States, in which the ownership of television sets is most widespread, the importance of televised political advertising easily lends itself to overstatement. Television is less important for local than for national campaigns. The standard study of U.S. elections in the presidential election year of 1988 found that television accounted for less than a tenth of the total sum spent on all electoral campaigns for public office (Alexander and Bauer 1991, 98).

In other economically advanced countries, the proportion of political spending accounted for by TV is probably less than in the United States—partly because parties and candidates can get free advertising time, partly because some countries (such as the United Kingdom) ban paid political advertisements on TV, and partly because a large share of political spending goes to pay for the national and local offices and staffs of political parties.

Second, television does not yet rule the world. In many parts of Africa and Asia, television sets and even radios can be quite hard to find outside cities. In countries such as Ghana, Kenya, and Bangladesh, rallies are still the best way for candidates to reach voters. Hence, the purchase of vehicles and electronic public-address equipment is a major expense.

Third, it is not at all obvious that the cost of the new politics, with its emphasis on mass media, professional image making, and opinion polling, is greater than the cost of the old politics. The old-fashioned electioneering revolves around vote buying, gift giving, and labor-intensive techniques of reaching individual electors, all of which tend to be very expensive. Indeed, evidence from a number of countries indicates that the venerable techniques of the old politics actually cost more than the thoroughly modern methods of media-oriented electioneering.

There has been a tendency for studies of trends in political spending to concentrate on national campaigns, rather than on the entire range of national and local campaigns; to ignore political parties' spending between elections; and to measure inflation according to movements in prices, rather than incomes. All these factors appear to have led to a premature judgment that there has been a widespread escalation of political expenditures.

Too often, reforms have been based on the assumption—convenient to the politicians who make the laws and vote in subsidies for themselves and their parties—that the core problem is the escalation of costs. This justifies the view that public funding provides a cure for corruption related to political funding.

In reality, there is probably no single, simple legislative "cure" for the problem. There will always be temptations and possibilities for politicians to evade controls and to introduce measures for partisan motives. Thus, an effective strategy should avoid utopian aims and claims. It arguably should comprise (a) constant vigilance; (b) a willingness to consider limited, practical objectives; (c) the realization that it is preferable to have fewer laws that are conscientiously enforced than to have too much law and too little enforcement; and (d) a choice of legislative and other measures that is based on the particular needs of each country, not merely on a set of vague international guidelines.

The Role of Legislators in Controlling Corruption Related to Political Finance

Members of legislatures play a considerable role in the task of controlling corruption related to the funding of election campaigns, political parties, and other forms of political financing. Because they or their parties have been obliged to raise money for their election campaigns, they may have been led into corrupt practices and may thus constitute a part of the problem. Alternatively, they may use their influence to control the problem.

First, it is important for would-be legislators to take special care about their fundraising practices as candidates. Admittedly, it may be hard to raise money honestly, but not as impossible as they may suppose. A principled candidate may be able to attract a following of volunteers who will carry out campaign tasks far better than those who do so merely for the pay. Candidates often struggle to raise campaign funds, yet are careless in the ways in which they spend their money. Much expenditure on political advertising is wasted and arguably ineffective. Careful and skillful planning may permit a candidate to use a smaller budget to greater advantage.

Second, once elected, legislators are frequently able to play a useful role in the formulation of political finance laws. Such laws are complex and technical; yet, they are often enacted in haste and without sufficiently detailed examination. Unclear definitions of terms such as "election campaign," "political party," or "expenditure" frequently make laws unenforceable. The generality of some international codes means that they are of limited value to the legislator and are no substitute for careful preparation by those responsible for drawing up drafts and amendments.

For this reason, individual members of a legislature may play an especially positive role if they (and their helpers) make a close study of legislation introduced in other countries and of the loopholes and disadvantages encountered by such legislation.

Third, legislators may help to ensure that a law is workable by putting pressure on the government to make financial provision to allow the enforcement of the law by the relevant authorities. Too often, a new law will impose heavy administrative responsibilities on an enforcement authority without at the same time providing the resources needed by the authority to permit it to carry out its new work.

Fourth, legislators have the job of calling the government to account for any failure to enforce political finance laws. For example, laws requiring the submission and publication of financial statements by parties and candidates are simply ignored with impunity. A legislator who asks pointed questions about the compliance of parties with the law may thereby put effective pressure on the government to ensure that the bodies responsible for collecting the financial accounts carry out their duties.

Bibliography

Alexander, Herbert E., and Monica Bauer. 1998. *Financing the 1998 Election*. Boulder, Colorado: Westview Press.

Hodess, Robin, ed. 2004. *Transparency International: Global Corruption Report 2004*. London: Pluto Press. http://www.transparency.org/publications/gcr/download_gcr/download_gcr_2004#download.

Lang, Steven. 2005. "Schabir Shaik on Trial." *SABC News* (January–February). http://www.sabcnews.com/features/schabir_shaik_trial/janfeb.html.

Open Society Justice Initiative. 2004. *The Use and Misuse of Administrative Resources in Russia: Monitoring the Campaign for the December 2003 State Duma Elections*. http://www.justiceinitiative.org/activities/ac/cfm/russia.

Pinto-Duschinsky, Michael. 2002. "Financing Politics: A Global View." *Journal of Democracy* 13 (4, October): 59–86. www.moneyandpolitics.net/researchpubs/pdf/Financing_Politics.pdf.

Reuters. 2004. "French Court Convicts Would-Be President Juppe." (January 30). http://www.washingtonpost.com/wp-dyn/articles/A62789-2004Jan30html.

Sithole, Emelia. 2004. "French Conservatives Rally behind Convicted Juppe." Reuters (February 1). http://www.washingtonpost.com/wp-dyn/articles/A3338-2004Feb1html.

Transparency International. 2006. "Political Corruption." In CORIS database. www.corisweb.org/article/archive/263.

Walecki, Marcin. 2004. "Political Money and Corruption." In *Transparency International: Global Corruption Report 2004*, ed. Robin Hodess. London: Pluto Press. http://www.transparency.org/publications/gcr/download_gcr/download_gcr_2004#download.

Wyatt, Caroline. 2004. "France's Chirac Stands by His Man." *BBC News,* British Broadcasting Corporation (February 3). http://news.bbc.co.uk/2/hi/europe/3453993.stm.

13

Legislative Ethics and Codes of Conduct

Riccardo Pelizzo and Rick Stapenhurst

Introduction

In the course of the past two decades, both the international community and the scholarly community paid increasing attention to the causes and the consequences of corruption.[1] As chapter 2 has shown, corruption is often a symptom of a deeper institutional weakness, and to reduce corruption, it is necessary to eliminate the conditions that favor the existence of corrupt practices and other forms of misconduct.

The establishment of ethics regimes, by adopting either ethics codes or codes of conduct, represents a valuable anti-corruption tool. In fact, by creating ethics regimes, parliaments (a) establish a standard for parliamentarians' behavior, (b) clarify what forms of behavior are acceptable and what forms are improper, (c) create an environment that is less likely to tolerate misconduct and other forms of unethical behavior, and, by doing so, (d) create an environment in which parliamentarians are less likely to engage in corrupt practices.

The purpose of this chapter is to discuss how some parliaments have attempted to create ethics regimes and to show how such regimes may be used to promote good governance and, by doing so, to create a system of disincentives for corrupt practices.

This chapter is organized in the following way. The first section provides a fairly detailed discussion of the ethics regimes and of how ethics regimes can contribute to fighting corruption and other forms of misconduct. Particular attention is paid to the fact that ethics regimes can be established by adopting codes of conduct, codes of ethics, or ethics rules. It discusses what are the most important differences between these institutional tools. Building on this discussion, the second section shows that while codes of conduct are generally more specific than ethics codes, they vary with regard to how specific are their provisions. The third section argues that the effectiveness of codes of conduct is affected by a variety of factors, such as the existence and severity of sanctions; the institutionalization of the code (which refers to which institution is in charge of administering those sanctions); cultural factors (attitudes, values, and norms); and the training of parliamentarians. The

---

[1] This chapter is an adaptation, in part, of Pelizzo and Stapenhurst (2004).

fourth section draws some conclusions and formulates suggestions as to what the international community could do to contribute to the establishment of successful ethics regimes and, by doing so, to eliminating corruption.

The Need for an Effective Ethics Regime

In a democratic system, each citizen has the right to exercise as much influence on the political process as any other citizen. In fact, in democratic regimes, each citizen has the right to cast his or her vote at the elections and to influence, through the vote, the composition of the legislature and the selection of the government.

Yet, as soon as corruption emerges, two problems appear. The first is that those citizens who have more financial means at their disposal and use these to corrupt elected officials acquire additional influence over the political process. This is a violation of the spirit of democracy: that citizens should exercise equal power on the political process.

However, corruption creates a second, and not less menacing, problem for democracy because corrupt politicians could utilize illicitly obtained resources for their electoral campaigns, thus acquiring an advantage over the other candidates and improving their chances of being elected. By so doing, corrupt candidates distort electoral competition and prevent the people's will from being properly expressed; this poses a direct threat to democracy.[2]

However, corruption is not the only threat to democracy. Any form of legislative misconduct undermines the public trust in the democratic system, and by doing so, it poses an indirect threat to the democratic system. As Seymour Martin Lipset pointed out more than four decades ago, the single most important condition for making democracy survive is that democratic system's legitimacy (Lipset 1959, 69–108).

Surveys around the world show that legislatures around the world are facing a "democratic deficit"—that there are low, and generally declining, levels of public trust in legislatures. As figure 13.1 indicates, the legislature ranks as the least publicly trusted institution in certain Latin American countries, although in others it ranks much more favorably.

Similarly, public opinion polls around the world consistently rate public trust in politicians as low.

The creation of an ethics regime represents an attempt to regulate the behavior of legislators and to rebuild the public trust in the political system. The question is: can this work? And, if so, how can an ethics regime be established? What are the basic elements of an ethics regime?

Creating an Ethics Regime

To develop citizens' trust in the political system, legislators understand the need for ethics reforms. The adoption of an ethics regime is intended to serve both an internal and external function. Internally, the enforcement of an ethics regime is intended to improve the ethical standards and performance of elected officials. Externally, it is intended to regain the confidence of the public.

---

[2] A discussion of corruption and misconduct can be found in Skelcher and Snape (2001, 72–78).

Figure 13.1 Parliaments: Misgoverned or Honest Institutions?

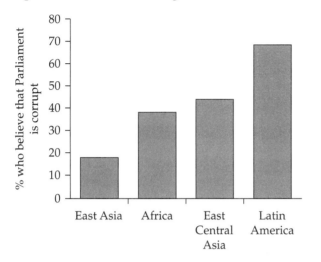

Sources: WBI diagnostics and survey data, various countries, 1998–2006.

Codes of Ethics and Codes of Conduct

Ethics regimes are created by adopting codes of ethics, codes of conduct, ethics rules, or all of the above. But what is a code of conduct? What is a code of ethics? How do they differ from each other?

Codes of ethics "are usually products of professional associations. They serve as a quality assurance statement to society and provide a set of standards for appropriate conduct for members of the profession that issues the code. Codes of ethics for those in government service challenge employees to identify with shared professional values that describe appropriate actions about acting rightly in the service of the public good" (Bruce 1996, 23).

Codes of conduct are quite different. They ". . . are more concrete and practical . . . for they represent executive orders or legislatively defined and enforceable behavioral standards with sanction for violation. They contain a list of the kinds of behavior required in a given set of circumstances and provide direction to those whose conduct they govern. Codes of conduct contain minimalistic prohibitions to unquestionably subversive or criminal acts. They are designed to protect the government employee, the client, and/or the public at large" (Bruce 1996, 24). In sum, there is a major difference between codes of conduct and codes of ethics.

Legislative Codes of Conduct

As was previously noted, codes of conduct represent one way in which parliaments and parliamentarians have attempted to establish effective ethics regimes. A formal code of conduct has been adopted by the legislatures of Chile, Fiji, Germany, Grenada, Israel, Japan, the Philippines, Poland, the United Kingdom, and the United States of America, while the Indian Lok Sabha has a customary code of conduct.[3]

---

[3] On this point, see the dataset of the Inter-Parliamentary Union. This dataset can be found at www.ipu.org. The Chilean Code of Conduct can be found on the Web site of the Chilean Congress: www.camara.cl/aindex/browsers/codigo_conducta.pdf.

A legislative code of conduct is a formal document that regulates the behavior of legislators by establishing what is considered to be an acceptable behavior and what is not. In other words, it is intended to promote a political culture that places considerable emphasis on the propriety, correctness, transparency, and honesty of parliamentarians' behavior. However, the code of conduct is not intended to create this behavior by itself. As Skelcher and Snape (2001, 73–74) pointed out, "compliance with codes of conduct . . . encourages a decision-making environment in which fraud and corruption should be less prevalent. But they cannot stop such offences."

How Specific Are the Provisions of a Code of Conduct?

Even though codes of conduct are more specific than codes of ethics, there is considerable variation in how specific their provisions can be. They may ask members of the legislature to disclose their interests concerning tax returns, sources of patrimonial income, investments, sources of income of the business of a partner or shareholder, ownership interest in a business, real estate interests, offices or directorships, creditor indebtedness, leases and other contacts with public entities, compensated representation before public entities, fees and honoraria, professional or occupational licenses, reimbursement of travel expenses from private sources, deposits in financial institutions, cash surrender value of insurance, private employer or nature of private employment, professional services rendered, identification of trusts by trustee, identification of trusts by beneficiary, names of immediate family members, and financial interests of spouse and children (NDI 1999, 5). The disclosure of interests before debating an issue related to those interests is a relatively common protection against conflicts of interest.[4]

In addition to asking legislators to disclose their interests, codes of conduct may impose some additional restrictions. Some apply while the legislator is in office, and some of them apply even after the legislator's tenure in office. The list of restricted activities include the following items: use of public position to obtain personal benefit, providing benefits to influence official actions, use of confidential government information, postgovernmental employment for two years, receipt of gifts by officials or employees above a certain value, receipt of fees or honoraria by public officials or employees, representation of private clients by public officials or employees, financial conflicts of interest, nepotism, political activity by employees, competitive bidding, outside employment or business activities by public officials or employees, and travel payments from nongovernment services.

Are There Complementary Factors That Can Contribute to the Effectiveness of Codes of Conduct?

Several factors may contribute to the effectiveness of legislative codes of conduct, including the existence of sanctions, institutionalization, cultural attitudes, and training. Each of these will be considered in turn.

---

[4] A discussion of the conflicts of interest can be found in Zimmerman (1994, 17–46).

Sanctions

There is some variation in the severity of the sanctions established for the violation of a code of conduct. Violations of the code of conduct can be punished with various sanctions such as censure, reprimand, fines, loss of seniority, and expulsion. (The data are presented in table 13.1.)

There is some variation in the severity of the sanctions established for a violation of the code. In Fiji, for example, the violation may be punished by the loss of mandate; in most other countries, there is a gradation of sanctions, ranging from reprimand and fine up to loss of mandate and (in the case of the Philippines) imprisonment.

Table 13.1 *Codes of Conduct and Sanctions*

Country	Sanction	Sanctions administered by
Fiji	Loss of mandate	n.a.
Grenada	Warning, reprimand, order to withdraw, suspension	House of Representatives
	Loss of mandate	High Court
India	Reprimand or admonition, imprisonment, suspension, expulsion	House of the People
	Disqualification from membership on grounds of defection	Speaker of the House
Israel	Remark, warning, rebuke, severe rebuke	The Knesset Ethics Committee
	Suspension from office	The Knesset Ethics Committee
	Loss of mandate	The Knesset
Japan	Admonition to abide by the standards of conduct, admonition to refrain from presenting at the House for a certain period of time, admonition to resign from the chairmanship of a committee	Deliberative Council on Political Ethics
Philippines	Imprisonment, disqualification to hold public office	n.a.
United Kingdom	Committal, reprimand or admonition, suspension from the House, expulsion	House of Commons
United States of America	Censure, reprimand, fines, loss of seniority, expulsion	House of Representatives

Source: Bruce 1996.

Sanctions are generally administered by one of the following bodies: independent commission, parliamentary ethics committee, parliament, speaker of the parliament, or court.[5]

Are sanctions effective? The question has two levels of answers. The first concerns whether sanctions are effective in eliminating misconduct while the second is whether sanctions affect the citizens' perception of the morality of legislators.

Although there is no evidence as to whether sanctions are able to curb corruption and other forms of misconduct, there is some evidence on whether (and how much) sanctions affect public officials' perceived morality. The evidence was gathered by a survey conducted by Willa Bruce in 1993 shows that "a clearly worded code of ethics with sanction" is the best way to curb corruption in government; at the same time, however, the survey also found that citizens' perception was influenced by the existence of a code of conduct rather than the presence or severity of sanctions (Bruce 1996, 27).

Institutionalization

A further difference can be observed between the various codes of conduct concerning the institutionalization of the code (that is, which institution is in charge of sanctioning those members who violate the code). In general, there are two principal variations: an independent commission (as in the case, for example, in Alberta, New South Wales, and Ontario) and an internal parliamentary body (either a parliamentary committee, as in Japan, or a parliamentary commissioner, as in the United Kingdom [see annex at end of this chapter, "Case Study of the House of Commons"]). In the case of extreme sanctions, cases may be referred to the High Court (as in Grenada) or to the Speaker of the House (as in India).

Attitudes, Culture, and Successful Codes of Conduct

In the political science literature, several phenomena are explained based on political culture, which is commonly defined as "the values and attitudes shared by a group." The literature on parliamentary ethics is no exception in this respect: it also emphasizes the role of political culture.

The analysis of the role of political culture with regard to parliamentary ethics must be twofold. First, it is necessary to study whether the existence of a specific political culture is conducive to the enactment of ethics reforms; second, it should be questioned whether the existence of a specific political culture affects whether, and to what extent, ethics reforms are successful.

A study conducted by Marshall R. Goodman, Timothy J. Holp, and Karen M. Ludwig (1996, 51–57) revealed that there is no detectable relationship between

---

[5] A discussion of some of the institutions that can administer sanctions can be found in Dr. Andrew Brien (consultant) (1998–99), "A Code of Conduct for Parliamentarians?" Research Paper 2, Department of the Parliamentary Library, Parliament of Australia. In addition to the solutions identified in this Research Paper, the data presented in table 13.1 suggest two additional options. One is that extremely severe sanctions, such as the loss of mandate, are decided by a high court (as in the case of Grenada). The other is that sanctions may be imposed by the speaker of the house (as in the Indian case).

political culture and whether ethics reforms are enacted. Attempts to create ethics regimes are generally a response to other forces, such as media investigations, scandals, and falling levels of public trust.

On the other hand, scholars have underlined that cultural factors, such as the existence of a common political culture, are a necessary condition for the success of ethics reforms. As Skelcher and Snape (2001, 74) pointed out, the success of an ethics regime requires the existence of a homogenous political culture. A code of conduct functions properly under three (cultural) conditions: (a) when the individuals, whom the code is intended to regulate, share the same attitudes and values;[6] (b) when those individuals have a shared view of what are the problems that the code is supposed to eliminate; and (c) if the individuals have a shared view of how those problems can be eliminated.

Yet, this is not always the case. A recent study of the ethical standards of the British MPs has revealed not only that is there no common set of values and attitudes but also that there are quite different views among MPs concerning ethical standards. According to Mancuso (1993, 179–82), "there is a multiplicity of ethical standards operative in the House [of Commons]. The conventional view that a common standard guides the behavior of MPs is simply incorrect." British MPs condemned corruption and criminal behavior. They also "condemned activities such as bribery, blatant misappropriation of public funds, and other clear statutory violations," but Mancuso went on to say, "in the problematic grey areas of constituency service and conflict of interest, the ethical consensus begins to unravel. . . . [Indeed,] on many important issues, there is stark dissensus among MPs as to what constitutes acceptable behavior, and many are engaging in activities that other[s] find reprehensible."

Mancuso pushed her analysis a step further. By investigating MPs' tolerance for conflicts of interest and constituency service and the relationship between the two types of tolerance, she was able to identify four distinct ethical types, which she defines as "puritans, servants, muddlers, and entrepreneurs." Puritans have little tolerance for both conflicts of interest and constituency service; servants tolerate constituency service, but not conflicts of interest; muddlers tolerate conflicts of interest, but not constituency service; and entrepreneurs will tolerate any kind of activity that is not explicitly forbidden.

The fact that there are quite different views regarding ethical standards among legislators has important implications, and it is something that reformers should take into consideration before enacting ethics reforms. If there is no consensus among MPs about what constitutes improper behavior, about the nature of the ethics problems, and about what changes should be made to make the ethics regime work, then any ethics reform is likely to face substantial problems. In other words, to make ethics reforms work, it is of prime importance to promote a common set of civic attitudes and ethical values among MPs.

---

[6] This means that for the proper functioning of a code of conduct adopted in a given parliament, the members of that parliament must have a set of shared values and attitudes. The fact that legislators in another country's parliament have a different set of values is absolutely not relevant, provided that if a code of conduct were adopted in this second parliament, its members should share a common set of attitudes and values. In other words, what is relevant for the success of a conduct code is cultural homogeneity within countries, not between countries.

Training

The training of legislators represents one way in which a common set of civic attitudes and values can be promoted. Such training—by clarifying what is misconduct; presenting findings of studies concerning the roots of misconduct; showing that misconduct undermines the legitimacy of democratic regimes (and indeed may threaten their survival, at least in newly established democracies); raising the awareness of the importance of eliminating misconduct; and identifying ways in which misconduct can be eliminated—can play a crucial role in making ethics reforms and ethics regimes succeed.

Conclusions and Recommendations

Ethics reforms and the establishment of ethics regimes serve two purposes. Ethical regimes are typically created with the intention of preventing corruption and misconduct. They do so by creating incentives for parliamentarians and legislators to perform their functions in an ethical manner. This is what we have called the "internal function." Ethics regimes and ethics reforms also serve an "external function": they can help reconstruct public confidence in elected officials and parliamentary institutions.

There are some steps that parliamentarians and legislators can take to avoid dilemmas in their conduct:

- First, parliamentarians can propose and promote the adoption of clearly worded codes of conduct. In doing so, parliamentarians must keep in mind that the successful establishment of an ethics regime depends to a large extent on the clarity of a code's dispositions. The code should specify what forms of behavior are acceptable, what forms of behavior are not acceptable, and what sanctions will be adopted to punish violations of the code.
- Second, it is of importance that the dispositions of the conduct code are reasonable and set a standard of behavior that parliamentarians can actually respect. If the dispositions of the code are unrealistic, they cannot be enforced, and the adoption of the code will at best be useless and at worst further undermine public confidence in politicians.
- Third, parliamentarians can propose and promote the adoption of specific parliamentary committees called "ethics committees." Such committees can perform two functions: to clarify the meaning of the code's dispositions and to ensure that the code dispositions are enforced consistently and impartially. This point has an obvious corollary: that ethics committees should not be used in a partisan way to get rid of political opponents and to promote the interests of a particular party. Doing so will ultimately lead to the failure of the newly established ethics regime.
- Fourth, parliamentarians should refrain from engaging in any activity that may damage their personal reputation and the reputation of the parliament. Genuine commitment to preserving the parliament's reputation is the most important condition for making ethics reforms succeed.

Bibliography

Bruce, Willa. 1996. "Codes of Ethics and Codes of Conduct: Perceived Contribution to the Practice of Ethics in Local Government." *Public Integrity Annual* 17: 23–30 (Council of State Governments [CSG], Lexington, KY).

Goodman, Marshall R., Timothy J. Holp, and Karen M. Ludwig. 1996. "Understanding State Legislative Ethics Reform: The Importance of Political and Institutional Culture." *Public Integrity Annual* 17: 51–57 (Council of State Governments [CSG], Lexington, KY).

Lipset, Seymour Martin. 1959. "Some Social Requisites of Democracy: Economic Development and Political Legitimacy." *American Political Science Review* 53 (1): 69–108.

Mancuso, Maureen. 1993. "Ethical Attitudes of British MPs." *Parliamentary Affairs* 46 (2, April): 179–91.

NDI (National Democratic Institute for International Affairs). 1999. "Legislative Ethics: A Comparative Analysis." Research Paper 4, NDI, Washington, DC.

Pelizzo, Riccardo, and Rick Stapenhurst. 2004. "Legislative Ethics and Codes of Conduct." Working Paper 37237, World Bank Institute, Washington, DC.

Skelcher, Chris, and Stephanie Snape. 2001. "Ethics and Local Councilors: Modernising Standards of Conduct." *Parliamentary Affairs* 54 (1): 72–78.

Zimmerman, Joseph. 1994. *Curbing Unethical Behavior in Government*. 17–46. London: Greenwood Press.

Case Study of the House of Commons: How Can Parliamentary Codes and Registers of Members' Interests Help?

Sir Philip Mawer

Introduction

In a democratic system, parliament plays a vital role in a nation's life. It is therefore important to ensure a parliament whose Members are held in high esteem by the public they serve. Sustaining high standards of conduct among Members is a key part of encouraging that confidence in parliament that is essential to the health of a democracy and the effectiveness of a system of government.

Over the years, the United Kingdom (U.K.) House of Commons has evolved and developed a system for encouraging the maintenance of high standards among its Members. The system is intended to ensure accountability through openness and transparency. It emphasizes prevention and the fair and impartial resolution of complaints.

This paper examines the system for ensuring accountability in the House of Commons. Although the House passed a resolution as long ago as 1695 declaring bribery of Members of Parliament (MPs) a "high crime and misdemeanor," the arrangements for encouraging high standards have been much strengthened since the mid-1990s. Following a series of allegations against Members, a new Parliamentary Code of Conduct and enhanced rules on registering Members' interests were approved. These represented a significant step forward in making explicit the standards expected of Members and making Members' interests transparent.

Recent independent review has found that the system for regulating standards in the House of Commons is generally effective and that the overwhelming majority of Members seek to, and in practice do, uphold high standards of propriety.

Context

As mentioned above, the House of Commons recognized, more than three centuries ago, that bribery of its Members was wrong. Beyond that, though, the predominant assumption in the House until recently was that Members were gentlemen (they were predominantly men) and that they could be relied on to observe the normal standards of the day of decent behavior. To the extent that they were found wanting, the ultimate remedy for the most part lay in the ballot box—with the risk that a Member who erred would not gain reelection.

This approach is buttressed by the limited extent of individual legal privilege attached to being a member of either House of the U.K. Parliament. For the Commons, this essentially extends only to things said or done during proceedings in the House. So a member is protected from, for example, defamation proceedings for anything he or she says in the House. But unlike in some other parliaments, a Member does not enjoy a general immunity from civil or criminal proceedings.

However, complaints of breaches of privilege or of expected standards continue to be regulated by the respective House rather than the courts. Parliament has resisted—and continues strongly to resist—any intrusion by the courts into its own internal processes. This is essentially on the grounds that a sovereign parliament must retain jurisdiction over its own affairs.

Much of the recent debate in the United Kingdom around these issues has concerned the question of whether regulation of these matters by Parliament alone can continue and, if not, what should replace it.

Development of the Present Arrangements

The impetus for the existing regulatory framework in the Commons for policing Members' conduct came from a succession of scandals that broke over the past 30 years. In 1975, for example, the first Register of Members' Interests was created following the Poulson case, in which several members were criticized, and one left the House, over nondeclaration of pecuniary and other benefits.

Rules regarding the registration of MPs' interests subsequently developed gradually through experience and were codified. They were first published in 1992.

The arrangements were further developed in the mid-1990s following a series of allegations against MPs of

- persistent failure to register benefits in cash or in kind and
- tabling questions to government ministers in return for payment.

The then Prime Minister, John Major, established a Committee on Standards in Public Life, which reported in May 1995. It recommended

- a new Code of Conduct for MPs;
- a more informative and detailed Register of Members' Interests; and
- the appointment of an independent Parliamentary Commissioner for Standards, who would maintain the Register and investigate allegations of misconduct by MPs.

These recommendations were refined by a specially constituted Select Committee of the House of Commons. The Select Committee also recommended new arrangements for institutional oversight, involving setting up a Committee on Standards and Privileges, the functions of which would include consideration of complaints against Members and advice to the House on conduct matters.

Key Elements in the Present Arrangements

(1) The Parliamentary Commissioner for Standards

The Parliamentary Commissioner for Standards (the Commissioner) is the independent element in the system for regulation of standards in the House of Commons. The role of the Commissioner is to advise the House and individual Members on matters of conduct; to oversee the maintenance of the Register of Members' Interests (and of other registers covering parliamentary journalists, Members' staff, and all-party parliamentary groups); and to receive, and if he or she thinks fit, investigate complaints against Members for breaches of the Code and Rules. The Commissioner reports on complaints and other aspects of his or her work to the Committee on Standards and Privileges (see below).

The Commissioner is expected to act independently and impartially. He or she is appointed by resolution of the House for a five-year, nonrenewable term.

Much of the emphasis of both the Commissioner and the Committee in recent years has been on trying to prevent problems before they arise. This is being done through providing written guidance and advice to Members, arranging talks and workshops, and providing confidential advice to individual Members. It is hoped that by doing so, standards of compliance will be enhanced, and the scope for complaints reduced in consequence.

(2) The Committee on Standards and Privileges

The Committee oversees the work of the Commissioner. It advises the House on changes to the Code and the Rules on registering interests. It also adjudicates in cases where the Commissioner has reported to it on a complaint and advises the House if it thinks a penalty appropriate.

The Committee is made up of 10 back-bench Members of the House (not government ministers). Unusually, to emphasize the House's wish to approach these matters in a nonpartisan way, the membership of the Committee is drawn equally from the government and opposition parties. It is chaired by a senior opposition back-bench Member.

(3) The Code of Conduct

The Code of Conduct for Members was first approved by the House on July 24, 1996. It was recently reviewed, and an amended version was adopted by the House on July 13, 2005.

The purpose of the Code of Conduct is described as follows:

> To assist members in the discharge of their obligations to the House, their constituents and the public at large by:
> a) Providing guidance on the standards of conduct expected of Members in discharging their parliamentary and public duties, and in so doing
> b) Providing the openness and accountability necessary to reinforce public confidence in the way in which Members perform those duties.

The Code applies to Members in all aspects of their public life. It does not seek to regulate what Members do in their purely private and personal lives.

In summary, the Code requires Members to

- uphold the law and the constitution;
- act always in the public (not their personal) interest and to resolve at once any conflict between the two in favor of the former;
- strengthen confidence in Parliament, not bring it into disrepute;

- observe the seven principles of public life, as set out in the first report of the Committee on Standards in Public Life;
- never accept a bribe, act as a paid advocate, or misuse allowances and other payments;
- observe the House's rules (for example, regarding the registration or declaration of interests).

The provisions of the Code are cast in wide terms. They state broad principles. It is the task of the Commissioner and of the Committee on Standards and Privileges to interpret and apply them in individual cases.

Although many complaints against Members were initially about paid advocacy, in recent years most have concerned either alleged failures to declare or register interests, or the alleged abuse of allowances paid to Members.

(4) The Register of Members' Interests

The Rules on registration and declaration of interest that underpin the Code have been developed over the years by resolutions of the House. The main purpose of the Register of Members' Interests is "to provide information of any pecuniary interest or other material benefit which a Member receives which might reasonably be thought by others to influence his or her actions, speeches or votes in Parliament, or actions taken in his or her capacity as a Member of Parliament."

The registration form specifies 10 categories of registerable interests. These include directorships; other forms of remunerated employment; sponsorships; gifts, benefits, and hospitality; overseas visits; overseas benefits and gifts; land and property; and shareholdings. Apart from the specific rules, there is a more general obligation upon members to keep the overall definition of the Register's purpose in mind when registering their interests.

The purpose of registration is openness, to give other Members and the public an opportunity to know about interests that may reasonably be thought likely to influence a Member's actions in his or her parliamentary capacity, and to make their own assessment of their significance. Registration of an interest does not imply any wrongdoing.

The Register is compiled afresh at the start of every Parliament or, as in 2002, following a major revision of the Rules. One bound, printed edition is published every year, and the text is also available on the House of Commons Web site at www.parliament.uk. In addition, the Register is updated every six to eight weeks to include fresh information supplied by Members. The text of the updated editions is also published on the Web site, and is available, by appointment, for inspection in hardcopy form.

How Complaints Are Handled

Complaints may be lodged by other MPs or members of the public, including members of the press. Any allegation that a Member's conduct is incompatible with the Code or Guide to the Rules on registration of interests must be submitted to the Parliamentary Commissioner in writing and signed.

A number of would-be complainants make initial contact through e-mail. A complaint must be sufficiently supported by evidence to warrant at least preliminary inquiry. If so, they are advised to write, forwarding their evidence so that their complaint can be considered.

On receiving a complaint, the Commissioner decides whether it does in fact fall within his or her terms of reference. Many fall outside the scope of the regulatory framework (for example, because they concern how an MP has handled a constituent's case or the complainant is simply taking issue with something the Member has said).

Complaints about the actions of a Member who is a minister, where those actions are taken purely in his or her ministerial capacity, also fall outside the Commissioner's remit. These are matters for the Prime Minister.

If a complaint involves an allegation of criminal activity, the Commissioner will encourage the complainant to refer the matter to the police or, if appropriate, make such a reference himself.

If the Commissioner is satisfied that the complaint is within his or her terms of reference and that there is enough evidence to merit at least a preliminary enquiry, he or she will refer the matter to the Member concerned for his or her response.

In the light of that response, it may be clear that there is no prima facie case, in which event the Commissioner will dismiss the complaint and inform the Member, the complainant, and the Committee on Standards and Privileges accordingly.

If, however, the complaint does seem to merit further investigation, the Commissioner conducts an enquiry. Although the Commissioner has no formal investigative powers, this is less of a problem than it would appear in practice because the Committee on Standards and Privileges has made clear that it expects Members to cooperate fully with the Commissioner and the Committee itself has power to send for persons, papers, and records and to order Members or others to appear before it. Indeed, failure by a Member to cooperate with an investigation is itself a breach of the Code.

In conducting an enquiry, the Commissioner seeks to be fair and impartial throughout. For example, the Commissioner shares the draft of his or her findings of fact with the Member concerned to take into account any comments the Member may make before finalizing his or her report to the Committee on Standards and Privileges.

At the conclusion of the investigation, the Commissioner reports the outcome to the Committee, including his or her view as to whether the complaint is substantiated.

The Committee considers the report and may agree or disagree with the Commissioner's conclusion. It also considers what penalty, if any, to recommend that the House impose. The Committee makes a published report to the House, to which is attached the Commissioner's report to the Committee of his or her investigation.

The Committee may indicate in its report that the Member concerned should apologize in public, on the Floor of the House, for his or her actions. Whether it does so or not, it may recommend further action to the House, if necessary. The House as a whole must approve that action, with or without modification, which may include

- a formal reprimand by the House,
- forfeiture of the Member's salary for a specified period,
- the suspension of the Member concerned from membership of the House for a specified period (which also involves loss of salary for that period), or
- expulsion of the Member.

Independent Review

The whole system for regulating standards of conduct in Parliament has been scrutinized twice by the independent Committee on Standards in Public Life since it was first established.

On the last occasion in 2002, the Committee found the fundamental structure of the system to be sound, but made a number of recommendations for strengthening the arrangements further. The House of Commons accepted virtually all of these recommendations which have since been implemented.

Lessons from the House of Commons Experience

How then does experience in the House of Commons suggest that parliamentary codes of conduct and registers of members' interests can help in the fight against corruption?

Essentially, they provide a framework within which Members and the public can know what behavior is expected of Members of Parliament. They can serve as a means of encouraging the observance of high standards and of helping to develop a culture of compliance.

They reflect an insistence on openness and accountability in the conduct of public affairs. In themselves, however, they are not enough. They should be accompanied by proactive systems for offering advice and guidance, and by effective means of enforcement that include an independent element. It is no good having codes and registers in place if these are merely fig leaves disguising unacceptable behavior.

Do codes of conduct and registers of members' interests—at least as we know them in the House of Commons' context—work?

Of course, in one sense we can never know whether they work because we cannot know how many instances of misconduct they have prevented or how many instances of misconduct have occurred but never come to light because they have not been the subject of complaints.

We do know in the U.K. context, however, that the climate in Parliament has altered radically since the present arrangements were introduced in 1995. The House of Commons is no longer seen as a "hiring fair," and there have been no recent generalized allegations that Members were engaging in paid advocacy or lobbying for reward on behalf of outside interests. The number of Members registering an arrangement as a paid parliamentary consultant has dropped dramatically. Codes of conduct have also been introduced by the three devolved U.K. assemblies: the Scottish Parliament, the Welsh Assembly, and the Northern Ireland Assembly.

While allegations of "sleaze" in public life occasionally resurface, recent research by the Committee on Standards in Public Life has indicated that public concern appears to have shifted from "sleaze" (that is, allegations of minor impropriety) to "spin" (that is, concerns about whether government is being entirely honest with citizens).

The general view would still be that expressed in 1995 in the first report of the Committee on Standards in Public Life: "We believe that the great majority of men and women in British public life are honest and hard working, and observe high ethical standards."

This view was reinforced in the Committee's Sixth Report, which noted the generally very high standards in the United Kingdom. And in its Eighth Report, in 2002, the Committee stated: "We endorse the view that standards in the House of Commons are generally high, and that the overwhelming majority of Members seek to, and in practice do, uphold high standards of propriety."

Conclusion

Issues of standards and accountability are complex, and it would be unrealistic to expect parliamentary codes of conduct and so forth alone to resolve them effectively. They can only ever be part of a solution, which must depend at least as much on encouraging the right attitudes about ethical behavior in society as a whole.

However, the experience of the House of Commons shows that a clear statement of what we expect of MPs, effectively and independently policed and firmly enforced by the House itself, can play a useful part in helping establish and maintain that public confidence in parliamentary institutions that is vital to the well-being of parliamentary democracy itself and therefore of our society.

Part VI
International Parliamentary Links

14

Building Parliamentary Networks

John Williams

In today's global environment, corruption is not confined within national borders—it crosses regions and the globe. In recognition of this, many international organizations are introducing programs and conventions to address corruption's international nature—such as the United Nations Convention against Corruption (2003).[1]

Any network or organization that seeks to be successful must have a clear vision of why it exists and what it is trying to accomplish. This is true not only for parliamentary organizations or networks but also for anyone who is attempting to bring people together in any grouping. Those who are successful in bringing people with competing issues and agendas together and build the largest coalition—whether it be a small group or a parliamentary network—are often the most successful.

Nowadays, the information and tools required to stem corruption and bribery in international business transactions and in international money laundering are often available only through regional and international cooperation. As such, the need to share information and cooperate across borders has increased, and the ability to network has also become more important—especially for parliamentarians.

This paper will briefly examine the different typologies of networking and knowledge sharing available, including that of networks specifically intended for parliamentarians and their needs. Two examples of parliamentary networks will be discussed—the Global Organization of Parliamentarians Against Corruption (GOPAC) and the Parliamentary Network on the World Bank (PNoWB)—and this paper will conclude with a discussion of the lessons learned in building effective parliamentary networks.

Evolving Forms of Networking and Knowledge Sharing

To understand parliamentary networks, it is necessary to place them within the current discourse on networking. As the number of networks has increased in recent years, so has the number of ways to describe them. There are knowledge networks, communities of practice, global public policy networks, advocacy networks, and parliamentary networks—to name but a few.

---

[1] Its preamble states that ". . . corruption is no longer a local matter but a transnational phenomenon that affects all societies and economies, making international cooperation to prevent and control it essential."

The International Institute for Sustainable Development defines *network* as "... a combination of persons (or organizations) usually dispersed over a number of geographically separate sites, with appropriate communications technology to link them."[2] A *knowledge network*, however, comprises a "... group of expert institutions working together on a common concern—strengthening each other's research and communications capacity, sharing knowledge bases, and developing solutions that meet the needs of target decision makers at the national and international levels" (Creech and Willard 2001, 15).

Communities of practice are "groups of people who share a concern, a set of problems, or a passion about a topic, and who deepen their knowledge and expertise in this area by interacting on an ongoing basis" (Tam 2002, 1). Participation is voluntary, and interactions are unstructured. Leadership tends to emerge from within, rather than being appointed. Communities of practice complement existing structures by promoting collaboration, information exchange, and sharing of best practices across boundaries of time, distance, and organizational hierarchies.

Global public policy networks create a transnational public discourse around policy issues that require a global approach (Benner, Witte, and Reinicke 2003). In many cases, networks that perform functions other than advocacy start in a similar fashion (that is, by placing issues prominently on the global agenda) before moving on to the other phases of the policy cycle. The transnational linkages formed during the advocacy process will likely assist these networks as they move toward implementing policy solutions.

Finally, *advocacy networks* are groups of individuals or organizations (or both) working together with a common goal of achieving change in policies, laws, or programs for a particular advocacy issue.

The difference between these network types lies with membership and ultimate purpose. While knowledge networks tend to identify groups or institutions as their membership, communities of practice and advocacy networks are more open in that they welcome both individuals and organizations. In ultimate purpose, knowledge networks and global public policy networks seek to find and share solutions among their members, while communities of practice and advocacy networks are more concerned with the process of sharing information, rather than a specific outcome. What remains common among them, however, is the networks' interest in sharing knowledge and expertise and the belief that the collective is more powerful than the individual.

Given this as an understanding, how can we define parliamentary networks? Can they be considered one of the network types discussed, or are they deserving of their own category?

Most parliamentary networks are best described as one type of global public policy network, albeit a powerful one. They typically are transnationally based and formed around a common policy issue that requires a global approach (for example, corruption, as with GOPAC). Members advocate for placing issues on the global agenda and share information and knowledge to seek out and implement policy solutions.

What Are the Roles of a Parliamentarian?

Before one can explore the nature of parliamentary networks, one must understand the fundamental responsibilities of a parliamentarian. It is clear that these responsibilities are universal, no matter which parliament one may be a Member of.

---

[2] www.iisd.org/networks/research.asp.

Essentially, a parliament has four fundamental responsibilities in the exercise of the oversight of government:

- To debate, modify, approve, or reject legislation
- To debate, modify, approve, or reject authority for government to raise revenues through taxation and other means
- To debate, modify, approve, or reject proposed expenditures by government
- To hold the executive accountable for its governance of society

Unfortunately, in many cases, parliamentarians believe that their role is to support the government at any cost if they are a member of a governing party or to oppose the government at all costs, regardless of the merits of the government's proposals.

In a properly functioning democracy, a government is accountable to the parliament as a whole, where the members bring a diversity of opinion to the debate, but are still required to exercise their considered judgment on the proposals by government and the performance of government.

Why Parliamentary Networks?

Parliamentary networks tap into a rich resource—parliamentarians—who are in a position to gain access to centers of power and to influence other nations where civil society organizations cannot (Andreychuck and Jennings 2003, 14). These networks often provide an outlet to parliamentarians for involvement in issues from which they have been excluded (for example, initiatives against corruption, WTO processes, and international aid). Because they are elected, parliamentarians have a moral authority and a legitimacy that give weight to their interventions and involvement (Parliament of Canada 2002). Parliamentarians are the ones who have been chosen by their citizens to represent their views and to demand accountability from governments who theoretically report to parliament.

Anyone who has been a parliamentarian or worked with parliamentarians knows the vast number of international boards, groups, and organizations that exist. Numerous groups and associations of parliamentarians deal with a divergent number of issues, from developing world debt relief, to environmental change and control, to issues of agriculture and agri-food.

Dilys Cossey, Manager of the Parliamentary Project of the International Planned Parenthood Foundation's European Network, argues that parliamentarians are effective communicators who have the ability to attract publicity. Their opinions are actively sought; thus, if parliamentarians from different parties or countries " . . . sing from the same hymn book, it makes a greater impact than the opinion of one politician" (Cossey 2000).

In sum, the creation of a network involving parliamentarians can have a number of advantages:

- Joint value creation among the group: developing new insights through the interaction of different perspectives and approaches
- Fostering change in policies and practices
- Capacity development for all members[3]

---

[3] www.iisd.org/networks/.

From the perspective of decision makers, parliamentary networks allow them to interact with their peers and can simplify the task of seeking reliable information and advice. For those with expertise in a certain field of public policy, it provides an opportunity to develop or further extend their international involvement in that field (Andreychuck and Jennings 2003, 16). Because party lines and the short-term need to win elections can be an impediment to true debate and consideration of the long-term global issues in a national parliament, parliamentary networks can provide the opportunity to explore issues in greater detail over an extended period of time. However, at the heart of these networks are people working together.

Networking around an issue such as corruption has the added benefit of giving its participants a global and regional voice. Such a voice, plus association with like-minded colleagues in other countries, can be particularly comforting when carrying out the often lonely fight against corruption in countries where a corrupt executive dominates parliament. Parliamentarians may additionally draw ideas from other countries and avoid the pitfalls that others have experienced by sharing information and lessons learned with their peers.

Parliamentary associations such as the Inter-Parliamentary Union (IPU), Commonwealth Parliamentary Association (CPA), and La Francophonie have been in operation for many years, providing an opportunity for parliamentarians to gather and discuss matters of common interest. Over the years, these mainstream associations have also provided important technical assistance to many young parliaments (for instance, by sending experienced parliamentary staff to assist newer legislatures in organizing their legislative support services).

In most of these cases, however, networking has been on an institutional basis: members are selected as representatives of their national parliaments. A key implication of such membership is that either the political head of parliament or the party leaders ultimately select actual members for participation in interparliamentary meetings. This tends to reduce both continuity and commitment on the part of participants. Moreover, it can be interpreted as a reward for other services rendered—thus the objective of the process of selection often can be something other than the policy purpose of the network (Ulrich 2004). For example, where parliamentary leadership is dominated by a corrupt executive, such a selection process for representatives on an anti-corruption network can have the effect of undermining the purpose of the network.

The danger of an executive-dominated selection process—and its consequent impact on a network—is greatest with single-purpose networks. And it is single-purpose or "focused" networks that are now emerging to complement the better-known multipurpose networks such as the IPU. Examples of such networks include Parliamentarians for Global Action (www.pgaction.org), the Parliamentary Network on the World Bank (www.pnowb.org), the Parliamentary Forum for the New Partnership for Africa's Development (NEPAD) (http://www.parlanepad.org/), and the Parliamentary Network for Nuclear Disarmament (http://www.gsinstitute.org/pnnd/).

Participation in policy-focused networks is most obviously effective if it includes those parliamentarians with an interest and commitment to the policy focus. Where continuity of membership is important, such as where policy issues are being examined or an active program of work is being pursued, individual membership is simply more effective. However, these organizations can suffer from a different kind of discontinuity as the result of elections. Establishing active country and regional chapters can mitigate such risk.

Example One: Global Organization of Parliamentarians Against Corruption (GOPAC)

GOPAC is a network focused on the single purpose of fighting and preventing corruption through strengthening integrity in governance. Comprising parliaments, parliamentarians, and former parliamentarians from countries around the world, GOPAC is a network that aims to provide information, tools, and relevant training to its membership and endeavors to support and counsel members in their personal initiatives in fighting corruption. Established in Ottawa at a global conference held at the Parliament of Canada in 2002, GOPAC is managed by an internationally representative board of directors and executive committee.

The GOPAC Global Secretariat, based in Ottawa, Canada, serves as an international point of contact, while each regional chapter is also represented by its own secretariat. National chapters of GOPAC work with the regions and the Global Secretariat toward improving integrity in parliament. GOPAC chapters exist in all regions of the world.

Conceptually, GOPAC perceives its work as being organized into three fundamental concepts: peer support, education, and goal-oriented results. In the past two years, the work of GOPAC, its regional and national chapters, and its membership have led to significant areas of impact throughout the globe in all three of these areas:

- *Peer Support.* GOPAC members, through either their regional/national chapters or the Global Secretariat, have worked together to share information and lessons learned and to provide support for their colleagues around the world. Members have frequently traveled outside of their countries to provide support to nascent chapters overseas—as in the case of the Latin America Chapter's travel to Africa and the African Parliamentarians' Network Against Corruption (APNAC) Chair's travel to other African nations—to provide encouragement to their colleagues in developing their own anti-corruption networks.

GOPAC has also been useful in providing support to colleagues facing a strong executive, as in the case with a parliamentarian from Mozambique who received support in the form of friendship and information sharing from her colleagues in Mexico.

- *Shared Learning.* Sharing lessons learned and best practices among the membership and to the larger community has also been an area of focus for the organization. The GOPAC Global Secretariat aims to keep communication channels open through the sharing of information, using the GOPAC Web site (http://www.parlcent.ca/gopac/index_e.php); the parliamentarian's handbook; the GOPAC CD-ROM (as developed with the World Bank Institute), the *GOPAC Newsletter*; and event reports, papers, and documentation. All of the information tools are shared with the GOPAC membership, GOPAC chapters, and have also been distributed to parliaments and civil society organizations such as Transparency International (TI). Also, all information tools have been reviewed and approved by the GOPAC Board of Directors to ensure their relevance to a parliamentary audience.

The majority of the information produced by GOPAC is for the purpose of education and training in good governance and anti-corruption issues. The ultimate purpose is to develop in its members expertise in a variety of areas relating to issues of good governance and to strengthen their capacity to effectively seek solutions.

- *Results.* Although only two years in existence, GOPAC has delivered some preliminary results[4] in the form of legitimacy to reformers (discussed below), establishing relationships with like-minded organizations, and the shared learning described above.

GOPAC members in Kenya, before the 2003 election, were mostly opposition members working against the corrupt Moi regime. The 2003 general election results for the APNAC members were, in some respect, linked to the legitimacy and respect the citizenry had for the organization. Of the 21 original members of the APNAC-Kenya chapter of GOPAC, eight were appointed to the new government's cabinet—including both the current Chair, Musikari Kombo, who is the current Minister of Local Government, and the Deputy Environment Minister—and Nobel Peace Prize winner—Wangari Maathai.

GOPAC and its chapters have also established solid relationships with other like-minded organizations. The Australasian, Kenyan, Middle East/North African, and South Asian chapters founded their secretariats within TI's local offices. In the case of the Latin American chapter, it signed a cooperation agreement with the Organization of American States (OAS) to work together on anti-corruption activities in the region, and the chapter also receives support from the Latin American Parliament (PARLATINO) in the form of office space and human resources.

In addition to those discussed above, the organization has established relationships with the United Nations Development Programme (UNDP), the International Compliance Association, the Latin American Financial Intelligence Council, the Commonwealth Parliamentary Association, GRECO, the Stability Pact, the Westminster Foundation, and the International Association of Business and Parliament.

Effective Parliamentary Networks: GOPAC's Experience

Since its creation, GOPAC has expanded its field of knowledge in regard to networking among parliamentarians—much of which is included in the Lessons Learned section below. The majority of what GOPAC has learned has been in the area of partnering with individual parliamentarians based in varying geographical locations, with different languages, cultures, and political structures. As stated in Creech and Willard (2001, 2), 98 percent of the work in networks is in managing relationships.

GOPAC has found that the organization has benefited from being focused on a single, yet universal, issue around which it can coordinate its members and activities. The universality of the experience of corruption has, in a sense, created a common language among GOPAC members that has allowed them to connect despite their differences.

Other lessons learned by GOPAC include the need for providing consistent and concise information to the membership, which ensures that members are engaged and have a sense of ownership over the agenda. The high value of e-communications

---

[4] This, in addition to a membership that continues to grow in all regions of the world, as well as the creation of new regional/national chapters.

can only be enhanced by periodic face-to-face meetings, an understandable and accessible reporting structure, and resources to carry out all of the above.

Example Two: Parliamentary Network on the World Bank

The Parliamentary Network on the World Bank (PNoWB, or the Network) was created with the aim of engaging the parliaments of the world in the global discourse on development and increasing the influence that parliamentarians can wield in relation to issues of development cooperation. With more than 400 members in 90 countries of the world, PNoWB members come from World Bank Member States; however, they represent themselves and their constituents—not their parliaments, governments, or countries. Legally independent from the World Bank, PNoWB is a nonprofit and nonpartisan organization incorporated under French law.

The mission of PNoWB follows the guiding principles of accountability, advocacy, networking, partnerships, and progress review:

- *Accountability.* To facilitate and encourage direct dialogue between parliamentarians and multilateral development institutions to promote greater transparency of policies and practices, in particular of the World Bank, and to also encourage collective accountability
- *Advocacy.* To provide the PNoWB members with a platform for coordinated parliamentary advocacy on international development issues
- *Networking.* To encourage concerted action, early debate, and exchange of information among parliamentarians on major issues of international development, finance, and poverty eradication
- *Partnerships.* To take initiatives to further cooperate and encourage partnerships among parliamentarians and policy makers, the academic community, the business sector, and nongovernmental organizations on development issues
- *Progress Review.* To promote the development of parliamentary mechanisms and practices for the effective democratic control of development assistance in all its phases

PNoWB conducts a number of activities at the international and national levels. At least once a year, the Network organizes a major international conference, while its regional chapters (East Africa, India, and the Middle East) further PNoWB's mission to increase accountability and transparency in international development while maintaining their own regionally sensitive agendas.

PNoWB also facilitates field trips for parliamentarians from donor countries to visit projects in developing countries. At the same time, the Network organizes visits from parliamentarians from developing countries to parliaments in countries with well-established democratic traditions. The organization engages in consultations with the World Bank and other international financial institutions on their respective projects, programs, and research activities. Finally, its members dedicate time to working groups (such as the HIV/AIDS working group, the Parliamentarians Implementation Watch on the Millennium Development Goals, and a trade working group).

In both of these case studies, we have observed that while the parliamentary network may not have the technical expertise that bodies such as TI or the World Bank do, they do have the ability to bring parliamentarians from every corner of the globe together on issues of shared interest and importance. This allows the parliamentary network to partner with an organization that possesses technical knowledge to work together on bringing attention to a larger issue.

Organizations that do possess technical knowledge and information are often unable to communicate their point to parliamentarians because they often attempt to communicate "to" parliamentarians, instead of "with" parliamentarians at a shared level of communication. Therefore, parliamentarians are often more open and willing to accept and share a message that is communicated in a collaborative manner.

We must return to the roles of a parliamentarian—essentially, the ability to hold government accountable for its programs and spending and the role of oversight and accountability. A democratic government must answer for its decisions in parliament, and it may only carry out its program once parliament grants its approval.

Similarly, a democratic government must also answer for not carrying out initiatives, and this is where parliamentary networks can be most effective. For example, governments that fail to ratify international conventions may be held to account by parliamentarians for their failure to sign. Parliamentarians speaking on their own in a given country may not have much success in bringing public attention to the issue, but the assistance of a parliamentary network (that is, peer support) may give the parliamentarians the support they need to bring attention to the issue and to hold their government to account.

Lessons Learned

Based on the study of other networks, the experiences of the founding members of GOPAC and the PNoWB, and the research completed by the International Institute for Sustainable Development (www.iisd.org), nine guiding principles exist regarding parliamentary networks:

1. *Focus.* Deepening the exchange of information and analysis in one area enables parliamentarians to play a more influential role than with superficial exchanges on several topics. A focused network committed to demonstrable results is likely to attract members dedicated to action and results.
2. *Leadership.* Establishing effective networks requires a single individual who is able to attract a representative core team to give it direction and engage a strong network of parliamentarians. Leadership is the ability both to articulate a broadly shared vision and to enable colleagues to more effectively deliver on that vision in a way that engages all members. Without such leadership, a network is more likely to die out after a few initial exchanges.
3. *Results.* Although interesting deliberations and formulating well-articulated resolutions can be satisfying activities for networks, actual delivery of practical results—things that affect the well-being of people—is the greater motivator.
4. *Access to Appropriate Support.* Networks of parliamentarians can best deliver results if they have access to effective secretariat and expert services. Expert services are needed to ensure that the political leadership is informed by expertise in the policy substance. Secretariat services are those that ensure effective deliberation and decision making on one hand and effective implementation on the other. Organizational management skills are also essential

for building and maintaining networks because they need structure, work-plans, timelines, and deliverables (Creech and Willard 2001, 23).

5. *Alliances.* The objectives of any policy-oriented parliamentary network will likely complement well the objectives of other organizations. Forming alliances with such organizations allows resources to be leveraged and, more important, possibilities to be expanded.

6. *E-Deliberation.* While deliberating through information technology networks has not yet replaced the need for face-to-face deliberation, it can become an essential complement and save on the time and cost of travel. Use of information technology also reduces the time and cost of access to resources in the development of plans, written products, and declarations.

7. *Scheduling.* IISD suggests to keep in mind the following when relying on online communication technology for communications and e-deliberation: longer time schedules when operating in a language in which all participants may not be comfortable, regional holidays and seasons, and adding the use of teleconferencing to add information richness that maintains stronger relationships at the core of the network (Willard 2001).

8. *Resources.* Multiple sources of resources reduce the risk of becoming an agent of another organization's interests. Sustainable funding affords an organization the luxury of devoting fewer resources to the search for funding. On the other hand, the search for funding can help ensure responsiveness to contemporary interests.

9. *Continuity.* Parliamentary networks are particularly vulnerable in view of the generally short career offered by elected office. Each of the foregoing factors can contribute to continuity. Clarity of focus (and results), committed partners, multiple funders, access to secretariat and professional staff, and the access and use of technology ensure a network a continuing stream of participants.

It is clear that in an increasingly interconnected world, the ability of people to network and coalesce around certain issues is extremely valuable. Those parliamentary networks that are able to overcome the challenges of working around the world (and the lessons learned, as listed earlier) will have the ability to grow and become useful tools in promoting certain policy issues. They are useful to allow parliamentarians to acquire the knowledge and ability to speak and act forcefully on issues of importance and shared interest.

However, those networks that are unable to meet the challenges presented to them, are unable to focus on delivering results (as opposed to talking about results), and have a diffuse area of focus (or an unclear mandate/mission statement) will fall into disuse and eventually wither away. There are many examples of groups that have failed, even after receiving grants and contributions of funds from various sources, including governments. Unfortunately, because of the pitfalls that these groups encounter, often these funds have been squandered and lost. It is hoped that the discussion of lessons learned in this paper will minimize this in the future.

There have been many groups that have come together, with grand-sounding mission statements, but were unable to deliver results, and have come and gone with little or no impact. It is the challenge of those involved with parliamentary networks to ensure that these organizations grow at an appropriate rate, to have clear goals to achieve, and to meet those goals and deliver results. After all, parliamentarians exist to serve those who elect them, and if they fail at achieving results, then they fail their electors and their citizens.

Bibliography

Andreychuck, Raynell, and Marlene Jennings. 2003. *Globalization and Governance: Contemplating the Global.* Ottawa: The Library of Parliament (December).

Benner, Thorsten, Jan Martin Witte, and Wolfgang H. Reinicke. 2003. "Global Public Policy Networks: Lessons Learned and Challenges Ahead." *Brookings Review* 21 (2, Spring): 18–21. http://www.brookings.edu/press/review/spring2003/benner.htm.

Canada, Parliament of. 2002. "Parliamentary Diplomacy: The Emerging Role of Parliamentarians in Diplomacy." Symposium on Parliamentary Diplomacy, April 29. Parliamentary Research Branch, Library of Canada, Ottawa. www.parl.gc.ca/information/InterParl/Associations/Francophonie/April2002/Report-e/cover-e.htm.

Cossey, Dilys. 2000. "Advocacy with Parliamentarians in Europe." *Choices* 28 (1). www.iisd.org/networks/.

Creech, Heather, and Terri Willard. 2001. *Strategic Intentions: Managing Knowledge Networks for Sustainable Development.* Winnipeg: International Institute for Sustainable Development.

Tam, Vicky Carpio. 2002. "Assessing the Value of Communities of Practice: Summary of Findings." Excerpt from MBA thesis, Simon Fraser University, Burnaby, British Columbia, Canada, sent to Canadian government agencies (September). http://www.km4dev.org/index.php/articles/downloads/241.

Ulrich, Martin. 2004. *Effective Interparliamentary Networks: Observations and Examples.* Ottawa: Parliamentary Centre.

UN (United Nations). 2003. "United Nations Convention against Corruption." UN Office on Drugs and Crime, Vienna. http://www.unodc.org/pdf/crime/convention_corruption/signing/Convention-e.pdf.

Willard, Terri. 2001. *Helping Knowledge Networks Work.* Winnipeg: International Institute for Sustainable Development.

Afterword

Denis Marshall

The consequences of ignoring or tolerating corruption are described in depth in this volume; but, in summary, corruption is a clear threat to development, democracy, and international security. It distorts economic development and subverts political decision making, stunting growth and creating political instability. Corruption is closely linked to failing public institutions and failed policies, undermining the legitimacy of governments. It drains national finances, acting as a major disincentive to serious foreign investment, as well as destroying the work ethic of citizens. Corruption can have a profoundly negative impact on patriotism and commitment to the national goals and ideals. But, above all, it deepens poverty. These factors combined show why combating corruption is an issue for both Commonwealth and non-Commonwealth parliaments and parliamentarians alike.

A Commonwealth Perspective

The communiqué[1] from the Commonwealth Heads of Government meeting in Malta (November 2005) includes the following paragraph on corruption:

> Heads of Government reiterated their commitment to root out, both at national and international levels, systemic corruption, including extortion and bribery, which undermine good governance, respect for human rights and economic development. They acknowledged that comprehensive preventative measures, including institutionalising transparency, accountability and good governance, combined with effective enforcement, are the most effective means to combat corruption.

The majority of Commonwealth citizens live on incomes of approximately US$2 per day, and they especially deserve the best from the nation's finances. Sadly, the latest Corruption Perceptions Index (2005) from Transparency International (TI) shows that corruption is still rampant in many Commonwealth countries—including Bangladesh, Cameroon, Guyana, Kenya, Nigeria, Pakistan, Papua New Guinea, and Sierra Leone. On the positive side, Australia, Barbados, Botswana, Malta, New Zealand, Singapore, and the United Kingdom are ranked toward the top of the survey,[2] but the bulk of the population of the Commonwealth resides in countries at the bottom of the list.

Of course, corruption is not an issue solely for the developing world—in many developed countries, it has taken a long time for their system of government and

---

[1] The communiqué can be accessed at http://www.thecommonwealth.org/Templates/Internal.asp?NodeID=147565.
[2] www.transparency.org/cpi/2005/cpi2005_infocus.html.

parliament to become relatively free and clean. There are examples of both political and financial corruption in mature democracies: a judicial inquiry in Canada on a scheme to promote federalism in Quebec exposed corrupt mismanagement that resulted in the minority government losing a confidence vote in the House of Commons and an election on January 23, 2006. However, it is fair to conclude that good governance and leadership in developing countries is increasingly being judged by efforts to tackle corruption.

Wider International Cooperation

Globalization has been trumpeted as either the solution to a vast range of problems or an uncontrolled juggernaut threatening many of the world's poorest individuals and countries. There can be no doubt that it has heralded ever-faster financial transactions, and monitoring financial movements is one feature of tackling corruption. The OECD estimates that some $80 billion change hands worldwide every year through corruption, making it a question of global competitiveness as well as an internal issue.

A plethora of important international anti-corruption conventions have therefore been agreed on in the past few years, including the United Nations Convention against Corruption (UNCAC), the OECD Convention on Combating Bribery of Foreign Public Officials in International Business Transactions, and the African Union Convention on Preventing and Combating Corruption.[3] Commonwealth Heads of Government in Malta welcomed the imminent entry into force of the UNCAC and urged Member States that had not already done so to become parties to the Convention and to strengthen the fight against corruption by the adoption of principles and policies, as appropriate, that emphasize good governance, accountability, and transparency. For global initiatives to work, however, there must be implementation and scrutiny at home. Parliamentarians must hold their governments to account by urging ratification of these international conventions. Transparency, accountability, and good governance are the principles in the campaign for effective democratic—and ethical—government.

The Parliamentary Dimension

The end of the Cold War necessitated a shift from a bipolar emphasis on regime type to an emphasis on regime performance and multilateral cooperation. Increasingly, therefore, democracy is being measured not in terms of its *breadth,* but in its *depth.* Unfortunately, a number of democratic governments still have undemocratic practices. Within the Commonwealth Parliamentary Association (CPA), there is a greater focus on the need to provide substance to democratic values through the institution of parliament in the consolidation of democratic reforms.

Corruption is a parliamentary issue on two levels. First, parliamentarians everywhere must set an example and uphold high standards of propriety. Public coffers are not Members' or the government's personal funds to finance irresponsible spending. Lawmakers must be beyond reproach: "We can't demand standards of others that we are not prepared to live up to ourselves. Without 'clean hands,' what

---

[3] For an overview of the most influential anti-corruption conventions, see http://www.u4.no/themes/conventions/intro.cfm.

right do we have to question the actions of others? And what credibility do we have to pursue issues our electors care about?"[4] Respect for politicians and for political institutions is ultimately dependent on the collective ethical behavior of individual Members.

Second, Members are elected to improve the lives of the people who elected them. Of course, parliaments often lack the experienced Members and the financial and human resources necessary for them to do what they were elected to do; therefore, the work and initiatives of NGOs and multilateral organizations such as TI, the World Bank, and the OECD, as well as parliamentary organizations such as the CPA and GOPAC, are of great importance. One lesson learned from the World Bank Institute's work with parliamentarians is the importance of networks in developing capacity and improving effectiveness of parliaments and parliamentarians in developing countries.[5] By helping to establish, or working within, broad anti-corruption coalitions, parliamentarians can aid their own professional development and increase mutual understanding.

Political Will

One key message of this volume is that parliaments can play an indispensable role across many aspects of an anti-corruption strategy. Naturally, there must be political commitment at the highest level; malpractice at any level will undermine trust in the political system as a whole. However, leadership is a necessary but not sufficient condition for controlling corruption if for no other reason than that tackling corruption can unleash opposition to reform. President Olusegun Obasanjo has expressed a strong personal commitment to tackling systemic corruption in Nigeria, and the first bill that was passed into law after he was elected into office was *The Corrupt Practices and Other Related Offences Act*. Unfortunately, the problem of corruption in Nigeria is still present, and there has not been one high-level conviction during Obasanjo's term as president.[6] Sahr Kpundeh and Phyllis Dininio conclude in chapter 4 that political will, as it applies to combating corruption, is most effective when it "is institutionalized and not dependent on the personality and intentions of particular persons."

A robust system of checks and balances and strong political institutions are therefore critical not only to combating corruption and promoting good governance but also to restoring trust and confidence in democratic politics. In the past, anti-corruption efforts have tended to focus on the executive branch or on the oversight role of the legislative branch, but parliaments can play an indispensable role across many aspects of an anti-corruption strategy.

The four conceptual roles or functions of parliaments (legislative, oversight, financial, and representative) are discussed in more detail below to illustrate how

---

[4] Hon. David Kilgour, "The Responsibility to Act Against Corruption," speech given to the Transparency International Symposium, "Toward Effective Implementation of the OECD Anti-Bribery Convention," May 12, 2003.

[5] For a review of activities of several such networks worldwide at the individual, regional, and global levels that are making a difference in the ability of parliamentarians to address corruption in their countries, see Meaghan Campbell and Frederick Stapenhurst, "Developing Capacity through Networks: Lessons from Anticorruption Parliamentary Coalitions," Capacity Development Brief 10 (Washington, DC: World Bank Institute, January 2005).

[6] "The Fat of the Land," *The Economist*, October 29–November 4, 2005, pp. 69–70.

parliaments can become part of the solution. A wide range of options are available: from enacting and complying with ethics codes, conflict-of-interest rules, and financial disclosure laws to the disclosure of parliamentary votes, opening committee meetings to the media, and public hearings to taking part in parliamentary anti-corruption networks, workshops, and task forces and supporting diagnostic surveys and assessments.

Legislation

Parliaments can enact a range of legislation to help curb corruption (see box 1). First, corruption must be criminalized, but laws must be clear and unambiguous: too many rules, laws, and regulations can be counterproductive and even encourage corruption. In chapter 5 on Parliament and Anti-Corruption Legislation, Jeremy Pope says that the first question a lawmaker must ask is whether a new law is needed at all. He distinguishes between three categories of laws: laws that punish the corrupt, laws that contribute to an administrative and social environment in which corrupt acts are less likely to take place, and laws on areas in which corrupt actions would be likely to occur if the legislation is not "corruption-proofed."

Possession-of-unexplained-wealth laws can require individuals to establish the origins of wealth that is beyond the capacity of their known sources of income. This can lead to constitutional problems—in Zambia, for example, this type of provision was held to be unconstitutional because it infringed on the right of the individual against self-incrimination. The *Transparency International Source Book 2000* suggests that a better approach would be to make special legislative provisions that state that the court may draw conclusions "in the absence of a satisfactory explanation by the accused."[7] A publicly available register of Members' interests enables the assets of parliamentarians to be verified, and this could be protected by legislated penalties for noncompliance and willfully inaccurate statements.

Linked to this is legislation on recovery of assets. In this area, there has been some progress internationally: the UNCAC contains a separate chapter on Asset Recovery, which seeks to reconcile the needs of countries seeking to return illicit assets with the legal and procedural safeguards of the countries whose assistance is sought. Following the Commonwealth Heads of Government Meeting (CHOGM) in Abuja, Nigeria, in 2003, a Working Group was established on Asset Repatriation. The Working Group was mandated to examine the issue of the recovery of assets of illicit origin and repatriation of those assets to the countries of origin, focusing on maximizing cooperation and assistance between governments. It found that some of the chief challenges to successful asset recovery and repatriation were excessive immunity of politicians and other civil servants from prosecution for corruption-related offenses: "[I]n many instances, this immunity extends not only to nonliability, in the case of serving members of the legislature, but extends to inviolability, or complete freedom from arrest, for any offence."[8]

---

[7] Jeremy Pope, "Confronting Corruption: The Elements of a National Integrity System," in *Transparency International Source Book 2000* (Berlin, Germany: TI, 2000).

[8] Bernard Turner, "Supporting Legislation and Action on Recovery of Stolen Assets and Money Laundering," paper prepared for the OECD Development Assistance Committee (DAC) Development Partnership Forum, "Improving Donor Effectiveness in Combating Corrution," organized by OECD and TI, December 9–10, 2004.

Box 1 *Parliament and the Fight against Corruption*

Parliamentarians must take the lead in the fight against corruption and must work with the executive, the judiciary, political leaders and parties, civil society, donors, and the media.[a]

Parliamentarians should maintain high standards of accountability, transparency, and responsibility in the conduct of all public and parliamentary matters and should adopt codes of conduct and values for themselves and the public service.

Parliamentarians must be aware of the strong linkage between poverty and corruption: poverty helps to entrench corruption, and corruption deepens poverty.

There must be zero tolerance for corruption at every level.

Parliaments should reexamine and, where necessary, amend anti-corruption legislation to reinforce the powers of anti-corruption agencies.

a. Extract from recommendations of a CPA/DFID "Regional Workshop to Strengthen Legislatures in Commonwealth West Africa," The Gambia, August 8–12, 2005.

Whistle-blower protection—legislation to prevent people from being penalized for disclosing information about malpractice where the disclosure is in the public interest—is a further tool at parliament's disposal. For example, a private Members' bill was introduced in the U.K. Parliament in July 1998. The Public Interest Disclosure Act came into force a year later after it received the crucial support of the British government. The Act has been used to protect whistle-blowers from reprisals and also enables those victimized for revealing corrupt practices to be compensated.[9]

Parliament can also legislate to ensure that the executive is bound to the principle of the Rule of Law, and the judiciary acts as a check or balancing mechanism. As the *Commonwealth (Latimer House) Principles on the Accountability of and the Relationship between the Three Branches of Government* state, "Best democratic principles require that the actions of governments are open to scrutiny by the courts, to ensure that decisions taken comply with the Constitution, with relevant statutes and other law, including the law relating to the principles of natural justice."[10]

Laws to foster free and fair elections are crucial in building trust and respect in the political system. In chapter 11, Riccardo Pelizzo argues that holding elections might not be sufficient for a regime to be democratic. An example is the denial of full voting rights to the majority African population in many former British colonies in Africa: one could not describe them as democracies, but their legislatures could be described as parliaments. However, faith in any electoral system is paramount: the system must be fair and be seen to be fair. The elimination of corruption, therefore, should be a fundamental objective of any system.[11]

Serious irregularities may include the stuffing of ballot boxes, a flawed counting process, falsified results, intimidation of voters by local officials, and denial to international observers of access to polling stations. However, dubious election practice

---

[9] For further information on the Public Interest Disclosure Act and whistle-blower legislation around the world, consult www.pcaw.co.uk/legislation.

[10] Agreed on by Commonwealth Law Ministers and endorsed by the Commonwealth Heads of Government Meeting, Abuja, Nigeria, 2003. The principles are available for download on the CPA Web site: www.cpahq.org/activities/PIRC/pircpublications.

[11] The Administration and Cost of Elections (ACE) Project provides a globally accessible information resource on election administration. See www.aceproject.org.

is not confined to any one region or to those countries where elections have not been regularly held. A judge investigating vote rigging in Birmingham's 2004 local elections upheld allegations of postal fraud relating to six seats won by Labour and ordered new elections. The Fitzgerald Royal Commission in Queensland, Australia, established in 1987, exposed endemic corruption in the Australian state, including the manipulation of constituency boundaries by political parties.

Whatever the system in place, boundaries should not be drawn in a way that favors one party or interest over another, a practice commonly described as "gerry-mandering," a term that derives from the activities of a former Massachusetts governor in the United States. In the United States today, election boundaries are still commonly drawn to suit party interests. Arnold Schwarzenegger, the Republican governor of California, recently put a package of measures in a ballot to California's voters. These included a proposal to move the power to draw political districts from the legislature to a panel of retired judges. The proposal was defeated.

A strong government bias in state-run media is dangerous both before and after elections. Research from the World Bank suggests that there is a strong correlation between freedom of the media and control of corruption; corruption is also associated with absence of civil liberties. In chapter 8, John Smith describes how the 1995 Ugandan Constitution enabled the media, for the first time in the country's history, to challenge government and expose corruption. Laws to foster freedom of the press and expression and freedom of information are therefore essential. The CPA, in association with other Commonwealth organizations and the World Bank Institute, has worked to develop a set of recommendations for parliament and the media that would lead to an "informed democracy."

On September 1–2, 2005, more than 40 parliamentarians, including government ministers and senior parliamentary officials from seven Commonwealth Pacific countries, met in Fiji with a team of experts assembled by the CPA and the Commonwealth Human Rights Initiative (CHRI) to discuss issues related to freedom of expression, especially in the context of the specific needs of Pacific countries. Participants agreed that free public access to information held by government and public institutions is good for economic and social development because it leads to a more efficient economy and better public sector performance, increasing investor confidence in the country's economy and reducing waste and corruption. It also promotes government accountability and public participation in governance and development and prevents governments from gravitating toward despotism.[12]

Other types of legislation that parliaments can enact to curb corruption include legislation ensuring the right to form civil society organizations (CSOs) and granting them tax exemption, as well as laws on procurement and financial disclosure, rules on conflict of interest, and ethics codes. The purpose of conflict-of-interest rules is to prevent legislators from using their public position for personal gain. Rules can cover employment/income restrictions while in parliament, employment restrictions after serving in parliament, and the right to vote on legislation where the member may have an interest at stake. In South Africa, for example, a Member cannot participate in a debate when he or she has a "direct and specific pecuniary interest" in the matter being debated or voted on. Some countries restrict employ-

---

[12] For further details of the CPA's work in this area, consult www.cpahq.org/topics/default.aspx?id=12.

ment of former members to limit their ability to exert undue influence or pressure on their former colleagues. The benefits of a strong ethical environment are increased public confidence in the institution of parliament and greater fairness and consistency for all Members, while maintaining good conduct and standards.

Parliament can also enact laws promoting a professional, meritocratic civil service. Merit should be rewarded; civil servants could, for example, be rewarded for unmasking corruption. The OECD says that the lower the pay of a civil servant, the more likely he or she will accept a bribe, and a similar point could presumably be made for parliamentarians. According to the Commonwealth Parliamentary Salaries and Allowances Survey (2005),[13] the basic pay of a Member in Malawi is less than half the amount paid to a secondary schoolteacher, whereas a Kenyan Member's basic salary equals that paid to a head of a civil service ministry. Members receive allowances for attendance, housing, entertainment, and their constituency expenses. The use or misuse of expenses and parliamentary allowances is a sensitive issue in all jurisdictions.

Parliament and Finance

Anti-corruption relies on financial integrity, and parliaments can strengthen their financial role by increasing their level of expertise through legislative committees focused on different policy areas or by strengthening parliamentary research capacity or ties to independent think tanks, private sector economists, and academics. Within the Westminster model, members are usually limited to debating the estimates and are not allowed to move amendments to increase the budgeted allotment or to propose that the vote be reduced. In some parliaments, the practice of reviewing detailed budget estimates before the passage of the government's annual budget has been abandoned—even when government's expenditures have increased.[14] Parliaments could and should improve access to supporting documentation on budget proposals and ensure adequate time to analyze budget proposals. An OECD Best Practice suggests that a minimum of three months is required for meaningful legislative analysis and scrutiny. In too many parliaments, however, the process is opaque, with little discourse between parliament and the executive. To play a more effective role in fighting corruption and ensuring transparent and accountable government, as well as the efficient delivery of public services, there should be effective legislative participation in the budget process (see box 2).

Oversight

Strong parliamentary oversight is an essential part of combating corruption and ensuring good governance generally. There are numerous oversight tools in parliamentary systems to ensure that programs are carried out legally, effectively, efficiently (value for money), and for the purposes for which they were intended. There should be sufficient opportunity for ministers and leaders of government to

---

[13] This and past surveys can be found online on www.cpahq.org.
[14] Gordon Barnhart, *Parliamentary Committees: Enhancing Democratic Governance* (London: CPA, in association with Cavendish Publishing Limited, 1999).

Box 2 *Parliament and the Scrutiny of the Executive: The Budget Process*

Parliamentarians must take seriously their responsibility for oversight and authorization of the executive's budget.[a]

Parliament should be formally consulted during the budget-setting process.

All parliamentary committees should be involved in scrutinizing the estimates.

Parliament should routinely monitor the execution of the budget and should approve any additional appropriations.

Parliaments should have a budgetary research capacity.

a. Extract from recommendations of a CPA/DFID "Regional Workshop to Strengthen Legislatures in Commonwealth West Africa" (The Gambia, August 8–12, 2005).

---

be publicly accountable during parliamentary question time. The capacity of oversight committees to review policy, programs, and operations should be increased where necessary, and all subordinate legislation must be scrutinized to ensure consistency with parliamentary acts. Parliaments should promote the independence and adequate staffing of the supreme audit institution, anti-corruption commissions, and other specialized agencies. Earlier, Rick Stapenhurst and Jack Titsworth highlight the role and nature of supreme audit institutions and identify six features as crucial to their success: supportive environment; clear mandate; independence; adequate funding, means, and staff; sharing of knowledge and experience; and adherence to international auditing standards.

Parliaments can establish public accounts committees (PACs) to ensure that governments are accountable for their use of funds and resources. CPA is widely regarded as leading the field in supporting public accounts committees and in producing seminal material, much of this in cooperation with the World Bank Institute.[15] CPA is now broadening the scope of its work with the WBI to include the financial scrutiny role of all parliamentary committees with an oversight role of government departments. The CPA has already produced guidelines on how parliament and the media can act as a powerful oversight engine against governments. To perform their respective duties, parliament and the media must work together, although a degree of mutual suspicion will always be an essential part of the relationship.[16] But just as a parliament's oversight powers might not exist in practice, too many governments are reluctant to promote a diverse media landscape, ensure the protection of journalists, support freedom of information, and push for media accountability.

---

[15] For an examination of the work of PACs and recommendations to improve governance outcomes through more effective use of PACS and auditors general, see David McGee, *The Overseers: Public Accounts Committees and Public Spending* (London: CPA, in association with Pluto Press, 2002).

[16] Nixon Kariithi, "Parliament and the Media: Securing an Effective Relationship," a report on the proceedings of the Indian Ocean Rim Conference on "Parliament and the Media," Cape Town, South Africa, April 14-18, 2002 (Washington, DC: CPA and World Bank Institute, 2002).

Representation

A parliament must be endowed with institutional powers and practical means to express the will of the people by legislating and overseeing government action.[17] Democracy also requires a parliament that represents the people, not one controlled by the president, the prime minister, or the military. A parliament representing all parts of society is essential, and political parties can also assist this process by adopting transparent rules that regulate the selection of party leaders and candidates and to strengthen the party bureaucracy.

Political party finance and related corruption pose one of the greatest threats to democratic and economic development worldwide.[18] Corruption in politics, particularly during election periods, compromises a critical asset of democracy: the faith and support of ordinary citizens in the political system. When political parties fail to appeal to voters or suffer from weak institutional capacities, they often turn to vote buying as a means to secure support. This in turn creates competitive election spending, driving up the cost of getting elected. As a result of high campaign costs, political parties become increasingly dependent on wealthy donors or, in the case of incumbents, on the wrongful use of state resources. Consequently, the basic underlying principles of democracy are undermined, and public confidence in the political process is eroded. In some cases, already limited public funds are diverted for private gain. The open disclosure of political campaign funding is one important anti-corruption safeguard.

A recent study on political party financing by the National Democratic Institute for International Affairs shows corruption relating to political party financing as a serious threat to democracy and economic development. The report concludes that legal reform aimed at tackling corruption—if supported by donors—will be effective only if accompanied by adequate enforcement mechanisms and parallel efforts to promote accountability and internal democracy within political parties.[19]

Over the past several years, party financing scandals have shaken countries in every region of the world, drawing increased international attention to the problem. In response, government officials and activists have launched public awareness campaigns and introduced legislative initiatives designed to restrict spending or improve disclosure about the sources of party funding and the expenditure of campaign funds. The success of these efforts varies and typically depends on a combination of legislation, enforcement regimes, sustained political will for reform, and public pressure to demand more accountability in politics.

Conclusion

Previous contributors to this volume have shown that it is essential to build a sound social and political foundation for reform, targeting the institutions of the state, the

---

[17] United Nations Development Programme, *Human Development Report 2002* (New York and Oxford, U.K.: Oxford University Press, 2002).

[18] Introduction to NDI's "Africa Political Party Finance Initiative." http://www.ndi.org/worldwide/cewa/finance/finance.asp.

[19] S. Bryan and D. Baer, eds., *Money in Politics: A Study of Party Financing Practices in 22 Countries* (Washington, DC: National Democratic Institute for International Affairs [NDI], 2005).

private sector, civil society, the political system, and public administration. In short, any strategy to tackle corruption must be holistic, focusing on preventive measures as well as enforcement. A comprehensive set of measures to promote horizontal accountability is needed, including anti-corruption legislation, investigative bodies, internal reporting and whistle-blowing, independent prosecutors and judiciary, competent law enforcement, ethics codes, audit systems, and legislative oversight. Vertical accountability must be fostered through free and fair elections; transparent funding of political parties; publication of proceedings, hearings, and votes in parliament; free media; ability to form civil organizations; and public awareness of the corruption issue.

Parliaments can play an indispensable role across many aspects of an anti-corruption strategy through their legislative, oversight, financial, and representative functions. A wide variety of tools may be considered—some of which may be more effective in one parliament than another. While no one step will be able to effectively eliminate corruption, a combination of measures can guard against corruption in government. Above all, there must be acceptance that any democratic system must recognize the three broad principles of openness, accountability, and integrity.

In practice, however, parliament's ability to curb corruption will depend to a large extent on how independent it is from direct government control. For example, governments in many countries are reluctant to relinquish their ministerial control of both the finances of the parliament and its administration. In other countries, the parliament is simply used as a rubber stamp for the government program and is only called to sit at the whim of ministerial authority. In short, too often it is the government that controls parliament and not the other way around. In these countries, parliament must be strengthened to ensure that it acts as the principal institution of democracy, holding governments to account and ensuring that resources are not diverted from the millions of people in poverty. This is the challenge facing all stakeholders working toward good governance and development.

Contributors

Phyllis Dininio

Phyllis Dininio is an affiliate scholar at American University's Transnational Crime and Corruption Center and a consultant to international, governmental, and nongovernmental organizations. Her publications include the *USAID Handbook for Fighting Corruption* (1998), the World Bank's *Improving Governance and Controlling Corruption* (coeditor, 2006), the U.S. Integrity Assessment and Scorecard for Global Integrity (2004), and several articles and book chapters on corruption. A recognized expert in the anti-corruption field, she regularly presents corruption overviews to foreign delegations for the U.S. State Department, serves as a governance adviser for the Development Gateway, is an external reviewer and contributor to Transparency International's *Global Corruption Report*, and has provided advice on fighting corruption to senior officials at the U.S. National Security Council. She holds a Ph.D. in Political Science from Yale University, an M.A. in Political and Economic Development from the Fletcher School, and a B.A. in Economics and Sociology (magna cum laude) from Harvard University.

John Heilbrunn

John Heilbrunn is an assistant professor for the Graduate Program in the International Political Economy of Resources at the Colorado School of Mines and a research associate of the Centre d'Études d'Afrique Noire of the Institut d'Études Politique, Bordeaux. Before joining the faculty at the Colorado School of Mines, Heilbrunn was a senior public sector reform specialist at the World Bank. He has considerable experience as a consultant to multilateral and bilateral donors. Heilbrunn has published a number of articles on African development, corruption and governance, and postconflict state reconstruction. He holds an undergraduate degree from the University of California, Berkeley, and a Ph.D. from UCLA.

Nicholas Hopkinson

Nicholas Hopkinson is a director at Wilton Park, a think tank and conference center affiliated with the U.K. Foreign and Commonwealth Office; previously, he was deputy director at Wilton Park (2002–5) and a member of the academic staff (1987–2002). He studied International Politics, Queen's University, Kingston, Ontario (B.A. with Honors) and International Affairs, Carleton University, Ottawa (M.A.) and was awarded a Graduate Diploma from the Johns Hopkins School of Advanced International Studies (SAIS), Bologna, Italy. His publications include a book (*Parliamentary Democracy*, Ashgate/Commonwealth Parliamentary Association, 2001); more than 100 Wilton Park Papers and reports on (among other things) parliamentary democracy and EU issues; and articles in the *Brown Journal of World Affairs, Euromoney, Kluwer,* and *Databank.* He has edited all Wilton Park reports since 2005 and during 1993–2001, during which time he was also editor of *Current Issues in International Diplomacy and Foreign Policy* (The Stationery Office).

Michael Johnston

Michael Johnston is the Charles A. Dana professor of political science, as well as division director for the social sciences, at Colgate University, Hamilton, New York. He has been studying issues of corruption, reform, and development for more than 30 years and has served as a consultant to a variety of international organizations. He received his Ph.D. from Yale University in 1977. His most recent book is *Syndromes of Corruption: Wealth, Power, and Democracy* (Cambridge University Press, 2005).

Niall Johnston

Niall Johnston has been director of development and planning, and now director of programs, since 2003. Previously, he was resident director in Sierra Leone for the National Democratic Institute and political development coordinator in Bosnia and Herzegovina for the Organization for Security and Co-operation in Europe. He has worked extensively in parliamentary and political affairs and was a key adviser in the establishment of the Northern Ireland Assembly following the 1998 Belfast Agreement.

Daniel Kaufmann

Daniel Kaufmann is a leading expert, researcher, and adviser to countries on governance and development and has pioneered survey methodologies and capacity-building approaches for good governance and anti-corruption programs around the world. He currently heads groups on Global Governance and Knowledge for Development within the World Bank Institute. Previously, he held positions at the World Bank that include managing a team on Finance, Regulation, and Governance; heading capacity building for Latin America; and serving as lead economist both in economies in transition and in the Bank's Research Department. He was the World Bank's first Chief of Mission to Ukraine and also a Visiting Scholar at Harvard University.

Daniel Kaufmann is a member of the World Economic Forum (Davos) faculty. His research on economic development, governance, the unofficial economy, macroeconomics, investment, corruption, privatization, and urban and labor economics has been published in leading journals. He is a frequent speaker on governance issues in major forums: examples include the recent keynote presentation at the First Global Forum on Media Development and the Annual Goodman Lecture at the University of Toronto in 2005. A Chilean national, he received his M.A. and Ph.D. in Economics at Harvard and his B.A. in Economics and Statistics from the Hebrew University of Jerusalem.

Kimmo Kiljunen

Kimmo Kiljunen is currently serving as an MP with the Social Democratic Parliamentary Group in Finland, where he has resided for more than 10 years. He acts as a vice chair to the Grand Committee (European Affairs) and the Finnish delegation to the Organization for Security and Co-operation in Europe (OSCE) Parliamentary Assembly, and he is a member of the Foreign Affairs Committee and vice chair of the Parliamentary Network on the World Bank. He received his M.S. from the University of Helsinki and his Lic.Phil. and Ph.D. from Sussex University. He has also held positions with UNICEF in Nairobi and has acted as a coordinator for the United Nations Development Programme in New York.

Sahr Kpundeh

Sahr Kpundeh is a Senior Public Sector Specialist working with the Governance team at the World Bank Institute and with the Public Sector Reform and Capacity-Building Unit in the World Bank's Africa Region. He is currently responsible for leading the Bank's public sector reform program in Kenya, as well as for developing and implementing governance learning programs for client countries. Previously, he was a program officer for the Panel on Issues in Democracy and States in Transition at the National Academy of Sciences in Washington, DC.

Frannie A. Léautier

Frannie A. Léautier is the vice president of the World Bank Institute. She assumed this position in December 2001. Previously, she was the chief of staff for the president of the World Bank Group, responsible for providing oversight and guidance to the staff of the president's office in all aspects of their work, as well as helping to enhance coordination of the president's office with other units throughout the Bank.

Ms. Léautier, who is recognized as a leading expert in infrastructure strategy formulation in developing countries, joined the World Bank Group in 1992. She has held several positions in the World Bank Group, including as a transport economist in the Latin America and Caribbean and the South Asia Regions and as a research economist in the Development Economics Department. She served as sector director for Infrastructure in South Asia during 1997–2000 and held the position of director for the Infrastructure Group, comprising the merged practices of Transport, Water and Sanitation, Urban Development, and Energy.

Ms. Léautier received both her M.S. in Transportation and her Ph.D. in Infrastructure Systems from the Massachusetts Institute of Technology (MIT). Before joining the Bank, she taught at the Center for Construction Research and Education and at the Department of Urban Planning, both at MIT. She is a recipient of a number of excellence awards (including Best Manager) from the World Bank Staff Association and of an International Finance Corporation/Policy Support Instrument (IFC/PSI) Senior Management Performance Award in recognition of her leadership in reinvigorating the intellectual thinking about the infrastructure sectors and providing strategic direction in these sectors. A Distinguished Engineering Accomplishment Award has been conferred on her by Tanzania's Engineers Registration Board. She is associate editor for the *Journal of Infrastructure Systems* and a member of a number of international committees on infrastructure development.

Daniel Lederman

Daniel Lederman is senior economist in the World Bank's office of the chief econo-mist of the Latin America and Caribbean Region (LCRCE) and in the Development Economics Research Group. An economist and political scientist by training, he has written extensively on issues related to financial crises in emerging markets, violent crime, the political economy of economic reforms, institutional reforms, economic growth, and international trade. He received a B.A. degree in Political Science from Yale University (1989), where he studied economics and political science. He then went on to receive his M.A. (1991) and Ph.D. (2001) in International Economics and Politics from the Johns Hopkins University, School of Advanced International Stud-ies (SAIS).

Norman V. Loayza

Norman Loayza is currently lead economist in the Research Department of the World Bank. He received his B.A. from Brigham Young University in Economics and Sociology and his Ph.D. from Harvard University in Economics in 1994. Since then, he has worked at the Research Group of the World Bank, with an interruption of two years (1999–2000) when he worked as a senior economist at the Central Bank of Chile. He has taught postgraduate courses and seminars at the University of the Pacific in Lima; the Catholic University of Chile; and in Nairobi, Buenos Aires, Helsinki, Mexico City, El Cairo, Rio de Janeiro, and Madrid. With an area of interest in economic and social development, including economic growth, private savings, financial depth, monetary policy, and poverty alleviation, he has edited five books and published more than 30 articles in professional journals.

Rod Macdonell

Rod Macdonell is the new senior editor of *Federations*. Before joining the Forum of Federations in December 2005 as senior director of public information and educa-tion, he was the executive director of Canadian Journalists for Free Expression, based in Toronto. He also worked for the World Bank Institute in Washington, DC, designing training for journalists in developing countries and delivering that train-ing both by video conferencing and in person in numerous countries in Africa, Southeast Asia, Latin America, and Central and Eastern Europe. He previously worked for the *Canadian Press* new agency and as an investigative journalist for the *Montreal Gazette,* and he taught courses in the press and the law at Concordia Uni-versity's Journalism Department in Montreal. He was the winner of three Judith-Jasmin Awards, Quebec's highest award for journalism. He has a law degree from Université de Sherbrooke in Quebec.

Denis Marshall, QSO

Denis Marshall, QSO, has been secretary-general of the Commonwealth Parliamen-tary Association since 2002. Prior to that, he was a Member of the Parliament of New Zealand during 1984–99. A government minister for six years with a range of portfolios, he has also chaired various select committees, including Transport and Environment, and Primary Production.

He is recognized as a leading expert in parliamentary and public sector processes and has considerable experience in Commonwealth and parliamentary affairs.

In his term as secretary-general, he has promoted work with key international and regional organizations in programs aimed at good governance, accountability, and—most important—poverty reduction. He has initiated the Association's work with partner organizations to provide sustained technical assistance in a number of countries (such as Guyana, Malawi, and the Solomon Islands).

Fred Matiangi

Fred Matiangi is currently the deputy chief of party of the Kenya Parliamentary Strengthening Program, funded by the U.S. Agency for International Development (USAID) and implemented by the State University of New York's Center for International Development. He previously worked with the Institute for Education in Democracy in Kenya as head of programs and research and taught in the English Department at the University of Nairobi. In addition, he has consulted for a number of governance institutions in Kenya, including Transparency International (Kenya chapter) and the Kenya Leadership Institute.

Sir Philip Mawer

Sir Philip Mawer began his professional life as a career civil servant, rising to become principal private secretary to Conservative Home Secretary Douglas Hurd. Thirteen years ago, he joined the Church of England as secretary-general of the General Synod and, in 1999, became director of the Archbishops' Council. During his time at the Home Office, he demonstrated a flair for handling politically sensitive briefs.

At the General Synod, Sir Philip Mawer was involved in the handling of delicate issues such as the ordination of women, the role of bishops in the House of Lords, and what he described as "unthinking racial discrimination" in the church and elsewhere. In 1995, he challenged the findings of the Commons Select Committee on Social Security, chaired by senior Labour MP Frank Field, on the funding of clergy pensions.

Sir Philip Mawer was educated at Hull Grammar School and Edinburgh University, where he read in Politics.

Riccardo Pelizzo

Riccardo Pelizzo received his Ph.D. from Johns Hopkins University and is currently an assistant professor of political science at the Singapore Management University. He has published in several scholarly journals, including *Comparative European Politics*, *Legislative Studies Quarterly*, *Party Politics*, and *West European Politics*.

Milica Pesic

Milica Pesic is executive director of Media Diversity. Previously, she was a presenter and editor at *TV Serbia* for more than 10 years and has reported for the *BBC* and *Radio Free Europe*. She was a founder of the *AIM* independent news agency (the only network of independent journalists from Southeastern Europe during the Yugoslav wars) and the Reporting Diversity Network.

Melica Pesic holds an M.A. in International Journalism from City University, London. She has lectured at King's College and City University in London and at Toronto University in Canada and delivered guest lectures at the Concordia and Carleton Universities in Canada, the University of Michigan and St. Lawrence University in the United States, and the Tirana University in Albania.

Milica Pesic has conducted media training for the UN, EC, Council of Europe, UNESCO, OSI, Freedom Forum, and IFJ and is a regular commentator on political and media issues in Southeastern Europe for the *BBC* and *CNN*.

Michael Pinto-Duschinsky

Michael Pinto-Duschinsky is senior research fellow in politics at Brunel University, England; chair of the International Political Science Association's research committee on political finance and political corruption; and a member of the board of directors of IFES (International Foundation for Election Systems). He is a former fellow of Pembroke College, Oxford, and of Merton College, Oxford. During 1992–98, he was a founding governor of the Westminster Foundation for Democracy. He is the author of many works on political finance, including *British Political Finance*, "Financing Politics: A Global View," and "Political Finance in the Commonwealth." He has advised international organizations, governments, and public bodies in 26 countries on issues relating to the reform of political finance and on related constitutional subjects.

Jeremy Pope

Jeremy Pope is director of policy for Tiri (the governance-access-learning network). His publications include *Confronting Corruption: The Elements of a National Integrity System* (now in more than 25 languages), *Best Practices in Combating Corruption* (Vienna: OSCE, 2004) and the *United Nations Handbook on Practical Anti-Corruption Measures for Prosecutors and Investigators* (Vienna: UNODC, 2004). Following a career in governance at the Commonwealth Secretariat, he was founding managing director of Transparency International (TI), where he developed the organization's intellectual property and its approaches to the corruption issue. He continues to mentor national chapters of TI informally. He has worked on human rights and governance in more than 50 countries, served as personal adviser on corruption matters to three presidents, and was adviser to James Wolfensohn when the World Bank's policy on corruption was reformed.

John Smith

John Smith works at the International Finance Corporation. He has a background in mass communications and worked as a journalist and media relations specialist in Uganda for nine years. He has also worked as a consultant for the World Bank.

Rodrigo R. Soares

Rodrigo Soares is an assistant professor of economics at the University of Maryland and at the Catholic University of Rio de Janeiro (PUC-Rio). He received his Ph.D. in Economics from the University of Chicago in 2002. His dissertation, "Life Expectancy, Educational Attainment, and Fertility Choice: The Economic Impacts of Mortality Reductions," earned him the 2003 Brazilian National Award for Ph.D. Dissertations in Economics (Prêmio Haralambos Simeonidis). His research focuses on development economics, ranging from health and population economics to corruption, institutions, and crime. His work has appeared in various scientific journals, including *American Economic Review, Journal of Development Economics, Economic Development and Cultural Change,* and *Economics and Politics.*

Recently, Rodrigo Soares was awarded—together with co-authors Gary S. Becker and Tomas J. Philipson—the Kenneth J. Arrow Award from the International Health Economics Association for the best paper published in the field of health economics during 2005.

Rick Stapenhurst

Rick Stapenhurst is a member of the Governance team at the World Bank Institute. He joined the World Bank in 1996 and has concentrated on anti-corruption, legislative strengthening, and media development. He has written extensively on issues relating to anti-corruption and legislative strengthening; his most recent publications include *The Role of Bilateral Donors in Fighting Corruption* (Washington, DC: World Bank, 2001) and *Curbing Corruption* (Washington, DC: World Bank, 1999). He has also written numerous articles and working papers that have been published by the World Bank and in the business and academic press. A dual Canadian-South African citizen, he completed his doctorate in Business Administration in 1989 and has master's degrees in both Business Administration and Development Studies.

Before joining the World Bank, Rick Stapenhurst was the director of the Multilateral Development Banks unit at the Canadian International Development Agency and an adjunct professor in international marketing at the University of Ottawa and at McGill University.

Katia Stasinopoulou

Katia Stasinopoulou is currently a policy adviser for a political party at the European Parliament, where she works for the Alliance of Liberals and Democrats for Europe. She previously worked as a political assistant at the European Parliament, where she focused on constitutional and foreign affairs. She also consulted for WBI's Parliamentary Strengthening Program, where she drafted and evaluated reports aimed at enhancing capacity building for parliamentarians and parliamentary staff. She completed her postgraduate studies with the Johns Hopkins University School of Advanced International Studies and with the London School of Economics.

Severin Strohal

Severin Strohal is currently working for the UN Department of Peacekeeping Operations in Kosovo. He has also held a position with UNDPKO in New York. Severin previously worked consulted for WBI's Parliamentary Strengthening Program, where he drafted and evaluated reports aimed at enhancing capacity building for parliamentarians and parliamentary staff. He completed his postgraduate studies with the School of International and Public Affairs, Columbia University and his undergraduate studies at the University of Essex in the United Kingdom.

Jack Titsworth

Jack Titsworth has degrees from both the University of British Columbia and the London School of Economics. He worked initially as a development administrator with the Canadian University Service Overseas and the Canadian International Development Agency in Asia and Africa. Subsequently, as an adviser in governance, he has worked in the area of public sector reform and anti-corruption with the World Bank, the Department for International Development (U.K.), and the UNDP in Africa.

Martin Ulrich

Martin Ulrich is a senior associate at the Parliamentary Centre in Ottawa, Canada. In this capacity, he also serves as the executive secretary of the Global Organization of Parliamentarians Against Corruption (GOPAC). Before joining the Parliamentary Centre, he served in policy and executive positions in the government of Canada, principally at the Treasury Board Secretariat.

Joachim Wehner

Joachim Wehner teaches public policy at the London School of Economics and Political Science. He previously worked at the Institute for Democracy in South Africa (IDASA) and as a consultant on public finance and governance issues, mainly in African and Eastern European countries. His research interests include public budgeting, legislatures, and federalism.

John Williams

John Williams was first elected as a Member of Parliament to the House of Commons, Canada, on October 25, 1993. He was reelected to the House of Commons in 1997, 2000, 2004, and 2006. He served as the chair of the House of Commons Standing Committee on Public Accounts during 1997–2005. He is also the chair of GOPAC, an international organization of parliamentarians focused on improving the effectiveness of parliament as an institution of oversight and accountability. He is also the chair of the Canadian chapter of GOPAC: Canadian Parliamentarians Against Corruption (CanPAC).

Appendix 1

Global Governance and Parliamentary Influence

Kimmo Kiljunen

Introduction

"Transparency" and "accountability" are two of the current buzzwords in modern international relations jargon and are perceived as key elements to positively manage globalization and reconnect decision makers to civil society. Certainly when Mike Moore, the former Director-General of the World Trade Organization (WTO), met the Finnish Parliamentary Subcommittee for the WTO, those concepts were his first topics for discussion. Transparency to him meant including parliamentarians in the work of the international organization he was directing, and consequently, the WTO has started to develop a parliamentary forum, co-organized by the European Parliament and the Inter-Parliamentary Union (IPU). Yet the WTO is just an example of a broader trend: the former President of the World Bank, James Wolfensohn, and the United Nations Secretary-General, Kofi Annan, similarly called for increased parliamentary involvement in their institutions and took concrete measures to follow up on these promises. In 2000 for example, the first parliamentary conference on the World Bank was held in The Hague. Since then, they have become an annual fixture under the leadership of the Parliamentary Network on the World Bank. Finally, Kofi Annan has received a report from a panel led by the former Brazilian Prime Minister, Enrique Cardoso, to examine ways to reinforce the relationship between the UN and parliamentarians.

These represent new and significant developments. Yet what explains the eagerness of international leaders to attach parliamentary bodies to their institutions? Major factors were the antiglobalization protests in Seattle, Prague, Geneva, and Cancun. They undoubtedly served as a reminder of the democratic deficit from which international organizations suffer and illustrated how suspicion rather then trust links global decision makers and civil societies. It seems that it is the Members of Parliament, elected at the ballot box, who might, as representatives of the citizens, be the natural agents to address this problem.

Nonetheless, the challenges are manifold. As this appendix will illustrate, a successful structure for parliamentary involvement would require specialized international legislative committees, an efficient division of labor, and a stronger national parliamentary participation in international affairs.

The Challenge of Globalization

The call for more democratic international governance has become ever louder in recent years, as the phenomenon of globalization has become a presence in so many areas of our lives.

The world economic and social system is integrating in a qualitatively new tempo and intensity, increasing mutual interdependence. At a constantly growing speed, goods, services, technology, information—as well as people—cross the borders. This phenomenon has been driven by a revolutionary progress in transportation and communication technology. The significance of distances is disappearing. Decision making has been affected, too: many central issues of society have become common to all of humankind. Environmental problems, capital flows and trade, population growth, security, international crime, migration, and refugees are phenomena that can no longer be addressed within the framework of any single state. Global, but also transparent and accountable, decision making is needed.

The neoliberal agenda has been regarded as the political catalyst for globalization. For neoliberal policy, the process of globalization is both means and objective in opening of market forces and for the abolition of political regulation. This again increases competition and production. For neoliberal thinkers, globalization is a predetermined, inevitable process, leaving us with the task to adjust to it. Although such a development would without a doubt result in the concentration of production factors, the widening of income disparities, and the narrowing of political influence, it is argued that this is a price to be paid to create a competitive and efficient economy.

There is, of course, opposition to the neoliberal approach that criticizes it for being inhumane and endorsing inequalities. For some opponents, the democratic state must be a safeguard for the social needs of people and not a promoter of the markets' interests. Instead, the economy is to be seen as an instrument, and its altar should not demand the sacrifice of human well-being. Such opposition calls for the renaissance of the nation-state, the closing of borders, and an isolation from the influence of the global economy. Traditional values and parochial interests become the guiding protecting principles against globalization. The criticism of globalization encompasses the entire political spectrum. The isolationist point of view may be equally endorsed by a traditional conservative and a radical leftist. It is manifested at its worst as an expression of xenophobia and racism or at its best as a fair concern for the future of the welfare state and local communities. Common to these concerns is the agreement on isolation from the effects of globalization.

Yet there are other options. Instead of merely adjusting to globalization or seeking isolation, globalization should be captured. The shrinking world, the strengthening of economic integration, and the decrease of the relative influence of the nation-state should be recognized, but at the same time, globalization ought to be governed and supervised. The exercise of public authority is as necessary to the governance of the world system as it is for the governance at the national level: global markets must be regulated, and there must be global rules of behavior. Supranational political cooperation, multilateral agreements, and strong transnational institutions are required. Such a structure has yet to be devised. However, the example of the European Union (see box A1) illustrates the feasibility of democratic supranational governance and the importance of such structures to fight corruption and ensure accountability. The different options will be discussed below.

> **Box A1** *The Example of Supranational Governance in the European Union*
>
> Because representative democracy has so far been confined to nation states, globalization is a major challenge to democratic decision making. There is no patent model to follow for the establishment of supranational democracy, and it is only in its earliest stage. On a regional level, such a structure has been taken furthest in Europe today, where the European Union features the first directly elected supranational parliament in world history. It has on several occasions illustrated its oversight powers, most spectacularly in March 1999, when it dismissed the whole European Commission under Jacques Santer for corruption, fraud, and mismanagement. With the ratification of the new EU Constitution, it will emerge as a fully fledged legislature. As of now, an intergovernmental body, the Council of Ministers, acts as the upper chamber and primary legislator. The European Parliament serves as the lower house and is still finding a role for itself in the prospective two-chamber system.
>
> Although it is frequently and misleadingly stated, the EU is not progressing toward a federal state. Instead, its evolution is in essence sui generis. As globalization advances, national sovereignty is no longer what it used to be, which creates a growing need for shared sovereignty. The first institutions to fulfill such a role in the post-nation-state world system emerged from the EU.

International Parliamentary Assemblies and Cooperation

Key to the establishment of an effective structure is interparliamentary cooperation. Foreign policy, generally dominated by the executive, traditionally refers to decision making between states and to their relations within international organizations. The role of parliaments has usually been limited to domestic policies and the exercise of internal legislative and budgetary authority. However, because of globalization and the unprecedented manner in which different cultures, religions, and civilizations meet, international and domestic affairs cannot be any longer separated. Because decisions taken by bodies such as the WTO and the World Bank impact on the work of national parliaments, and because they must ratify the bi- and multilateral agreements their governments enter, parliaments must be fully informed and aware of the issues concerned. As Members of Parliament become involved in a broad range of international activities, international connections between legislatures help to exchange information and experiences, to effectively influence topical global matters, to propose initiatives, and to increase the transparency and accountability of governments and international organizations.

As mentioned above, international organizations initially tended to serve purely as forums for intergovernmental cooperation and lacked direct parliamentary involvement. Yet, again, as globalization proceeds, parliamentary involvement has gradually grown, both quantitatively and in substance within regional and global bodies. The examples for active contribution of parliamentary assemblies to such organizations are numerous: they include the Nordic Council, the Council of Europe, the Organization for Security and Co-operation in Europe (OSCE), Arctic cooperation, the North Atlantic Treaty Organization (NATO), the Western European Union, and cooperation in the Baltic Sea area. All these organizations have an established parliamentary assembly or hold regular parliamentary conferences. In some cases, the existing assemblies also function as parliamentary forums for other international organizations (for example, the Parliamentary Assembly of the Council of

Europe provides the parliamentary dimension for the OECD). Outside Europe, both the Commonwealth and its Francophone counterpart, La Communauté, have established parliamentary assemblies, while Latin America, Africa, and Southeast Asia—as well as the Islamic countries—likewise feature interparliamentary bodies of their own. The same goes for the Russian-led Commonwealth of Independent States.

Independent networks and associations for global parliamentary cooperation have also been established. In addition to the IPU, the oldest parliamentary organization in the world, they include (for example) the Global Legislators Organization for a Balanced Environment (GLOBE), the Organization of European Parliamentarians for Africa (AWEPA), World Women Parliamentarians for Peace, and Parliamentarians for Global Action (PGA).

A most recent development is the creation of parliamentary forums that relate to global organizations. The European Parliament and the IPU have arranged parliamentary conferences on world trade, addressing issues on the agenda of the WTO. A similar type of effort is under way for the Bretton Woods institutions. A Parliamentary Network on the World Bank (PNoWB) has been established and has arranged regular annual parliamentary conferences since 2000. Although the emergence of such parliamentary assemblies and networks constitutes a great step forward in rendering international organizations more accountable and transparent, the example of a similar development within the United Nations illustrates well the urgent need not only for a new qualitative role of such parliamentary institutions in political life but also for an effective division and coordination of labor (see box A2).

Box A2 *A Parliamentary Body for the United Nations?*

While many other international organizations have created specialized parliamentary bodies, the United Nations has not. Even though the need has been recognized, it is not entirely clear how such a body might look and work.

An activist organization, Parliamentarians for Global Action (PGA), already exists, comprising individual parliamentarians who focus their work on the substance of the UN agenda. Yet as an organization, it is not broadly representative.

An organization with a far wider membership basis is the Inter-Parliamentary Union (IPU). In recent years, it has tried to undertake more-substantive work and initiatives and was granted UN observer status in 2001. Hoping to institutionalize formal parliamentary meetings, the IPU organized a summit for Speakers in cooperation with the UN in 2000. The next one took place in 2005. In addition, as an observer, it has the right to be represented at the UN General Assembly, address its sessions, and distribute official IPU documents. As a result, it has organized regular meetings on the work of the General Assembly. So far, participants have been a mix of IPU delegates from their respective parliaments and of parliamentarians attending the UN General Assembly as members of their national delegations. Therefore, in many respects, the IPU has established a certain parliamentary link to the UN.

Yet to be successful, broader participation must be ensured and differentiated according to the issues discussed. Indeed, too often, only parliamentarians who are responsible for IPU affairs attend such meetings. In many ways, this might limit the potential aspirations of the IPU to play a broader role in relation to the UN. The IPU could, for example, act as a coordinator and invite parliamentarians who are actively involved on the concerned issues in their national parliamentary committees. This is important in relation not only to the General Assembly but also to the specialized UN agencies. Such coordination should ensure that, depending on the type of UN meeting, the conference is covered by parliamentarians for whom it is of special relevance. In the case that the IPU should not be available for such a task, a new UN entity could take up this role.

New Proposals

There have been a number of proposals to reform the global governance system. Two of them are of particular relevance to the role of parliaments in global decision making.

In April 2004, the International Labour Organization (ILO) Commission on the Social Dimension of Globalization, headed by Presidents Tarja Halonen of Finland and Benjamin William Mkapa of Tanzania, published its report and proposed two crucial steps that could be taken to increase transparency and accountability in international decision making:

1. The ILO report requested that all multilateral organizations, including UN agencies, should become more accountable to the public at large. In particular, national parliaments should contribute to this process by regularly reviewing decisions taken by their countries' representatives in those organizations.

2. Global parliamentary associations, regional parliamentary assemblies, and global parliamentary networks have aimed at increasing the performance and accountability of international agencies and organizations. Although their work and achievements are important, greater coordination is needed. Hence, the ILO report calls for the creation of a global parliamentary group that should develop an integrated oversight of major international organizations and ensure the coherence and consistency of global economic, social, and environmental policies.

In April 2003, the UN Secretary-General appointed a panel of eminent persons to study relations between the UN and civil society, and among other issues, examine the relations between the UN and Members of Parliament. The former president of Brazil, Fernando Enrique Cardoso, was invited to chair the panel, which submitted its report in June 2004.

To strengthen global governance, confront democratic deficit in intergovernmental affairs, and better connect the UN to global opinion, the Cardoso Panel called for more-effective interaction between parliaments and the UN. To this end, the report made four concrete proposals:

1. National parliaments should more regularly address UN issues by scrutinizing government management of UN affairs, overseeing its commitment to global agreements, and holding debates on major issues on the UN agenda. Frequently, governments agree to major global commitments without proper parliamentary scrutiny and previous debate. As a result, global initiatives, such as the Millennium Development Goals, do not obtain adequate attention in most parliaments, greatly reducing their potential impact.

2. Parliamentarians participating in the UN events, usually as members of government delegations, should be provided with a greater platform for action. Parliamentarians should have the opportunity to participate in debates preceding a General Assembly meeting or be allowed to speak to relevant committees and at special sessions of the Assembly. This would encourage the Members of Parliament to follow up on these debates with their national parliaments.

3. In addition, there is a need to create a functional international parliamentary mechanism similar to the standing or select committees of national parliaments. Such global public policy committees would build up substantive expertise, forward policy proposals, and scrutinize progress on

past agreements made by intergovernmental organizations and governments. They could submit reports to the secretary-general and heads of relevant specialized agencies. Up to 30 regionally representative parliaments should take part in such committees, and rotation of membership would be (perhaps) within five-year terms. At the initial stage, the committees would be informal and advisory, with somewhat ad hoc groups of countries. Later, they might become more formal, eventually leading to globally representative committees on all global priorities, with the right to submit policy recommendations and progress audits to the UN and Member States.

4. The Cardoso Panel suggests that a small elected representatives liaison unit should be formed within the UN, resembling the well-respected UN Non-Governmental Liaison Service. The liaison unit would provide information service for Members of Parliament and encourage UN-related debates in national parliaments. In addition, it would create opportunities for parliamentarians to take part in UN forums and eventually could become a secretariat for global public policy committees.

All these proposals would engage Members of Parliament more systematically in the work of the UN and other specialized agencies and therefore deserve to be tested.

Conclusion

The growing frustration of many citizens of this world with the international system and the perceived inefficiency of national democratic institutions to solve the problems of globalization can be addressed through increased parliamentary involvement in global governance.

As we have seen, a crucial step to greater engagement is global parliamentary cooperation. While keeping in mind that the parliamentary mandate is strongest for domestic politics, every effort should be made to integrate these two levels to optimize the legislatures' fulfillment of their responsibilities. On one hand, participation in international forums facilitates the parliamentarians' access to global information and knowledge and reinforces their ability to fulfill their domestic mandate. International organizations, on the other hand, could gain in transparency and accountability from a stronger association with national parliamentarians and their expertise. However, a division of labor among parliamentarians is needed. Otherwise, a limited group of parliamentarians, taking care of international affairs, might be overwhelmed by the burden of global work and commitments. Thus, to ensure that the best and most relevant parliamentary expertise is represented at a global level, it is necessary that specialized committees of national parliaments have a stronger role in selecting parliamentarians to participate in the UN and other international events.

Parliamentary events and bodies of international organizations are, however, of secondary importance from the perspective of representative democracy. The organizations are, as such, intergovernmental in character. The main emphasis of parliamentary influence must be on the national level. International parliamentary cooperation can help to strengthen legislative monitoring and scrutiny of the executive branch. There is a great need for legislators to more effectively guide the work of governments in international affairs. Ministers responsible for decisions in international organizations should therefore have to obtain a mandate from their respective parliaments. These are important steps. After all, it is not only protesters—but also parliamentarians—who should have a say in the emerging global governance.

Appendix 2

WBI-CPA Conferences at Wilton Park: Reports

Nicholas Hopkinson and Riccardo Pelizzo

Report on Wilton Park Conference 704

THE ROLE OF GOVERNMENT AND PARLIAMENT IN CURBING CORRUPTION IN CENTRAL AND EASTERN EUROPE

Introduction

1. Corruption will always exist. Because it cannot be eliminated totally, we can only try to curb and control it, rather than fight it. Although corruption is universal, states in transition, where democracy and a market economy have only recently been established, are particularly afflicted. For example, corruption is regarded as the most significant political challenge in most Central and East European countries.[1]

2. There are three levels of corruption: "grand" or high-level corruption, which affects the mechanisms of political decision making ("state capture") and decisions on large projects and public contracts; "functional" corruption, which affects central and local administrations; and "institutional" corruption, which influences administrative culture and economic and social activities. What separates state capture from conventional forms of political influence, such as lobbying, are the illicit, hidden, and preferential mechanisms by which the private interests interact with the state. In the civil service, corruption involves the misuse of an official position for actual or expected material reward or gain. Effectively, the individual does something he or she should not do, or fails to do something he or she is required to do. A corrupt act can occur on or off duty, but it must be related to the individual's employment or conduct of his or her position.

---

[1] Wilton Park reports are summaries of the main points and conclusions of the conferences. The reports reflect rapporteurs' personal interpretations of the proceedings-as such, they do not constitute any institutional policy of Wilton Park, the Commonwealth Parliamentary Association, or the World Bank Institute, nor do they necessarily represent the views of the rapporteurs.

3. What makes it difficult to curb corruption is that there is no obvious or immediately identifiable victim. On the face of it, the two parties, donor and recipient, both benefit, and neither would report a crime. However, it is citizens and economies that are the victims. Corruption frustrates economic development, a conclusion substantiated by many World Bank and Transparency International global studies, which correlate lower degrees of economic growth with the higher incidence of corruption. Corruption destroys the potential benefits of introducing democracy and market disciplines. As a result, investors, both domestic and foreign, are less willing to risk their capital. Investment in corrupt countries is 5 percent lower than in relatively less corrupt countries. There are also political and social costs. General public mistrust of parliamentarians, public servants, and state institutions reduce citizens' respect for authority and willingness to abide by the rule of law. Higher rates of crime in more corrupt countries in turn threaten national security, political stability, and economic development.

4. To create an economy and democratic society based on the principles of transparency, accountability, and responsibility, it is necessary to target different groups through a well-planned strategy and organized activities. No one is exempt from abiding by the rules. Joint action is needed in all spheres: creating the political will to develop the necessary legal and institutional framework; enforcing the rule of law by government and public administration; and working to raise public awareness about the culture of law and good governance. Any single action alone, no matter how effective, is insufficient to stop corruption in the long term. Only a well-planned strategy spanning a multidisciplinary range of activities can create a positive environment to curb corruption.

Political Will

5. To curb corruption effectively, the commitment of government and parliament is above all required. If there is an absence of political will at the top, there will be a general lack of commitment to enforce laws and punish the corrupt. Almost all national anti-corruption commissions point to political will as the main precondition for their effective operation. It is easy to see which countries sincerely want to curb corruption. Sometimes political will is real and sincere; sometimes it manifests itself as merely proclamations and slogans to attract voters. Exposing the danger of corruption and mounting public and civil society pressure can help generate political will and indeed even contribute to a change of government, as happened in 2002 in the Macedonian and Kenyan elections. Governments usually feel obliged to act when they are faced with a real threat of losing elections because they are perceived as corrupt, inept, ignorant, or all of the aforesaid. But sometimes the incumbent government can simply take the money and run, or abuse their power over the organs of state to secure reelection by preventing a free and fair election, arguably the most corrupt act of all.

6. In spite of acceptance by governments that corruption exists and is serious, and in spite of several expert recommendations for constitutional amendments, there has been a general lack of political will to implement recommendations and the necessary legislation to combat corruption. Failure to enact legislation has become one of the biggest obstacles to curbing corruption and organized crime in general. Mobilizing parliamentarians to take corruption seriously and to enact con-

stitutional and legislative amendments should be one of the first steps in establishing an efficient anti-corruption regime. But neither is passing a plethora of acts alone sufficient; acts must be implemented and given the necessary resources to make them work.

Government and Parliament

7. Legislation must be anticipatory rather than reactive. Policy makers must follow actively and anticipate new practices and trends in corruption. The executive, legislature, civil servants, and police are either unfamiliar with, or do not take, the results of expert research seriously enough. This suggests there is a need for closer cooperation between policy makers and experts. Standardization and harmonization of police, prosecution, and judicial statistics can improve information about trends in corruption. Preventive legislation would harmonize the actions of different agencies and would increase their efficiency. Parliamentarians should also ensure that anti-corruption legislation is in fact primarily aimed to reduce corruption. Nevertheless, shortcomings in legislation should not be an excuse for not implementing the law in one specific area or another. Uncoordinated reforms weaken the process. Establishing different organizations to curb corruption is not necessarily positive because it can mean spreading resources thinly and limiting their authority, thus preventing the necessary coordination.

8. The issue of who regulates the regulators is difficult to resolve. At the same time that the government is the economic regulator, wealth distributor, and one of biggest spenders (if not the biggest), it should be the custodian and enforcer of the rule of law. The independence and separation of the legislature, judiciary, and executive are essential to ensure checks and balances and accountability in a democracy. Accountability can be defined as "motivators" beyond your control that cause you to think and act in a certain way. Parliament is an institution of accountability, and it should hold the government to account. Parliament is not government, government members are not the government, and opposition members are not the only ones able to hold government to account for its actions. Government must come to parliament when it wants to introduce new programs and legislation. Parliament can approve, amend, or reject proposed legislation—without parliament's approval, the government cannot do anything. Parliament approves the raising of revenues for government through taxation, and government cannot amend income tax legislation without parliament's approval. Parliament also approves the government's budget and spending.

9. Ensuring accountability in government is more difficult than in the private sector because accountability in the latter is largely ensured through competition. If products do not satisfy customers, they will not buy them, so the firm must either adapt or go out of business. However, recent scandals such as Enron and Worldcom, exposing serious flaws in management practice and the independence of external auditors, and concern about excessive top management pay in the United Kingdom and elsewhere demonstrate that corporate governance worldwide also needs improvement. Public sector bodies don't have to compete because they are essentially monopolies. Parliamentary structures such as public accounts committees (PACs), performance reporting, and estimates committees to encourage accountability therefore have to be designed. PACs within parliament provide

political impetus to reports made by autonomous government auditors (for example, the Auditor General in Canada and the National Audit Office in the United Kingdom). Auditors' reports on the functioning of government, which must be timely, require organizational contexts and strategic outcomes to be clear; performance expectations to be clear and concrete; key results to be reported against expectations; and performance information to be supported, reliable, and demonstrable. If the "motivators" are changed, so will be the results. Decentralization, more local ownership of projects, and publishing how MPs voted can also improve the accountability of government.

10. Parliamentarians can help curb corruption by joining international groups. The Global Organization of Parliamentarians Against Corruption (GOPAC), for example, has been established, with an international secretariat in the House of Commons in Ottawa. If one Member stands up against corruption, the Member may be isolated, but if several parliamentarians band together, the cause is taken more seriously. A GOPAC regional chapter can be set up by identifying a group of 8–12 members nationally or regionally (or both) who are committed to fighting corruption. The group then constitutes itself as an interim steering committee (ISC) whose members then individually recruit four to five additional members each, bringing the total to 30 or more and identifying an NGO willing to act as a secretariat. The ISC then reviews the draft regional constitution and calls a meeting of all members, which adopts a constitution. Finally, funds are sought to run the secretariat, and a plan of action is developed.

11. Parliamentarians should not be immune from prosecution. If parliamentarians act incorrectly, the ultimate sanction usually lies in the ballot box, and members who err should in theory not be reelected. In the United Kingdom, a legal privilege attached to being a Member of the Parliament (MP) extends only to proceedings in the House of Commons. There is no general immunity from criminal prosecution. So a Member is protected from criminal proceedings only with regard to anything he or she says in the course of participating in proceedings in the House. But unlike in some other parliaments, a Member does not have total immunity from prosecution if he or she commits a criminal offense.

12. Consideration should be given as to what matters should be regulated by the courts and what should be regulated by parliament itself. In the United Kingdom, complaints of breaches of privilege or of expected standards continue to be regulated by Parliament itself. Parliament has resisted and continues strongly to resist any intrusion by the courts into its own internal processes.

13. Parliamentary codes of conduct and registers of members' interests can help curb corruption by providing a framework within which Members and the public can know what behavior is expected of Members. They can serve as a means of encouraging the observance of high standards and of helping to develop a culture of compliance, openness, and accountability. They must be accompanied by proactive systems for offering advice and guidance and by effective means of enforcement that include an independent element. In the United Kingdom, an independent Parliamentary Commissioner for Standards to maintain the Register of Members' Interests and investigate allegations of misconduct was recommended in 1995. A parliamentary code of conduct was established and applies to Members in all aspects of their public life. It does not seek to regulate what Members do in their purely private and personal lives. The code requires MPs to uphold the law and the constitution; act

always in the public (not their personal) interest; strengthen confidence in Parliament, not bring it into disrepute; observe seven principles of public life; never accept a bribe, act as a paid advocate, or misuse allowances and other payments; and observe the House's rules (for example, as regards the registration or declaration of interests). The main purpose of the Register is "to provide information of any pecuniary interest or other material benefit which a Member receives which might reasonably be thought by others to influence his or her actions, speeches or votes in Parliament, or actions taken in his or her capacity as a Member of Parliament." The registration form specifies 10 categories of interests, including directorships; other forms of remunerated employment; sponsorships; gifts, benefits, and hospitality; overseas visits; overseas benefits and gifts; land and property; and shareholdings. Apart from the specific rules, there is a more general obligation on members to keep the overall definition of the Register's purpose in mind when registering their interests. Registration of an interest does not imply any wrongdoing. Although initially many complaints were about paid advocacy, most now concern alleged failures to declare or register interests, or the alleged abuse of allowances paid to Members. Any allegation that a Member's conduct is incompatible with the code or guide to the rules on registration of interests must be sufficiently substantiated and submitted in writing and signed to the Commissioner (who, if proposals shortly to be considered by the House of Commons are approved, will serve a single term of between five and seven years). Complaints should fall within the Commissioner's remit. Many do not because, for example, they concern how an MP has handled a constituent's case or a possible allegation of criminal activity. If the complaint is within the Commissioner's terms of reference and there is enough evidence to merit at least a preliminary enquiry, the matter is referred to the Member concerned for his or her response. If, however, the complaint does seem to merit further investigation, the Commissioner has no formal investigative powers. However, the Select Committee has made clear that it expects Members to cooperate fully with the Commissioner, and the Committee itself has power to send for persons, papers, and records and to order Members or others to appear before it. The Committee also considers what penalty to impose and will recommend further action to the House, if necessary. The House as a whole must approve that action, which may include a requirement that the Member concerned apologize on the floor of the House in public, the suspension of the Member concerned from membership of the House for a period, or the expulsion of the Member.

Financing Political Parties

14. Adopting new legislation on the financing of political parties is one of the most urgent areas for attention if corruption is to be curbed effectively. Illegal political financing includes practices that contravene the law, unauthorized use of state resources, accepting money from disreputable sources (such as the Mafia), spending money to buy votes, and giving money in return for government favors. It is feared that criminals in Russia and India, in particular, are buying immunity from prosecution through donations to political parties. The Enron case in the United States might suggest that developed countries are not immune from state capture. The absence of control over financing political parties, combined with unsynchronized privatization, liberalization, and deregulation reform processes, as well as

high levels of black market activity and tax evasion, create ripe opportunities for corruption.

15. Political parties should be obliged to register their income and expenditure and establish efficient financial control of political expenditure. Some have suggested setting expenditure limits, ensuring sufficient state funding to avoid election campaigns being excessively reliant on private sponsors, and establishing an independent institution to monitor the financial management of political parties. However, recent experience in Germany, Italy, Spain, and elsewhere demonstrate that state funding does not necessarily reduce the scope for illegal contributions to political parties. Indeed, it can be argued that there are more political scandals where there are relatively high levels of state funding. Solutions therefore must be more carefully considered and tailored to prevailing national circumstances. For example, what is the optimum mix between public and private financing? More research and discussion of the financing of politics is needed, and a successor Wilton Park conference in 2004 focusing on this issue is envisaged.

The Public Sector

16. Reforming the public sector is one of the most important priorities in curbing corruption. Effective institutional and legal mechanisms in former socialist countries are weak largely because of neglect and mishandling in the socialist period. The public sector is highly susceptible to corruption as a result of its relatively low pay, the wide-ranging implications of the decisions it takes, and the substantial resources managed. Independent public service commissions should establish a code of conduct, train civil servants to become acquainted with professional codes of conduct, implement rewards for preventing corruption, rotate staff among positions that are particularly susceptible to corruption, restrict unnecessary discretionary powers, and introduce meritocratic standards and systems for promotion. Random auditing of civil servants can help ensure that ethical standards are maintained. Unfortunately, in poorer countries, even earning double the national average pay is insufficient to curb corruption because pay is still low and a spiral of public pay claims may result.

Police

17. The police, by virtue of their visible public role, their low pay, and their potential to use force, are particularly susceptible to becoming involved in corrupt (usually petty) acts. The police in Central and Eastern Europe are widely perceived by the public and the media as abusing their positions for personal gain. Ensuring effective scrutiny of police conduct in postsocialist countries is important because there was previously no public oversight of police operations. Breaches of police integrity are found in most police forces, despite variations in organizational structures, pay levels, codes of conduct, cultures, and roles. It is useful therefore to recognize unethical conduct in the police, which can include dishonesty; the deliberate misuse of duty time and sick leave; lying; theft; the use of unnecessary force; physical or psychological abuse; racial prejudice; judging people on the basis of stereotypes; acceptance of money, gifts, and special favors; enjoying unreasonable privileges; conversion of prisoners' property; securing false testimony; deliberate disregard for rules or laws; violation of civil rights; false arrest; illegal search; denial

of the due process of law and the right to bail; willful, discourteous conduct; failure to perform according to standards; ignoring violations; unwillingness to change inefficient practices and abide by agency standards; violating secrecy; violation of privileged communication; and misuse of public property, including willful disregard for the proper use of vehicles, equipment, and supplies.

18. Measures to curb corruption in the police center include creating the structure and systems to manage information and knowledge securely, effectively, and accountably; developing personnel policies and practices to ensure the hiring of staff of the highest integrity; providing effective management of the organization, with visible leadership to prevent and challenge unethical behavior; and developing proactive tactics and techniques to identify and detect corruption, dishonesty, and unethical behavior. Measures to protect whistle-blowers, reduce peer group secrecy, raise salaries, dismiss corrupt officials, and disclose assets should also be undertaken. Making the police an autonomous force, answerable to the head of state or another authority, but not the government, can enhance its status and effectiveness.

Judiciary

19. A fair and efficient legal system is based on its neutrality, equality, and nondiscrimination before the law; the legal consistency and coherence of its decisions; and its smooth functioning. Formally, constitutions and legislation guarantee the independence of the judiciary, but other measures are needed. The legislative and executive should do their best to allow the judiciary to work independently because their success depends on the smooth functioning of a self-governing judiciary. It is necessary to ensure that a judge is responsible and that there are transparent procedures for his or her appointment and removal. Judges should be selected with long terms of office according to the following criteria: first, selection should be undertaken by a self-governing, politically neutral, and legally independent body with a guaranteed status and procedure prescribed by itself; second, criteria must be prescribed in advance on the quality, capability, professionalism, and personal quality of the candidate; finally, the procedure must be transparent. In the Macedonian case, for example, the legislature and executive seriously undermined the independence of the judges. The independence of the Macedonian Republic Judicial Council was diminished by the fact that it did not make the final selection; it merely made proposals to Parliament. The parties in Parliament persevered in making selections through a parliamentary commission. After a long debate, this procedure was changed, and Council proposals were sent directly to Parliament, where dominant parties continued to influence selection.

20. The judiciary must be depoliticized. A judge's independence can be infringed if he or she serves in incompatible roles in legislative and executive functions, whether at the national, provincial, or municipal level. For example, engaging judges in election commissions before and during elections can infringe their neutrality.

21. The financial status and security of the judges should be improved to ensure their economic independence and standing in society. If judges have the same low salaries as other state employees, the temptation to accept bribes to improve his or her economy status increases. If public sector wages in countries in transition continue to decline, enhancing judges' career prospects, providing ongoing professional education, and ensuring adequate physical premises and resources can help.

For example, the Romanian government recently introduced an integrated information technology system, opened a legal library, and acquired computer hardware for 120 locations, including 10 courts of appeal. A software application has been created for the random distribution of cases to judges, which increases the potential for objectivity within the system. Exposing corruption in the judiciary is complex because legal procedures involve several stages and each stage presents specific opportunities for corruption. The independence of the judiciary should not become a cloak to hide corruption.

Anti-Corruption Commissions

22. The basic question is not whether there should be specialized agencies but rather how to make them effective. Governments must ensure that these agencies are independent, autonomous, secure from illicit influence, and have adequate means and knowledge to conduct their work. Anti-corruption commissions should have a mandate broad enough to gather all relevant information, as well as be protected from political, economic, and personal pressures, introducing at the same time strict rules of control over the interests, income, and property of their employees. Anti-corruption agencies must have the financial, material, and other resources necessary to perform their functions. Having segregated budgets can help ensure independence, but equally it can leave these agencies with a less secure financial basis.

23. Surveys have correlated lack of independence of anti-corruption agencies to high levels of corruption in individual countries. Some governments (for example, Hong Kong [China], Malta, and Singapore) establish such agencies outside their regular structures to highlight their determination to curb corruption seriously. However, there are so far few countries with such agencies, sometimes because some governments lack the political will and sometimes because many states lack the necessary financial resources. However, no one disagrees that specialized agencies must exist, and this is enshrined in the Council of Europe Criminal Law Convention on Corruption. Some countries designate representatives in charge of anti-corruption efforts across government within the existing state apparatus (often within existing law enforcement agencies). Usually, these agencies are positioned high in government to ensure that their positions and instructions carry the necessary weight. However, such bodies can give rise to concerns about duplication. In Romania, for example, it is argued that the anti-corruption framework should be streamlined by consolidating the anti-corruption bureau and abolishing the prime minister's control department.

Prosecution

24. Some countries have agencies specializing in the detection and prosecution of corruption, and they have investigative powers. Corruption is very difficult to detect and to prove. There have been too many international conventions and too few prosecutions. The weaknesses of both partners in corruption and investigators should be recognized. The corrupt are vulnerable in their communication with associates, their acts, illicit covering up of their actions, and handling of the proceeds. Investigators' points of weakness are not understanding the links, not knowing where to concentrate, being unable to obtain evidence and corroboration, revealing methods, and being unable to operate covertly. Success in making a con-

viction requires determination, training, and sufficient and effective tools. Regular investigators can do much to stop general types of crime, but they are often unable to prevent, detect, and prove corruption. Good legislation and honest judges are needed to ensure that cases are prosecuted effectively. Furthermore, prosecutors also must be well trained, equipped, and resourced. Other than specialist prosecutors, prosecutors are not prepared to counter the new forms of organized crime. Prosecutors require well-protected witnesses, watertight confessions, proactive special methods, plea bargaining, and reversals of the burden of proof to make convictions. Direct contacts between professionals in different countries can foster international cooperation.

25. National anti-corruption prosecutors' offices should be autonomous structures, independent of the courts and other public authorities, in which police officers and qualified specialists in the economic, financial, banking, customs, information technology, and other fields work together. They should carry out mandatory criminal prosecution of "classic" offenses such as bribe giving, bribe taking, influence peddling, receipt of undue advantage, deliberate overvaluing of businesses and assets for sale, deliberate undervaluing of privatizations, use of credits or subventions for purposes other than those for which they were granted, use of inside information to conclude financial transactions, money laundering, drug trafficking, fraudulent bankruptcy, and tax evasion. In financial areas, improvements in corporate governance, such as better managerial control and systems, the publication of transparent and accurate accounts, and greater minority shareholder activism, can help.

26. The use of "special" investigative measures can raise human rights questions about their possible abuse. However, many regard special measures such as wire tapping, bugging, intrusive and electronic surveillance, and undercover police work as covert rather than special. "False" or "fictitious" bribery is explicitly illegal in some countries because it presents problems of "entrapment." Although covert investigative methods should not exceed what is allowed by the European Convention on Human Rights and national constitutions, it is debatable whether it is wise to ban a potentially useful measure only because it might be abused. In their desire to have effective agencies, some countries have engaged different types of experts and functions that really should not be colocated in a single institution. There is no problem colocating police officers and prosecutors in the same institution, but to include judges may be problematic, especially in light of a defendant's right to a fair trial.

27. All authorities involved in curbing corruption should share their findings and information because it is much easier to investigate cases with prior knowledge of a suspect's financial situation. Although it is not normally difficult to collect general data, there can be considerable problems collecting information from tax and anti-money-laundering authorities. Some countries do not allow monitoring mechanisms to exchange financial information at all, or they allow it only with a prior judicial order.

Administration

28. Regulatory reform is required to ensure a level playing field between prospective domestic and international suppliers, a transparent legal and tendering framework, free and equal access to information, and carrying out tenders through electronic means so the public procurement process is transparent. In so doing, the

discretionary powers of officials awarding government contracts, privatizing state assets, and granting import and export licenses are limited. Autonomous public sector auditors should be free to monitor and investigate public administration. Citizens should be provided with adequate avenues of redress for alleged wrongdoing in public administration, and the judiciary should have a role in rectifying or punishing any wrongdoing.

Other Actors

29. Anti-corruption efforts should involve government, responsible nongovernmental organizations (NGOs), the media, and the international community. To date, cooperation among these groups has been insufficient.

NGOs

30. Generally, the resources available to NGOs do not provide them enough access to data and control to lead to significant influence over anti-corruption politics and activities. However, NGOs can on occasion increase the transparency of government actions. Perception indexes such as the Transparency International index raise awareness and can even force necessary legislative and regulatory change. However, they can cause governments to skew their actions just to please outsiders. For example, a government can announce the creation of an anti-corruption central agency or make high-profile arrests, but pressing attention to improving the judiciary can be neglected.

31. Sometimes, NGOs can easily become part of the web of corruption. Nevertheless, NGOs act much more as part of the solution than as part of the problem. There are several distinct means of influence available to NGOs. NGOs can lobby parliament and parliamentarians, participate in public consultations, and comment on draft laws. NGOs can initiate continual requests for information (which includes explanation, justification of certain activities, and the assumption of responsibility) within the legal acts and share this information with other NGOs, the media, and responsible state organs. NGOs can highlight an issue in public by identifying key problems and examining all relevant parameters connected to the problem. Many citizens simply accept that corruption in its many forms is a way of life or believe that life is impossible without corruption. Many believe that it is not in their power or even their own interest to do anything about it. Often people simply don't know the mechanisms and options available to them to avoid or prevent corruption. NGOs can help citizens obtain knowledge and skills with which to reduce the impact of corruption or avoid it altogether in branches of government.

32. NGOs should avoid acting in an inappropriate or amateur fashion lest they be discredited. NGOs should not overreach their mandate, a danger especially for countries in transition with imperfect democratic systems. NGOs can, even under the banner of the cause of transparency, unwittingly become part of political disputes. NGOs should not become involved in intra- and interparty disputes (allegations of corruption can be used for party political advantage and sometimes revenge). NGOs should not violate privacy, conduct campaigns approximating "witch-hunts," disrupt the effective functioning of the legal system, and violate the presumption of innocence. NGOs can be a model of action and existence without

corruption. This is the hardest way to act against corruption, but also the most accessible to citizens. If NGOs are to act as a model, they cannot, under any circumstances, use corrupt channels to influence or achieve a goal. The idea that "the end justifies the means" is fatal for any NGO trying to curb corruption. Consistent adherence to procedures and legally prescribed channels, despite the difficulties and complications in achieving the desired effect, is one of the best ways to curb corruption.

Media

33. Information is one of the most powerful tools for combating corruption. Secrecy and silence are the strongest tools corruption has, along with fear. If citizens are uninformed about corruption, they can do little to counter it. Although governments in democracies are and feel obliged to inform the public about most government activities, information is often only declaratory and without any additional regulatory mechanisms for its implementation. Public enquiries and the televising of parliamentary and political debates, municipal information centers, and Web sites should be encouraged and supported. Journalist associations should be strengthened because they can instill principles of sound and responsible journalism, protect journalists from political pressure and physical intimidation, and lobby for freedom of expression.

34. The media can reinforce the work of anti-corruption agencies and NGOs and act as an ally of the victims of corruption. Indicators of the effectiveness of the media as a pillar of integrity include existence of freedom-of-information laws and procedures; official secrets act; libel laws to censor the media and restrict dissemination of information; requirement of journalists to be licensed; stories critical of government; sufficient competition within the media; enforcement of antimonopoly laws within the media; equal treatment of national and foreign media to report stories and to operate freely; restrictions on the supply of materials and resources to enable the media to function without hindrance; transparency of media ownership; adequate pay of journalists; limited criminal libel actions against journalists; and adequate training of journalists.

35. The media should be independent of government, although it is possible to have independent autonomous state-owned outlets. Countries where the media shelter the government and public officials are likely to be more corrupt. Conflicts of interest can occur when a parliamentarian is also an owner, manager, or board member of a commercial media company. One of the more serious conflicts can occur when the media are owned or controlled by a leading parliamentarian or political figure. It is debatable whether re-registering the ownership of media interests in another family member's name or segregated trust or placing a company under someone else's direct control is sufficient to prevent potential conflicts of interest.

The International Dimension

36. International initiatives to curb corruption and bribery are all relatively new. Some are still not fully implemented, while others are still under negotiation (for example, the UN convention). It is too early for a complete assessment of whether the initiatives are working, but so far there is little concrete evidence of success, given the continued cases of corruption and the limited number of prosecutions.

Nonetheless, there is cautious optimism that the initiatives will eventually produce successful outcomes. More effort should be made to get the message out about initiatives that have been taken, but are not well known or understood. Auditors should be required to report evidence of corruption, bribery, and money-laundering offenses to prosecutors (in addition to company officials). There should be effective monitoring of all conventions, including the prospective UN convention. There should be an international hotline to which cases of apparent corruption, bribery, or money laundering could be reported and referred to the relevant authorities.

37. Institutional and small investors should promote action against corruption, bribery, and money laundering. National legislation such as the 1977 Foreign Corrupt Practices Act (FCPA) in the United States, although extraterritorial in their reach, have been effective in reducing U.S. corporate payments to foreign governments. As a result, the United States pushed for a multilateral convention in the Organisation for Economic Co-operation and Development (OECD), but the resulting convention does not cover foreign subsidiaries. Private sector and NGO officials should be included among those whom it is illegal to bribe. The private sector should be engaged in the adoption of codes of conduct, compliance codes, and personnel training to prevent corruption, bribery, and money laundering. Indeed, some larger companies would rather lose a contract because they have refused to give a bribe for fear in part of adverse publicity if the bribe is exposed and publicized. By contrast, medium and smaller companies are more likely to be engaged in bribe giving. Countries whose legislation is not as watertight as the U.S. FCPA are more likely to have their firms involved in corrupt actions. Whistle-blower protection should be introduced to protect private and public sector officials who report corruption, bribery, and money-laundering transactions. There should be education in ethical behavior orientated to preventing corruption, bribery, and money laundering, commencing at the primary school level.

38. International cooperation on the tracing, forfeiture, and confiscation of assets has increased over the past years, because of the efforts of countries accepting basic principles for cooperation and implementation of international documents. Without appropriate international cooperation, all efforts would achieve few results at great cost. It is nevertheless necessary to raise awareness for the need to introduce legislation on the confiscation of the criminal proceeds and related provisional measures for seizure and freezing. It is necessary to implement international standards, to facilitate efficient international cooperation, and to address the national dimension by introducing the necessary legislative amendments, institutional framework, and training programs and convening multidisciplinary conferences.

39. Legislation in Central and East European states should be considered more carefully before implementation. The European Union (EU) is adept at telling others what to do and what projects to accept, and accession countries shouldn't be equally so adept at telling the EU what it wants to hear. Implementing international instruments in new democracies is usually done under political pressure. Laws are drafted to ensure compatibility with international (usually EU) standards. The EU expert usually recommends his or her own country's model, and the law is drafted and ratified quickly. This often results in difficulties during and after implementation.

40. The European Commission has impressed on candidates the urgency to curb corruption so they can qualify for EU membership. However, the Commission itself should establish a dedicated unit with a forward-looking, coherent strategy, like the

Council of Europe, to aid the curbing of corruption in accession and candidate states. Recognition of corruption as a problem will become more apparent as up to eight Central and East European countries join the EU in 2004. Although there are deficiencies in the EU's approach to corruption, adoption of the EU's *acquis communautaire* is slowly, albeit imperfectly, helping reduce the scope for corruption in accession, candidate, and neighboring countries.

Conclusion

41. Curbing corruption in Central and Eastern Europe may be difficult and progress slow, but actions under way can and are helping. Initially, the focus was on curbing corrupt acts, but now a more holistic approach has developed. Curbing corruption requires a multidisciplinary response and cooperation between different institutions at the national and international levels. The diffuse nature and complexity of the problem should not reduce the will to counter it, for that alone would result in failure. Countries in Central and East Europe have had democratic institutions for only less than 15 years, and they should not lose sight of the fact that gradual improvements in democracy and the market economy will in the longer term go hand in hand with reduced levels of corruption.